Studies in Ancient Monarchies

Edited by
ULRICH GOTTER (Konstanz), MATTHIAS HAAKE (Bonn),
NINO LURAGHI (Oxford) und KAI TRAMPEDACH (Heidelberg)

Volume 8

Germanicus Caesar

History and Memory

———————

Edited by
Paweł Sawiński and Adam Ziółkowski

Franz Steiner Verlag

Umschlagabbildungen:
Links: King Tiglath-pileser III of Assyria. Stone panel, ca. 728 BCE.
From the Central Palace in Nimrud, now in the British Museum.
© akg / Bible Land Pictures
Mitte: Emperor Justinian. Mosaic, ca. 540 CE. Church of San Vitale, Ravenna.
© akg / Bildarchiv Steffens
Rechts: Alexander the Great at the Battle of Issos. Mosaic, ca. 100 BCE.
From the Casa del Fauno, Pompeii, now in the Museo Archeologico Nazionale di Napoli.
© akg / Nimatallah

Bibliografische Information der Deutschen Nationalbibliothek:
Die Deutsche Nationalbibliothek verzeichnet diese Publikation in der Deutschen
Nationalbibliografie; detaillierte bibliografische Daten sind im Internet über
dnb.d-nb.de abrufbar.

Dieses Werk einschließlich aller seiner Teile ist urheberrechtlich geschützt.
Jede Verwertung außerhalb der engen Grenzen des Urheberrechtsgesetzes
ist unzulässig und strafbar.
© Franz Steiner Verlag, Stuttgart 2023
www.steiner-verlag.de
Layout und Herstellung durch den Verlag
Satz: DTP + TEXT Eva Burri, Stuttgart
Druck: Beltz Grafische Betriebe, Bad Langensalza
Gedruckt auf säurefreiem, alterungsbeständigem Papier.
Printed in Germany.
ISBN 978-3-515-13440-8 (Print)
ISBN 978-3-515-13446-0 (E-Book)

Table of Contents

ADAM ZIÓŁKOWSKI
Introduction 7

PAWEŁ SAWIŃSKI
Proconsul of Augustus or of Tiberius?
Some Remarks on the Nature of Germanicus' imperium *and his*
First Imperatorial Acclamation 13

FILIP TATERKA
The Egyptian Voyage of Germanicus
An Egyptological Perspective 25

ADAM ZIÓŁKOWSKI
Rome's Aims in Germania in AD 14: Tacitus, *Annales* 1.3.6
An Attempt to Appraise a Queer Statement 53

JAKUB PIGOŃ
Ad spes Germanici coercendas
Germanicus and Piso in the Second Book of Tacitus' Annals. 73

MICHAŁ NORBERT FASZCZA
Roman Military Discipline and Germanicus' Political Position
A Note on D. 49.16.4.13 97

AGATA ALEKSANDRA KLUCZEK
Germanicus in Roman Numismatic Memory 117

LECHOSŁAW OLSZEWSKI
The Secret Life of Things
The statua loricata *from Ameria.* 147

Introduction

ADAM ZIÓŁKOWSKI

An unwritten law of historical writing dictates that great historical anniversaries engender conferences, colloquia and, ultimately, floods of publications. As far as the Roman history is concerned, the first two decades of this century were under this aspect dominated by grand jubilees linked with two greatest revolutionaries in purple, Augustus and Constantine, the occasions being, respectively, the bimillenaries of the Teutoburg disaster (2009)[1] and of the death of the first emperor (2014),[2] and the one-thousand seven-hundredth anniversaries of Constantine's ascent to power (2006)[3] and of the legendary Edict of Milan (2013).[4] In 2019, another similar occasion presented itself with the bimillenary of the death of a historical person that, although of much lesser stature, is one of the best recognizable figures of the Empire, Germanicus Iulius Caesar.[5]

Germanicus is easily the principal might-have-been of the Roman history. Untimely demise at the age of thirty-three prevented him from reaching the imperial power and in the long run signed the death-warrant for his wife and two eldest sons; yet their murderer was forced to resign himself to be succeeded by the surviving son, and when that son, the last of the Iulii Caesares, succumbed to the assassins' blades, the imperial power fell ineluctably to Germanicus' brother, a half-wit till then considered unqualified for holding public offices, let alone reigning. How would the early principate evolve had Germanicus outlived Tiberius and been succeeded by sons grown up in relatively normal conditions, not by Caligula, gone mad from the horrible experiences of his youth, and the feeble-minded Claudius? The *manqué* reconqueror of Germania, according to Tacitus deprived by his jealous adoptive father of conclusive victory when the rebellious tribes were on the verge of giving up resistance, wouldn't he be allowed,

---

1   Varusschlacht (2009); Baltrush et al. (2012).
2   Goodman (2018).
3   Demandt/Engemann (2007); Van Dam (2011).
4   Melloni et al. (2013); Cuscito (2014).
5   Anniversary conferences of Germanicus' death (The Roman Society – London – 12 X 2019); Germanico Caesare a un passo dall'impero (Museo Archeologico e Pinacoteca – Amelia – 24–25 V 2019); Germanico, l'imperatore mancato (Roma/Lucus Feroniae – 11–12 X 2019).

or could he be prohibited, to continue the war till the enemies' final defeat if he had not twice committed the same blunder of exposing, with disastrous results, his Mediterranean-type fleet to the storms of the North Sea? He was credited by Suetonius and Tacitus with all the positive traits which Tiberius and later emperors so sadly lacked (including the old Roman persistence in extending the empire), becoming under their pens a paragon of princely virtues (Suet. *Caius* 4; Tac. *Ann.* 2.73, 3.4); exaggeratedly, perhaps, but his exceptional position in the Romans' historical memory two hundred years after his death and a hundred years after the said historians had written their laudations is corroborated by a *supplicatio* in his memory in the *Feriale Duranum*, his being the only thus honoured deceased person in the calendar who did not become emperor and/or was not divinized.[6] On top of all that, epigraphic discoveries of the last decades of the previous century, *Tabula Siarensis* and *Senatus Consultum de Cn. Pisone patre*, have given us not only new data on Germanicus, especially on his death and status in the *domus Augusta*, but also a precious insight into the working methods and reliability of Tacitus, our main source for the post-Augustan Principate. Germanicus may not have been a historical giant like his adoptive grandfather, but his figure lends itself like few others as the starting point for (re-)examining various aspects of the Roman history and historical memory during the first phase of the imperial régime.

The present volume has its origin in the conference "Germanicus: history and memory", held in the Kalisz branch of the University of Poznań on 6 December 2019. Its guiding idea, reflected in the title, was that Germanicus – the last hero of Rome's uninterrupted external expansion, in spite of having never reached the imperial power the key member of the first imperial dynasty as, respectively, father, elder brother and grandfather of the subsequent Julio-Claudian emperors, an embodiment of the ideal of a "good" imperial heir apparent, unspoiled by his unique position – was memorable in the literal sense of the word, i. e. worthy of remembrance, by later generations of educated Romans. The memory of his person was expressed in so many ways that to realize the concept in full our volume hosts papers by representatives not only of the classical quartet – history, classical philology, art history/archaeology and numismatics – but of Egyptology and Roman law as well.

The first strictly historical contribution, Paweł Sawiński's "Proconsul of Augustus or of Tiberius? Some Remarks on the Nature of Germanicus' imperium and his First Imperatorial Acclamation", a re-examination of the moot question of the date of Germanicus' first imperatorial acclamation, concerns the mainstay of the new régime, the total subordination to the *princeps* of the Roman army, sworn in his name, paid by him and commanded by his lieutenants of varying grades and in varying positions. All that, however, as became an autocracy which would not admit being one, had to

---

6   I am sceptical about restoring the name of the person in col.1.11–12 as Lucius Aelius Caesar (i. e. Hadrian's first designated heir) instead of Robert Fink's reading Lucius Seius Caesar (i. e. Severus Alexander's father-in-law), now defended by Iovine (2018), 65–78.

be expressed in and run with old Republican terms and procedures which inevitably were acquiring a new meaning in the process. The terms which probably underwent greatest change in spite of remaining ostensibly the same as before were *imperium* and *imperator*. In consequence, to defend his date of the event, the author had first to inquire into the equally debatable question of Germanicus' status as commander on the Rhine, which in turn raised such issues as the reliability of the contemporary evidence, i. e. essentially poems and inscriptions set up by low-ranking officers, in reflecting fine points of the Augustan arrangement.

As the title indicates, the second historical chapter, "The Egyptian voyage of Germanicus: an Egyptological perspective" by Filip Taterka, is the work of an Egyptologist, not a classical historian. Some of the questions his contribution deals with are those scholars usually ask with regard to Germanicus' visit to Egypt: his motives for going there, his alleged transgression of Augustus' *dominationis arcanum* which prohibited senators and high-ranking *equites* from entering the province without the emperor's permission, the peculiarities of Tacitus' account; what sets it apart is the posit, defence of which fills more than a half of the chapter, that Germanicus went to Egypt in search of hidden lore. An argument like this unavoidably requires assumptions and interpretations which will not necessarily be shared by every reader; some might also think that the author, like almost all those who have tackled this particular point, assumes too easily the historicity of Germanicus' visit to the oracle of Apis, not mentioned by Tacitus. He is, however, fully aware of the hypothetical character of the argument, and disarms the reader with an opening notification: "the following lines are not supposed to present an indisputably certain reconstruction of the events, but rather they should be treated as an attempt to revisit the question from a different perspective".

The last strictly historical chapter, "Rome's aims in Germania in AD 14: Tacitus, *Annales* 1.3.6. An attempt to appraise a queer statement" by Adam Ziółkowski, is a comment on a sentence from the beginning of the *Annales* (a follow-on of the report that in AD 13 Germanicus had been put at the head of eight legions on the Rhine), in which we read that at the time of Augustus' death the Germanic war was being waged but to wipe out the ignominy of the Teutoburg disaster, not for conquest or other "worthy benefits". This statement, unlike the other, ostensibly corresponding in substance, that Augustus added to his will a counsel that the empire should be kept within its present limits (*Ann.* 1.11.4), has attracted little attention of modern scholars. The author argues, by setting it against the rest of Tacitean narrative and other reports on the same subject-matter, that it does not reflect the attitude of Augustus at the time of his death, but presages the position of his successor, which would prevail barely two years later with the recall of Germanicus.

Every text on Germanicus is of necessity a Tacitean undertaking, but the chapter "*Ad spes Germanici coercendas*: Germanicus and Piso in the second book of Tacitus' *Annals*" by Jakub Pigoń, is so to the utmost degree. Tacitus' unsurpassed mastery in the art of insinuation and of building up an atmosphere of impending doom has been the favourite theme for students of the literary aspects of his works. Our author concentrates on Tacitus' depiction of the clash between Germanicus and his alleged murderer Piso; he identifies and analyses the wide range of sophisticated literary devices with which the historian on the one hand magisterially recreates the atmosphere of doubt, suspicion and helpless anger which surrounded, in Rome as well as in Antioch, the news of Germanicus' illness and demise, and on the other leads his reader from Germanicus' triumph to death in such a way as to make the prince's deathbed accusation of Piso and Plancina as his murderers most compelling, with Tiberius and Livia looming in the background as accomplices.

As the title proclaims, Michał Faszcza's "Roman Military Discipline and Germanicus' Political Position: a note on D. 49.16.4.13" is strictly speaking a note on a passage in *Digesta* by the Severan jurist Arrius Menander, which mentions Germanicus' issuing edicts which affected the status of the legionaries, i. e. Roman citizens. An apparently simple question of when, in what circumstances and on what basis Germanicus could engage in an activity which, as far as we know, was the exclusive prerogative of the ruling emperors, set in the context of what we know about the Roman military law (an "invention" of the Augustan reign) during the early Principate, leads to important conclusions about the nature and scope of one of the most characteristic features of the period that was the granting of extraordinary *imperium* to members of the imperial family, of whom Germanicus is a paragon.

In "Germanicus in Roman numismatic memory" Agata Kluczek discusses the presence of Germanicus in the Imperial coinage from the perspective of the coins' issuers. Although almost all the issues on which he was represented were struck well after his death, they were still being minted after the demise of his last descendant, in numbers whose total approached those of some emperors and exceeded by far those which commemorated other non-rulers. The author examines motives which led imperial and provincial authorities to issue coins depicting him and the influence the types which referred to his achievements had, certainly or probably, on the imagery of coins of the same categories commemorating later emperors, with the following summing up: "Germanicus, not an emperor, was present in the numismatic memory of the later generations of the Romans as if he had been one".

In the last chapter, "The secret life of things: the *statua loricata* from Ameria", Lechosław Olszewski proposes a new reconstruction of the history of the monumental bronze statue found in 1963 in Amelia (ancient Ameria) in Umbria. The statue's identification has never been in doubt, as its head belongs unmistakably to Germanicus' "Gabii" type; since, however, it does not match well the torso, it is pretty obvious that the original depicted a different member of the imperial family. Now, on the assumption that in those days only statues of those whose memory had been condemned (*memoria damnata*) were being reused, it is thought that the original depicted Caligula, whose head was replaced after his posthumous disgrace by that of his father. The author observes that in reality the reasons for the practice were varied and that it was often meant to honour further the person to whom the transformed statue was to be dedicated, thanks to positive associations which the original honoree brought up. An analysis of the iconography of the statue, especially of its armour, leads him to the conclusion that the person whom it originally depicted was most probably Caius Caesar, Augustus' eldest adoptive son.

In the end, it is worth asking in what direction the papers here presented go with regard to the question of what principally kept Germanicus' memory alive in the minds of the Romans of later generations. In theory, we are faced with an alternative: the victorious commander and paradigmatic triumphator of the imperial era or the crucial link in the chain of descendancy in the first imperial family. A second look shows a clear preponderance of the dynastic aspect. Even in "military" Chapters One, Three and Five the argumentation always returns to, or revolves around, the key point that is his extraordinary status, bestowed on him thanks to his position in Augustus' scheme of imperial succession. In Chapters Two and Four, this extraordinary status, familial and so official, is the starting point of the demonstration: Germanicus does what he does thanks to it, and dies as he dies because of it. Chapters Six and Seven, dealing with material objects and so more "objective" (at least in popular perception) than written sources, tell the same story, but even more clearly. Germanicus mattered not for the *signa recepta*, but as the embodiment of the dynastic principle, crucial for the Roman Empire as much as for any other monarchy, but in constant need of being recalled, probably as much to neutralise the republican heritage with its "choice of the best" (whether by the senate or the people in arms) alternative as to make up for the failure of successive imperial families to establish long-lasting dynasties.

***

The publication of this volume was financially supported by the Faculty of Pedagogy and Fine Arts in Kalisz, Adam Mickiewicz University in Poznań (ID-UB n° 59), the Faculty of Humanities and the Institute of History, University of Silesia in Katowice, the Institute of Classical, Mediterranean and Oriental Studies and the Research Discipline Council for Literary Studies, University of Wrocław, and Excellence Initiative – Research University, University of Warsaw.

Bibliography

Baltrush, Ernst et al. (eds.) (2012): 2000 Jahre Varusschlacht. Geschichte – Archäologie – Legenden. Berlin: De Gruyter.

Cuscito, Giuseppe (ed.) (2014): Costantino il Grande a 1700 anni dall' "Editto di Milano". XLIV Settimane Aquileisi, 30 maggio – 1 giugno 2013. Trieste: Editreg.

Demandt, Alexander / Engemann, Josef (eds.) (2007): Konstantin der Grosse. Ausstellungskatalog. Imperator Caesar Flavius Constantinus. Mainz: Philipp von Zabern.

Goodman, Penelope J. (ed.) (2018): Afterlives of Augustus AD 14–2014. Cambridge: Cambridge University Press.

Iovine, Giulio (2018): "New Textual Perspectives on Feriale Duranum (P. Dura 54)". In: Analecta Papyrologica 30, 65–78.

Melloni, Alberto et al. (eds.) (2013): Costantino I. Enciclopedia costantiniana sulla figura e l'immagine dell'imperatore del cosiddetto Editto di Milano 313–2013. Roma: Istituto della Enciclopedia italiana fondata da Giovanni Treccani.

Van Dam, Raymond (2011): Remembering Constantine at the Milvian Bridge. Cambridge: Cambridge University Press.

Varusschlacht im Osnabrücker Land. Ausstellungskatalog. 2000 Jahre Varusschlacht 1–3 (2009). Stuttgart: Wissenschaftliche Buchgesellschaft.

Proconsul of Augustus or of Tiberius?
Some Remarks on the Nature of Germanicus' imperium and his First Imperatorial Acclamation

PAWEŁ SAWIŃSKI

Keywords: Germanicus' independent imperium, imperium proconsulare, imperatorial salutation, domus Augusta

Germanicus' adoption by Tiberius, who had himself been adopted by Augustus, fundamentally changed his standing in the imperial family, as he then became the second candidate, after Tiberius, to succession from Augustus, which crucially influenced the course of his political career.[1] A few years after the adoption he began a spectacular career in the army, holding various military functions *ex mandatis Augusti*. In AD 7, he was dispatched to Pannonia and Dalmatia to help Tiberius suppress the great anti-Roman uprising of the tribes there which had broken out the previous year;[2] there he remained active until the year 9, most likely as a *legatus Augusti pro praetore*, receiving his first military decoration, the *ornamenta triumphalia*, for his service in the province.[3] Another area of Germanicus' military activity was Germania, where he was first sent with Tiberius in AD 11 and again in 13, to take command of eight legions stationed on the Rhine.[4] In this paper, I focus on two issues. The first concerns Germanicus' legal status during the campaign in Germania in the years 11 and 13–16, and the closely related question of when he was first granted an independent *imperium*. The second issue is connected with the dating of Germanicus' first imperatorial salutation. Considering the contradictory and terse nature of our sources, both these problems have occasioned heated debate among the scholars.

---

1   On Germanicus' place in Augustus' succession plans, see Sawiński (2018), 86–91.
2   Cass. Dio 55.31.1.
3   Cass. Dio 56.17.2. See also Hurlet (1997), 167; Kienast et al. (2017), 73.
4   Cass. Dio 56.25.2; Tac. *Ann.* 1.31.1–2.

I will start my analysis with the issue of status, as it is relevant to establishing the date of Germanicus' imperatorial salutation, since holding independent *imperium* was surely a prerequisite for each and every award of this kind; it bears emphasising that no member of the *domus Augusta* had earlier acceded to that honour without holding independent *imperium* first.[5] Generally, there are two opinions among the scholars. Some maintain Germanicus was granted his first independent *imperium* during Augustus' reign, whereas others think it only happened after Tiberius had come into power. The discussion results from disagreement between our two main sources, Cassius Dio and Tacitus – the only two authors to mention Germanicus receiving these prerogatives. Whereas Dio writes that Germanicus was granted *imperium proconsulare* in AD 11, before he was sent to Germania with Tiberius, Tacitus mentions him receiving those powers in September of AD 14, that is, after Augustus' death.

Μάρκου δὲ Αἰμιλίου μετὰ Στατιλίου Ταύρου ὑπατεύσαντος, Τιβέριος μὲν καὶ Γερμανικὸς ἀντὶ ὑπάτου ἄρχων ἔς τε τὴν Κελτικὴν ἐσέβαλον.[6]

In the consulship of Marcus Aemilius and Statilius Taurus, Tiberius and Germanicus, the latter acting as proconsul, invaded Germany. (transl. by E. Cary)

at Germanico Caesari proconsulare imperium petivit, missique legati qui deferrent.[7]

but he [Tiberius] asked proconsular powers for Germanicus Caesar, and a commission was sent out to confer them. (transl. by C. H. Moore, J. Jackson)

F. Hurlet, P. M. Swan, and Y. Rivière accept Dio's chronology.[8] For Hurlet, the crucial argument is Germanicus' first imperatorial acclamation, which he dates to AD 13 or early AD 14, resting his reasoning on the correct assumption that independent *imperi-*

---

5 In 10 or 9 BC, Drusus the Elder and Tiberius won their first imperatorial salutations for successes in Germania and Pannonia. See Syme (1979), 310–314; Rich (1999), 549. Both held *imperium proconsulare*, which they had been granted in 11 BC. See Cass. Dio 54.33.5; 34.3. *Contra* Vervaet (2020), 152 f., who argues that Drusus and Tiberius had the *imperium proconsulare* from as early as 12 BC, so from the very beginning of their activity in Germania and Pannonia. This thesis is debatable. We know they led campaigns there in the rank of *legati Augusti* in the years 12–11. Augustus' stepsons were both hailed *imperatores* by the army, but the emperor did not confirm those salutations. See Syme (1979), 310; Rich (1990), 213; Dalla Rosa (2014), 238. Then towards the end of AD 3 or at the beginning of 4, the title of *imperator* was given to Gaius Caesar, Augustus' son, for his successes during the campaign in Armenia. See Cass. Dio 55.10a. 7; CIL 5.6416; Syme (1979), 315; Faoro (2016), 208, 212. Also in that case Cassius Dio (55.10.18) confirms that Gaius had an independent *imperium*, one he had received in 1 BC for his mission in the East.
6 Cass. Dio 56.25.2.
7 Tac. *Ann.* 1.14.3. The interpretation of that passage by Koestermann (1963), 115, who maintains that the *imperium* then granted to Germanicus was *proconsulare maius*, is quite groundless, as it is common knowledge that he only received such powers in AD 17 for the mission in the East. See Tac. *Ann.* 2.43.1; *SCPP*, ll. 34–35.
8 Hurlet (1997), 168 f.; Swan (2004), 278; Rivière (2016), 133.

um was a prerequisite for being awarded this honour. In his opinion, Tacitus' text does not mention Germanicus receiving independent *imperium* for the first time, because the commander had had such prerogatives since AD 11. Unfortunately, Hurlet does not clarify how in that case the passage in Tacitus should be understood.[9] Y. Rivière has expressed a similar view, although he also thinks that Germanicus' *imperium* was lesser (*minus*) than the *imperium* Tiberius held when he was sent to Germania in the year 11.[10] However, as far as the formal aspect of the matter is considered, his assumption does not seem justified. If, following Dio, we take Germanicus to have been granted *imperium proconsulare* that year, then *de iure* his status in Germania was the same as Tiberius'. The superiority of his adoptive father stemmed in that case primarily from Tiberius' greater military experience and *auctoritas*, owing to which it was he who held the high command in Germania at the time. The informal hierarchy between them is reflected in Ovid's choice of words, when the poet, referring to the campaigns of AD 10–11, calls Tiberius dux and Germanicus proximus duci.[11]

P. Brunt and R. Syme, in their turn, accept the content of Cassius Dio's account while rejecting his chronology and believe that Dio made a mistake with his dating of Germanicus' first *imperium*. They argue that since Tiberius was then the high commander of the Rhine army, and Germanicus necessarily fought under his command, the latter is unlikely to have been granted the status of a proconsul during the same time. For that reason, they suggest that the date of the event should be moved to AD 13, when Germanicus replaced Tiberius as the commander of the legions stationed on the Rhine.[12] I do not find their argument convincing. As I have indicated above, Germanicus' having had the same proconsular standing as Tiberius did not rule out the latter's being in fact the supreme commander in Germania.

In yet another view, K. Bringmann assumes, drawing on Tacitus, that Germanicus first received independent *imperium* only after Augustus' death and on Tiberius' clear orders. Consequently, he decidedly rejects Dio's account, believing that either the author or a copyist made a mistake. He thinks, instead, that until the death of the first princeps, Germanicus conducted military operations in Germania in the rank of *legatus Augusti*,[13] a view I am convinced is completely unfounded, as Germanicus could

---

9   Hurlet (1997), 168 f., 171.
10 Rivière (2016), 133.
11 Ovid. *Tr.* 4.2.28. The word *proximus* is used in a similar sense by Velleius Paterculus (2.71.1; 127.1) to refer to Messalla Corvinus as being the closest in rank to Brutus and Cassius in the Republican camp, and to refer to Statilius Taurus, whom he describes as Augustus' second-closest aide (*adiutor*) after Agrippa.
12 Brunt (1974), 180, 185; Syme (1978), 57 f., 63; Syme (1979), 320.
13 Bringmann (1977), 227; in a similar vein, Lebek (1991), 122. With some reservations, also D. Kienast accepts Germanicus had the status of *legatus Augusti pro praetore* until Augustus' death. See Kienast et al. (2017), 73 f.

hardly have assumed command of the eight legions stationed in Germania as a mere imperial legate after his consulship of AD 12.[14]

To summarize, I do not believe that there are grounds for rejecting the version of Cassius Dio, who dates Germanicus' being granted his first independent *imperium* to the year 11. An argument in favour of that date might be Germanicus' first imperatorial acclamation, which most likely took place in the final years of Augustus' reign (see below), thus making it legitimate to suppose that Germanicus obtained his first independent *imperium* before the first princeps died. Additionally, P. Swan rightly points out that the earlier careers of members of the *domus Augusta* show they tended to be granted *imperium proconsulare* before attaining consulship, as the careers of Drusus the Elder (Germanicus' natural father) and Gaius Caesar (Augustus' son) indicate.[15] I see no reasons to suppose that Germanicus' *cursus honorum* was different.[16]

How then is one to interpret Tacitus account? Th. Mommsen tried to reconcile the two narratives: he thought the mention in Cassius Dio referred to Augustus conferring on Germanicus proconsular powers in AD 11, while Tacitus took note of the senate renewing that *imperium* after the first emperor's death, which in Mommsen's opinion automatically made Germanicus' prerogatives expire.[17] However, his view has been criticized by many scholars[18] who chiefly point out that, in Tiberius' case, Augustus' death did not require his *imperium* to be renewed; why then should such an extension be necessary for Germanicus?[19] Still, their counter-argument is disputable, seeing that Tiberius' *imperium* thoroughly differed from Germanicus' in its nature, and that the two men had different standing in the imperial family. In AD 13 Tiberius had his *tribunicia potestas* extended for another ten years, and a decree of the senate, sanctioned by the people, granted him *imperium aequum* to that of Augustus in all the provinces of the Empire, which was meant to ensure his smooth succession.[20] Therefore his *imperium* as Augustus' co-ruler and designated successor could hardly have required any renewal after the first princeps died. In contrast, Germanicus held a command in Germania *ex mandatis Augusti*, and in my opinion his position needed to be defined anew after Tiberius came into power, so the senate granted him *imperium proconsulare* at the new emperor's express bidding. From that moment on, therefore, Germanicus commanded the legions

---

14   From Tacitus (*Ann.* 1.31.2) we also know there were at the time two *legati Augusti pro praetore* under Germanicus' command, C. Silius and A. Caecina. That constitutes another argument against the claim that Germanicus was just an imperial legate then.

15   Drusus the Elder was granted *imperium proconsulare* in the year 11 and assumed consulship in 9, whereas Gaius Caesar received *imperium proconsulare* in 1 BC and held his consulship in the following year. See Kienast et al. (2017), 61, 67.

16   See Swan (2004), 278.

17   Mommsen (1887), 1158 (n3).

18   See esp. Goodyear (1972), 191; Brunt (1974), 179 f.; Syme (1978), 57.

19   Brunt (1974), 179 f.; Syme (1978), 57 (n2).

20   See Sawiński (2018), 108 f.

stationed in Germania *ex mandatis Tiberii*. Considering that he had eight legions under his command, Tiberius' actions are fully understandable. I am of the opinion that this is how we ought to interpret Tacitus' passage: in his account he gave special attention to Germanicus' being granted proconsular power for the second time by the new princeps, i. e. primarily as a result of the imperial purple passing on to a successor. I do not think, therefore, that it could have anyhting to do with the expiry of his imperium. If we accept Hurlet's supposition that the *imperium* conferred on Germanicus in AD 11 was to be valid for five years (*quinquennium*), then it cannot possibly have expired by AD 14.[21]

The problem of dating Germanicus' first imperatorial acclamation also inspires heated discussions among scholars. Epigraphic sources unambiguously confirm that Germanicus was hailed *imperator* twice,[22] yet whereas we know from Tacitus that the second acclamation took place in AD 15 in connection with his victorious campaign in Germania, the precise circumstances and date of the first are unknown.[23] In the debate on its date, present-day scholars very often invoke the inscription erected in honour of an equestrian officer C. Fabricius Tuscus, discovered in 1959 in the Roman colony of Alexandreia Troas.[24] The inscription, originally located on the plinth of a statue of Tuscus, lists in detail his *cursus honorum*:

C(aio) Fabricio C(ai) f(ilio) Ani(ensi)
Tusco, II viro, augur(i)
praef(ecto) cohort(is) Apulae et
operum quae in colonia iussu
Augusti facta sunt, trib(uno) mil(itum) leg(ionis) III
Cyr(enaicae) VIII, trib(uno) dilectus ingenuorum
quem Romae habuit Augustus et
Ti(berius) Caesar, praef(ecto) fabr(um) IIII, praef(ecto) equit(um)

---

21 Hurlet (1994), 277f. Hurlet's hypothesis of Germanicus' *imperium* expiring in five years might be supported by the earlier case of Agrippa, whose *imperium* was extended every fifth year, first in 18 BC, and then in 13. See Rich (1990), 168.

22 Among the sources confirming that Germanicus was hailed *imperator* twice, there is an inscription placed in his honour in Rome by the *plebs urbana* (CIL 6.909), and an inscription on the arch at Mediolanum Santonum dedicated to Tiberius, Germanicus and Drusus the Younger by C. Iulius Rufus, a priest of the cult of Roma and Augustus at Lugdunum. See CIL 13.1036; Rose (1997), 130. Goodyear (1981), 83 is incorrect, however, in his claim that Germanicus is also referred to as "IMP. II" on coins, as all we have is a single emission from Caesarea in Cappadocia (RPC 1, no. 3623), which does refer to him as an *imperator* ("IMP."), but without specifying the number of salutations.

23 Tac. *Ann.* 1.58.5–6. The possibility that Tacitus meant Germanicus' first acclamation there, and his second resulted from his actions in the East later, is unlikely, since during his eastern mission, Germanicus conducted no military campaigns that could have potentially won him an *acclamatio*. At any rate we know of no imperatorial salutation from the reigns of Augustus and Tiberius that was awarded for achievements other than military.

24 *Contra* Faoro (2016), 210 (n33), who does not believe the inscription lends any information which could help date Germanicus' first acclamation without, however, justifying that position.

alae praet(oriae) IIII, hasta pura et corona
aurea donatus est a Germanico
Caesare imp(eratore) bello Germanico,
d(ecreto) d(ecurionum).[25]

To Gaius Fabricius Tuscus, son of Gaius, of the Aniensis tribe, Member of the Board of
Two, augur, prefect of the Apulan cohort and of the works which were carried out in the
colony on the orders of Augustus, military tribune of Legion III Cyrenaica for eight years,
tribune in charge of the levy of freeborn men which Augustus and Tiberius Caesar held
in Rome, prefect of engineers for four years, prefect of cavalry of praetorian *ala* for four
years, granted an Untipped Spear and Gold Crown by Germanicus Caesar Imperator in
the German war, be decree of the town councillors (transl. by B. Campbell).[26]

Of particular importance are the final lines of the text, which inform us that Fabricius
Tuscus received from Germanicus two high-prestige military decorations (the *hasta
pura* and the *corona aurea*) for his service in the Germanic war. In his commentary
on the inscription, P. Brunt puts forward a somewhat forced claim that it must have
been set up before Augustus' death, which, he believes, is indicated by the lack of the
formula *divus Augustus*.[27] In other words, he thinks Fabricius held the last function of
his career (*praefectus equitum alae praetoriae*) in the years 11–14, and assumes that the
German campaign mentioned in the inscription, which gained Tuscus the honours
listed above, took place while Augustus still lived. Since the inscription explicitly refers to Germanicus as *imperator*, Brunt infers that the commander's first imperatorial
acclamation must have occurred before the death of the first princeps.[28] However, not
all scholars have accepted the date he proposes. W. Orth notes that the expression *divus Augustus* does not always come up in reference to Augustus in the inscriptions set
up after his deification.[29] R. Syme is equally sceptical of Brunt's arguments, stressing
that inscriptions need not have always rendered an emperor's official nomenclature
precisely, and pointing out that our inscription twice lists the first princeps as *Augustus* instead of *Augustus Caesar*. Unlike Brunt, Syme believes Tuscus held the function
of *praefectus equitum* in the years 13–16 and that the inscription refers to the German
campaign carried out after Tiberius had assumed principate (between AD 14 and 16).[30]
As can be seen, it is impossible to ascertain beyond doubt whether Fabricius Tuscus'

---

25 AE 1973, 501.
26 Campbell (1994), 14 f.
27 One other argument for dating the inscription to Augustus' times could be the fact it refers to
Tiberius as *Caesar* rather than *Augustus*.
28 Brunt (1974), 174–180. Other scholars who date the inscription to Augustus' times are Barnes
(1974), 25, and Goodyear (1981), 84.
29 Orth (1978), 58. Examples are provided by inscriptions from Opsorus (Dalmatia) and Boljetin
(Moesia Superior). See CIL 3.3148 and CIL 3.13813.
30 Syme (1979), 318. So Speidel (1975), 165.

inscription was made during Augustus' or Tiberius' reign, which means that every attempt to date Germanicus' first acclamation on its basis is no more than a speculation. Here I would like to point out one more thing; namely, it is also possible that, in the inscription, the expression *a Germanico Caesare imperatore* was used not in a technical sense, in reference to a specific imperatorial acclamation, but in its colloquial meaning of 'general',[31] the sense found fairly often in literary sources, including Velleius Paterculus.[32] Should that be the case, the inscription in question would prove quite useless for the discussion on Germanicus' first acclamation.

Despite there being no clear evidence in the sources, a large majority of scholars believe Germanicus' first acclamation to have taken place during the final years of Augustus' reign[33], although they differ on its date. The earliest is that put forward by E. Koestermann, who opts for AD 9, linking Germanicus' first acclamation with his activity on the Pannonian-Dalmatian front[34], but his proposal is quite unfounded. First, we do know that at that time Germanicus did not hold independent *imperium*, which was a necessary precondition for such an acclamation. Second, it seems unlikely for Cassius Dio – who meticulously lists the honours awarded to Germanicus, as well as to Augustus and Tiberius, for suppressing the uprising in Pannonia and Dalmatia – to omit such a prestigious accolade; and he reports that only Augustus and Tiberius each received another imperatorial salutation, whereas Germanicus was rewarded with *ornamenta triumphalia*.[35] Granting him that honour unambiguously indicates that his status then was that of *legatus Augusti pro praetore*.

D. Timpe, followed by F. R. D. Goodyear, supposes that Germanicus' first acclamation took place in AD 11, when he was sent with Tiberius to Germania to stabilize the situation after Varus' defeat; yet our sources, while pointing out that the Roman army did cross the Rhine then – so the campaign may have given occasion for Germanicus' first salutation[36] – disagree on the aims and extent of operations. While Velleius Paterculus writes in general terms of successful fighting in Germania during that time, Cassius Dio merely notes that bearing in mind the recent *clades Variana*, Tiberius and Germanicus refrained from major raids across the Rhine and so failed to achieve any significant military success.[37] Considering the character of Paterculus' narrative, in which each campaign of Tiberius is presented as a series of great victories, we ought to be suspicious about his account, especially since Dio's version portrays the campaign very differently.

---

31 An interpretation firmly rejected by Brunt (1974), 176; and Goodyear (1981), 84.
32 E. g. in reference to Tiberius as a commander under Augustus. See Vell. Pat. 2.113.2; 115.2; 121.1; and in reference to Varus as a *legatus Augusti pro praetore* in Germania. See Vell. Pat. 2.120.5.
33 *Contra* G. E. Bean, the only historian I know of who believes Germanicus' second acclamation of AD 15 was actually his first. See Cook (1973), 412.
34 Koestermann (1957), 429 (n3).
35 Cass. Dio 56.17.1–2.
36 Timpe (1968), 36 f., 45; Goodyear (1981), 84.
37 Vell. Pat. 2.121.1; Cass. Dio 56.25.2–3.

And if we do accept Dio's account of the cautious operations of the Roman military during that time, it seems unlikely that Germanicus' first acclamation occurred in AD 11.

In their turn, P. Brunt, T. D. Barnes, and R. Syme favour AD 13, when Germanicus assumed independent command of the eight Rhine legions. They believe that around that time he carried out a successful campaign across the river, which brought him his first acclamation, and provided the reason for adding to the number of imperatorial salutations of Augustus and Tiberius, who thus received their twenty-first and seventh acclamations respectively.[38] However, the problem is that, with the sources silent, we know of no campaign of AD 13 which could potentially have earned Germanicus his first title of *imperator*. Regrettably, Cassius Dio's narrative, in which we would expect notes of this kind, breaks off in the summer of that year, and the gap extends as far as the events surrounding Augustus' death. It is also difficult to determine which campaign of Germanicus is referred to in a short epigram preserved in the *Palatine Anthology* and attributed to Crinagoras:

οὔρεα Πυρηναῖα καὶ αἱ Βαθυαγχέες Ἄλπεις,
αἳ Ῥήνου προχοὰς ἐγγύς ἀποβλέπετε,
μάρτυρες ἀκτίνων, Γερμανικὸς ἃς ἀνέτειλεν
ἀστράπτων Κελτοῖς πουλὺν Ἐνυάλιον.
οἱ δ ἄρα δουπήθησαν ἀολλέες, εἶπε δ Ἐνυώ
Ἄρει τοιαύταις χερσὶν ὀφειλόμεθα.[39]

O Pyrennes and you deep-valleyed Alps that look down on the nearby sources of the Rhine, you are witnesses of the lightning that Germanicus flashes forth as he smites the Celts with the thunderbolts of war. In masses the foe fell, and Enyo said to Ares, "It is to such hands as these that our help is due." (transl. by W. R. Paton)

The text contains a mention of a great victory of Germanicus over barbarians (Κελτοί). Some scholars suppose it could be a reference to the suppression of a rebellion of some Gallic tribes in AD 13 which would have resulted in Germanicus being awarded his first imperatorial acclamation,[40] but R. Syme is sceptical of such an interpretation, pointing out that the only rebellion in Gaul during that time, mentioned by Velleius Paterculus (2.121.1), took place either toward the end of AD 11 or at the beginning of 12 and was pacified by Tiberius himself. Besides, in Syme's opinion suppressing a rebellion would have been too trivial a reason to grant an acclamation. Furthermore, he rightly notes

38 Brunt (1974), 178 (n50); Barnes (1974), 25 f.; Syme (1978), 58–63. Similar notions are expressed by Hurlet (1997), 171; Dalla Rosa (2014), 238 (n24); and Rivière (2016), 134, who all think Germanicus' first acclamation was a result of a victorious campaign in Germania which took place in AD 13 or early in 14.

39 *Anth. Pal.* 9.283.

40 See Barnes (1974), 25.

that in the texts of Greek authors the word Κελτοί can also mean Germans.[41] Therefore it is just as possible that it were Germanicus' victories over Germanic tribes that the poem actually praised. Unfortunately, nothing more can be said about it, neither what campaign was meant nor when it happened, so Syme's guess that the epigram refers to Germanicus' campaign of 14–16 is pure speculation as well.[42] In fact, the brief mention in the poem may just as well refer to an expedition of Germanicus carried out in Augustus' reign as to one of those conducted after Tiberius rose to power.[43]

The latest date for Germanicus' first acclamation has recently been put forward by D. Faoro, who believes that it may have been occasioned by a campaign which supposedly took place in the summer of the year 14, that is, shortly before Augustus' death.[44] I find his proposition unconvincing, since we learn from Tacitus that Germanicus spent most of that year in Gaul carrying out the census, and that it was there that he received the news of Augustus' death. Tacitus also reports that at the moment of the first princeps' death the legions sat idle in their summer camp, which indicates they had not conducted any significant military operations for months.[45] Thus it is most unlikely that in the final weeks before Augustus died, a campaign against the Germans took place which earned Germanicus his first imperatorial acclamation.[46]

As can be seen from the discussion summarized above, any attempts at determining the exact circumstances and date of Germanicus' first imperatorial acclamation can only be hypothetical. One supposition can be made with considerable likelihood: that it took place in the last few years of Augustus' reign and was occasioned by a campaign in Germania. Of the suggestions adduced above, I find AD 13 the most convincing, but with the sources silent, and especially with Cassius Dio's account for the second half of that year missing, it is impossible to say exactly what campaign against whom earned Germanicus the title *imperator* for the first time.[47]

---

41   See e. g. Cass. Dio 55.13.2; 28.5; 56.25.2.

42   Syme (1978), 58 f.

43   In an article published a year later, Syme (1979), 318 pointed out the epigram could allude to the Alpine expedition of Drusus the Elder in 15 BC; as we know from Suetonius (*Claud*.1.3), Drusus was posthumously granted the title of *Germanicus*. It is a dubious hypothesis; the potential reader could hardly be expected to guess the name *Germanicus* there meant Drusus the Elder rather than his son Germanicus Caesar. I also believe that if Crinagoras had wanted to allude here to the expedition against the Alpine peoples, he would not have omitted Tiberius, who led the campaign jointly with Drusus.

44   For detailed arguments in favour of that dating, see Faoro (2016), 210–212.

45   Tac. *Ann*. 1.31.2–4; 33.1; 35.1. See also Wolters (2014–2015), 206.

46   See Timpe (1968), 36–38.

47   See Wolters (2014–2015), 204 f. *Contra* Ziółkowski (see his article in this book), who argues that Germanicus received his first acclamation for the victorious campaign against the Marsi which took place in the autumn of AD 14. I am not convinced; I do not think it likely for Tacitus not to mention Germanicus' first salutation if his account of Germanicus' campaigns on the Rhine does take meticulous note of both Germanicus' second salutation of AD 15 and Tiberius' eighth of AD 16. See Tac. *Ann*. 1.58.5–6; 2.18.2.

To answer the question posed in the title of this article, it can therefore be said that Germanicus carried out military operations in proconsular rank under both Augustus and Tiberius. He earned his first independent *imperium* in 11 and, armed with it, acted in the Gallic provinces and Germania, first jointly with Tiberius in AD 11, and then from AD 13 on as the commander general of the Rhine legions. The campaign of AD 13 most likely brought him his first imperatorial acclamation; then after Augustus' death and until the year 16, he conducted campaigns in Germania as a proconsul and *auspiciis Tiberii*.

Bibliography

Barnes, Timothy D. (1974): "The Victories of Augustus". In: Journal of Roman Studies 64, 21–26.

Bean, George E. (1973): "New Inscription, no 50". In: Cook, John M. (ed.): The Troad. An Archaeological and Topographical Study. Oxford: Oxford University Press, 412.

Bringmann, Klaus (1977): "*Imperium proconsulare* und Mitregentschaft im frühen Prinzipat". In: Chiron 7, 219–238.

Brunt, Peter (1974): "C. Fabricius Tuscus and an Augustan Dilectus". In: Zeitschrift für Papyrologie und Epigraphik 13, 161–185.

Campbell, Brian (1994): The Roman Army, 31 BC–AD 337. A Sourcebook. London–New York: Routledge.

Dalla Rosa, Alberto (2014): *Cura et tutela*. Le origini del potere imperiale sulle province proconsolari. Stuttgart: Franz Steiner Verlag.

Faoro, Davide (2016): "Nota sulla cronologia delle acclamazioni imperatorie XV–XXI di Augusto e III–VII di Tiberio Cesare". In: Zeitschrift für Papyrologie und Epigraphik 199, 208–212.

Goodyear, Frank R. (1972): The Annals of Tacitus. Books 1–6, edited with a commentary. vol. 1: Annals 1.1–54. Cambridge: Cambridge University Press.

Goodyear, Frank R. (1981): The Annals of Tacitus. Books 1–6, edited with a commentary. vol. 2: Annals 1.55–81 and Annals 2, Cambridge: Cambridge University Press.

Hurlet, Frédéric (1994): "Recherches sur la durée de l'imperium des 'co-régents' sous les principats d' Auguste et de Tibère". In: Cahiers du Centre G. Glotz 5, 255–289.

Hurlet, Frédéric (1997): Les Collègues du Prince sous Auguste et Tibère. De la Légalité Républicaine à la Légitimité Dynastique. Roma: Collection de L'École Française de Rome.

Kienast, Dietmar et al. (2017): Römische Kaisertabelle. Grundzüge einer römischen Kaiserchronologie (6. Auflage) Darmstadt: Wissenschaftliche Buchgesellschaft.

Koestermann, Erich (1957): "Die Feldzüge des Germanicus 14–16 n. Chr.". In: Historia 6, 429–479.

Koestermann, Erich (1963): Cornelius Tacitus, Annalen, vol. 1, Buch 1–3. Heidelberg: Carl Winter.

Lebek, Wolfgang D. (1991): "Der Proconsulat des Germanicus und die auctoritas des Senats. Tab. Siar. Frg. I 22–24". In: Zeitschrift für Papyrologie und Epigraphik 87, 103–124.

Mommsen, Theodor (1888): Römisches Staatsrecht, vol. 2. Leipzig: S. Herzel.

Orth, Wolfgang (1978): "Zur Fabricius-Tuscus-Inschrift aus Alexandreia/Troas". In: Zeitschrift für Papyrologie und Epigraphik 28, 57–60.

Rich, John W. (1990): Cassius Dio. The Augustan Settlement (Roman History 53–55.9). Warminster: Aris&Phillips Classical Texts.

Rich, John. W. (1999): "Drusus and the Spolia Opima". In: Classical Quarterly 49 (2), 544–555.

Rivière, Yann (2016): Germanicus. Prince romain 15 av. J.-C. – 19 apr. J.-C. Paris: Perrin.

Rose, Charles B. (1997): Dynastic Commemoration and Imperial Portraiture in the Julio-Claudian Period. Cambridge: Cambridge University Press.

Sawiński, Paweł (2018): The Succession of Imperial Power under the Julio-Claudian Dynasty (30 BC – AD 68). Berlin: Peter Lang.

Speidel, Michael P. (1975): "Germanicus' Gardereiter. Ein neues Zeugnis zur Geschichte der niederrheinischen Ala praetoria und zur Entstehung der Singulares". In: Germania 53, 165–166.

Swan, Peter M. (2004): The Augustan Succession. An Historical Commentary on Cassius Dio's Roman History Books 55–56 (9 B.C. – A.D. 14). Oxford: Oxford University Press.

Syme, Ronald (1978): History in Ovid. Oxford: Oxford University Press.

Syme, Ronald (1979): "Some Imperatorial Salutations". In: Phoenix 33(4), 308–329.

Timpe, Dieter (1968): Der Triumph des Germanicus. Untersuchungen zu den Feldzügen der Jahre 14–16 n. Chr. in Germanien. Bonn: R. Habelt.

Vervaet, Frederik J. (2020): "*Subsidia dominationi.* The Early Careers of Tiberius Claudius Nero and Nero Claudius Drusus Revisited". In: Klio 102(1), 121–201.

Wolters, Reinhard (2014–2015): "Germanicusfeldzüge vor den Germanicusfeldzügen? Annalistische Rekonstruktionen *ante excessum divi Augusti*". In: Palamedes 9–10, 197–209.

The Egyptian Voyage of Germanicus*
An Egyptological Perspective

FILIP TATERKA

Keywords: Germanicus in Egypt, ancient tourism, Roman Egypt, ancient monuments

When in AD 17 Germanicus left Rome to set out for his journey to the East, where he was sent "in order to set the provinces beyond the sea in order",[1] he did not expect that he would never come back to the City. Although the main aim of Germanicus' mission seems to have been to deal with the problem of the royal succession in Armenia and to strengthen the easternmost limits of the Roman Empire,[2] on his way he stopped at various historically important sites. Among these Egypt undoubtedly presents a most special case as it was not only the longest of Germanicus' stops in his Eastern mission,

---

*   I should like to thank Paweł Sawiński for having invited me to the symposium on Germanicus and to contribute to this volume, which proved quite a challenge for a simple Egyptologist like me. I am indebted for both the kind reception in Kalisz and for all support in preparing this paper. My thanks go also to Michał Baranowski, Nicola Barbagli, and Adam Ziółkowski for their critical remarks and comments on the earlier draft of this paper as well as for numerous discussions we had on the way, and to Angela McDonald for revising my English. It goes without saying that I remain solely responsible for all interpretations as well as for all possible errors. The work on this paper was possible thanks to the support of the Foundation for Polish Science, which granted me the scholarship START in 2019.

1   [ἐ]πι τὸ καταστήσασθαι τὰς πέραν θαλάσσης επαρχίας: pOxy. 25 2435, rt., 10; Greek text after Weingärtner (1969), 73; cf. also Tac. *Ann.* 2.43 (*tunc decreto patrum permissae Germanico provinciae, quae mari dividuntur, maiusque imperium, quoquo adisset, quam iis qui sorte aut missu principis obtinerent* – "Then by a decree of the Senate the provinces which are divided by the sea were entrusted to Germanicus together with greater power, wherever he would go, than that of those who obtained them by a lot or by the princeps' dispatch"; all references to Tacitus' *Annals* follow the edition by Koestermann (1965) and TS. 1.15–16 (*proco(n)s(ul) missus in transmarinas pro[uincias] in conformandis iis regnisque eiusdem tractus ex mandatis Ti(berii) C⌈a⌉esaris Au[g(usti)]* – "Proco(n)-s(ul) sent into the transmarine pro[vinces] to set these in order together with the kingdoms of the same region by the order of Ti(berius) C⌈a⌉esar Au[g(ustus)]"; edition: Sánchez-Ostiz Guitérrez [1999]). All translations of ancient texts included in this paper were made by the author.

2   Tac. *Ann.* 2.43. For Germanicus' exploits in Armenia, see also Rivière (2016), 301–305.

but also it is his Egyptian voyage which is discussed in greatest detail by our main source on Germanicus' journey, namely the account of Tacitus, who dedicated three chapters of Book 2 of his *Annals* to Germanicus' stay in Egypt, out of a total of 14 relating his Eastern mission.[3]

Germanicus' travel to Egypt has inspired many discussions in scholarly literature, although two main interpretative approaches to the issue seem to dominate nowadays. The first one is a purely historical approach, which pervades especially in older literature, whose aim is to define the motives of Germanicus which led him to visit Egypt as well as the exact course of events which took place during his stay in the ancient land of the pharaohs.[4] More recent studies present a historical literary approach: that way, instead of trying to define what actually happened while Germanicus was visiting Egypt, scholars concentrate rather on how his Egyptian journey was presented in Tacitus' account and what might have been the possible motives of the Roman historian to recount it in such a way.[5]

As any discussion on the way a historical event is portrayed in a narrative source cannot be detached from the actual event, the aim of the present study is an attempt to combine both approaches, which in my opinion may lead to some interesting insights into the long-discussed problem of Germanicus' travel to Egypt.

Scholars have long noticed that Germanicus' portrayal in the *Annals* is overwhelmingly positive, which is rather surprising since Tacitus hardly ever speaks of the members of the imperial family in such terms.[6] Even if Tacitus knew of other traditions presenting Germanicus in a less favourable manner (as can be deduced from *Ann.* 1.35[7]) his overall image in Tacitus' work is close to an ideal. This stands in neat contrast to the Tacitean portrayal of Tiberius, who is described as a suspicious and malicious tyrant.[8] According to Tacitus, Tiberius preferred his own son Drusus to Germanicus[9] and his jealousy with respect to his adoptive son grew over time. Unfortunately, we

---

3   Germanicus' Eastern mission in recounted in Tac. *Ann.* 2.53–73 (excluding 2.62–68 which concern other matters), while his Egyptian voyage is related in 2.59–61.

4   The best illustration of this approach is the detailed study by Dieter Georg Weingärtner (1969), which has become an indispensable point of reference for all later studies on Germanicus' journey to Egypt.

5   See e. g. Gissel (2001), 278–301; Kelly (2010), 221–237; Manolaraki/Augoustakis (2012), 386–402; Ferenczi (2018), 269–276; Woods (2021), 1–14.

6   Gissel (2001), 279–281.

7   Rutland (1987), 155.

8   For this, see Shotter (1968), 194–214; O'Gorman (2000), 46–105; Williams (2009), 117–130. For the image of Tiberius in the works of Roman historians, see Baar (1990).

9   Tac. *Ann.* 2.43: *Tiberius ut proprium et sui sanguinis Drusum fovebat: Germanico alienatio patrui amorem apud ceteros auxerat, et quia claritudine materni generis anteibat, avum M. Antonium, avunculum Augustum ferens* ("Tiberius favoured Drusus as his own son, and as of his own blood: but the insensibility of the paternal uncle increased the love for Germanicus among the others as well as the fact that he surpassed Drusus due to the renown of his mother's family, having Mark Antony for a grandfather and Augustus for a maternal uncle".)

The Egyptian Voyage of Germanicus 27

are unable to say how strong Tiberius' negative feelings for Germanicus were or if he actually had such feelings for his adoptive son in the first place. Nevertheless, the position one accepts with respect to the existence of a disagreement between Tiberius and Germanicus influences the way one interprets the motives of the latter's Egyptian journey.

According to Tacitus, Tiberius was dissatisfied by Germanicus' visit to Egypt because his adoptive son disrespected the arrangements of Augustus (*instituta Augusti*) prohibiting senators and illustrious equites from entering Egypt without the princeps' permission.[10] The question of whether Germanicus was allowed to enter Egypt without prior consent from the princeps is certainly one of the most vividly discussed in the scholarly literature pertaining to his Eastern mission.[11] According to the classical interpretation, Egypt was singled out by Augustus in order to prevent a situation in which Rome could be threatened by withholding grain supplies. That way, all the senators and equites wishing to visit Egypt needed to obtain a special permission from the princeps himself,[12] which, according to Tacitus, Germanicus failed to even ask for. This leads to the question of whether he unconsciously ignored his duty towards his adoptive father or intentionally disobeyed Tiberius.

It does not seem likely, however, that Germanicus spontaneously decided to go to Egypt while already being in the East, as it would have been quite a detour, so his Egyptian journey must have been planned from the very beginning.[13] If so, it seems equally unlikely that Tiberius was unaware of Germanicus' plans which he must have accepted. As we shall see, the edicts issued by Germanicus in Egypt seem to attest to his loyalty to Tiberius, so it does not seem probable that he could have disobeyed a direct order of the princeps prohibiting him to enter the ancient land of the pharaohs. That is, of course, if there ever was such an order as in his other work, *The Histories*, Tacitus states that Egypt was kept as the property of the imperial house,[14] and since Germanicus was the member of the latter, he must have been exempted from the prohibition against entering Egypt allegedly issued by Augustus.[15] It seems therefore that

10   Tac. *Ann.* 2.59; Cass. Dio 51.17.1; Weingärtner (1969), 29–33.
11   For the summary of the views on this problem, see Hennig (1972), 349–365.
12   Levi (1924), 231–235; Hennig (1972), 351–353. Cf., however, Solazzi (1928), 296–302.
13   It is interesting to note that Germanicus might not have been the only Roman general to have visited Egypt during his Eastern mission as according to Oros. (7.3.4–5) the land of the pharaohs was visited earlier by Caius Caesar, Augustus' adopted son. See Arnaud (1994), 229–232. It is possible, however, that Orosius' assertion that Caius Caesar stayed in Egypt for some time results from the author's misinterpretation of Suet. *Aug.* 93.4, which he explicitly refers to, an error quite typical of Orosius (Michał Baranowski, personal communication). This would explain why Caius Caesar's voyage to Egypt is otherwise unattested (although his Eastern mission is mentioned by several authors) and any details thereof remain unknown.
14   Tac. *Hist.* 1.11.
15   It is possible that the story is artificially transposed into the past by Tacitus from the time of Vespasian who actually did order a blockade of the grain destined for Rome. Cf. Tac. *Hist.* 2.82; Ash

Germanicus not only had a right to visit Egypt whenever he wished, but, moreover, in this particular case, the princeps was fully aware of his plan to visit this province.[16]

On the other hand, however, Suetonius' account seems to indicate that eventually Tiberius did feel dissatisfied with his adoptive son's visit to Egypt. According to this author, "He [i. e. Tiberius] complained to the senate that he [i. e. Germanicus] went to Alexandria without consulting him while there was an immense and sudden famine".[17] How should we interpret this statement? According to Tacitus, after having arrived at Alexandria in early AD 19 (*M. Silano L. Norbano consulibus*) Germanicus "reduced the prices of the crops by opening the granaries".[18] In fact Tacitus informs us that it was precisely "care for the province" which was used by Germanicus as a pretext to visit Egypt in the first place (*cura provinciae praetendebatur*). This suggests that there were indeed some problems in Egypt, or at least in Alexandria, which Germanicus had to handle immediately upon his arrival at the city.[19] Some scholars have suggested that Germanicus' actions in Alexandria caused a drastic raise of grain prices in Rome, hence the critique expressed by Tiberius against his adoptive son, announced in the senate.[20] It has been rightly pointed out, however, that Germanicus did not touch the reserves of grain destined to be sent out to Rome, which would have been indeed a capital offence; instead, he released the grain stocks destined for the local population in Alexandria.[21] Whatever Germanicus did or did not do in Egypt thus had no influence on grain prices in the capital of the Empire.[22]

(2009), 95; for the date of Tacitean account on Germanicus' visit to Egypt, see Syme (1958), 470–472; Goodyear (1981), 387–393. I am indebted to Michał Baranowski for this suggestion.

16 A different interpretation was proposed by Goodyear (1981), 378 f., who suggests that Germanicus consciously disobeyed Tiberius due to the unhappy personal relationship between the two men, who could never truly understand each other. Yet another one was suggested by Capponi (2020), 126–131, who believes in the spontaneous nature of Germanicus' travel. According to her, Germanicus decided to go to Egypt after hearing the news of the fate of the prefect of Egypt Lucius Seius Strabo, who unexpectedly died on his way back to Egypt from Rome, where he was summoned to explain himself for putting Egypt in a state of economic crisis. According to Capponi, such a scenario explains why no prefect of Egypt is mentioned in our sources as it is Germanicus who acts as a prefect *interim* before the appointment of Caius Galerius in 19/20. Such a scenario is indeed ingenious, but rather speculative. Even if Capponi's new reconstruction of the succession of the prefects of Egypt is accepted (which is far from being proven), it does not necessarily mean that Lucius Seius Strabo's supposed unexpected death affected Germanicus' decision to go to Egypt in any way as the visit might have been planned in advance.

17 Suet. *Tib.* 52.2.

18 Tac. *Ann.* 2.59. The famine in Alexandria is corroborated also by the testimony of Flavius Josephus who additionally indicates that Germanicus' actions in Alexandria did not encompass the Jewish population of the city (Ios. *C. Ap.* 2.63).

19 Weingärtner (1969), 91–99.

20 Cichorius (1922), 382–385.

21 Van Ootenghem (1959), 250 f.

22 A different opinion was expressed by Capponi (2020), 131, who believes that Germanicus' actions in Alexandria could have destabilised the Empire and that Tiberius was justified in his dissatisfac-

It seems that Germanicus was extremely well received by the inhabitants of Alexandria, or at least by the Greek part of the city's population. This might have been partly caused by the respect which the inhabitants of Egypt had shown towards the members of the ruling family and partly by the rather easy-going behaviour of Germanicus as described by Tacitus. Although the author of the *Annals* claims that Germanicus consciously emulated Scipio Africanus,[23] it is noteworthy that he earlier stated that Germanicus presented this same kind of attitude towards the inhabitants of Athens in order to show respect for their ancient and honourable culture.[24] And such an attitude of one of the most powerful men in the Mediterranean world must have easily won him sympathy among both the Athenians and Alexandrians.[25] Moreover, the Egyptian material corroborates that Germanicus' behaviour is more than just a literary creation of Tacitus. Both pOxy. 25 2435, rt., and pSB 1 3924 (the so-called "Acclamation Edict") testify to the homage paid by the inhabitants of Alexandria towards Germanicus.[26] Moreover, the spontaneous nature of this homage is suggested by the testimony of a later edict by Claudius who, addressing the Alexandrians, states what follows:

φύσει μὲν εὐσεβεῖς περὶ τοὺς Σεβαστοὺς ὑπάρχοντες, ὡς ἐκ πολλῶν μοι γέγονε γνόριμον, ἐξέρετως δὲ περὶ τὸν ἐμὸν οἶκον καὶ σπουδάσαντες καὶ σπουδασθέντος, ὧν εἶνα τὸ τελευταῖον εἴπωι παρεὶς τὰ ἄλλα μέγειστός ἐστι μάρτυς ούμος ἀδελφὸς Γερμανικὸς Καῖσαρ γνησιωτέραις ὑμᾶς φωναῖς προσαγορεύσας[27].

By nature you are truly reverent towards the Augusti, as I came to know from many examples; in particular, you were eagerly interested in my house and your interest was reciprocated, of which, to name but one last instance, leaving others aside, my brother Germanicus Caesar, addressing you in unfeigned speeches, is the greatest witness.

---

tion. For a detailed analysis of Germanicus' actions in Alexandria with respect to grain prices, see Goodyear (1981), 372 f., 376 f.

23 Tac. *Ann.* 2.59; Weingärtner (1969), 99–108.

24 Tac. *Ann.* 2.53. In doing so Germanicus emulated not only Scipio Africanus, but also Mark Antony: Shuttleworth Kraus (2009), 112, and even Tiberius himself, who is said to have behaved in a very similar way during his "retirement" at Rhodes in 6 BC: Suet. *Tib.* 13.1; cf. Levick (1972), 779–813; Zanker (1988), 227. It has been suggested that the figure of Scipio Africanus is in fact a façade for Mark Antony whom Germanicus was actually emulating: Goodyear (1981), 377, although it seems rather doubtful. For Germanicus' respect for other cultures as portrayed by Tacitus, see Woods (2021), 9–13.

25 Germanicus' care for the local population is especially visible in the so-called "Requisition Edict" from pSB, 1 3924, 1–30, which forbids unauthorised requisitions of property on his behalf. For the text, see Hunt/Edgar (1934), 76, no. 211. The official requisitions on account of Germanicus' visit in Egypt are otherwise attested by oLouvre 9004; Wilcken (1963), 490 f., no. 413. See also Weingärtner (1969), 122–136.

26 For these texts, see Weingärtner (1969), 73–90, 108–119.

27 PLond. (1912), 23–27: Greek text after Hunt/Edgar (1934), 80, no. 212. The text dates from AD 41.

All these honours shown to Germanicus by the people of Alexandria[28] were consistently declined by him as is attested by his "Acclamation Edict" in which he states:

Γερμανικὸς Καῖσαρ Σεβας[τ]οῦ υἱὸς θεοῦ Σεβαστοῦ υἱωνὸς ανθύπατος λέγει· τὴν μὲν εὔνοιαν ὑμῶν, ἥν ἀεὶ ἐπιδείκνυσθε ὅταν με εἴδητε, ἀποδέχομαι, τὰς δὲ ἐπιφθόνου[ς] ἐμοὶ καὶ ἰσοθέους ἐκφωνήσεις ὑμῶν ἐξ [ἄ]παντος παραιτοῦμαι. πρέπουσι γὰρ μόνῳ τῶι σωτῆρι ὄντως καὶ εὐεργέτη τοῦ σύνπαντος τῶν ἀνθρώπων γένους, τῷ ἐμῷ πατρὶ καὶ τῇ μητρὶ αὐτοῦ, ἐμῇ δὲ μάμμῃ. τὰ δὲ ἡμέτερα ε[...] ἐστίν τῆς ἐκείνων με μὴ πολλάκις ὑμεῖν ἐνφανίζεσθαι[29].

Germanicus Caesar, son of Augus[t]us, grandson of the divine Augustus, proconsul declares: I gladly accept your favour, which you constantly show whenever you see me, but I refuse to hear [a]ltogether your acclamations which are despicable to me and suitable for a god. For they are appropriate exclusively to the one who is the saviour and benefactor of humankind in its entirety, my father and his mother, my grandmother. But our [...] is [...] their divinity, so if you do not obey me, you will force me to show myself to you not too often.

It has sometimes been suggested that Germanicus left in Egypt some inscriptions in which his name was encircled by the cartouche.[30] This would be an important piece of evidence for determining Germanicus' attitude towards Tiberius, as putting one's name in a cartouche was a strictly royal prerogative.[31] In the reality of the Roman Egypt it means that the only person allowed to inscribe his name in the cartouche would basically be the princeps himself.[32] Germanicus putting his name in the cartouche would

28   Hausmann (1995), 326 f., suggests that these honours found their expression also in the form of a statue of the type *capite velato* which was posthumously erected in Alexandria (statue Tübingen 90.8603), although this is uncertain as the statue might equally well represent Tiberius, as originally suggested. One should also mention a dedicatory inscription commissioned by three *magistri Larum Augusti*, most likely coming from the Egyptian capital, which evokes the name of Germanicus. Weingärtner (1969), 119–121.

29   PSB 1 3924, 31–45: Greek text after Hunt/Edgar (1934), 76–78, no. 211.

30   Poethke (1977), col. 553.

31   In the pharaonic period the two names of the fivefold royal titulary (the so-called throne and birth names) are inscribed in cartouches. From the Middle Kingdom on, royal wives and daughters also have their names inscribed in cartouches: von Beckerath (1999), 27–29. The only instance that I am aware of in which a royal son has his name encircled by a cartouche is Amenmose, the eldest son of Thutmose I of the 18th dynasty: Loyrette (1992), pl. XXIV, but the reasons behind this are obscure. In later periods the God's Adoratrices of Amun at Thebes inscribe their names in cartouches. Occasionally some gods can also have their names inscribed in cartouches, which emphasises their royal aspect as the ultimate sovereigns of the universe: Kaplony (1980), cols 610–626.

32   The only known exceptions are Sabina, wife of Hadrian, and Julia Domna, wife of Septimius Severus: Hoffmann (2015), 139–156. Rare instances of imperial sons having their names inscribed within a cartouche, (e. g. joint cartouches of Marcus Aurelius and his son Commodus in *Esna* nos 596, 597, 606, 616, 625, and 631, with other variants in *Esna* nos 567, 577, and 584 or *Esna* no. 496 representing the family of Septimius Severus, including the princeps himself, his wife Julia Domna, and their sons Caracalla and Geta, all four with their names in cartouches. Cf. Sauneron (1975) and (2009),

thus have been usurping a royal prerogative and declaring himself a living incarnation of the god on earth to openly challenge Tiberius' power or, if he had acted with the princeps' consent, it would have meant that Tiberius officially appointed him to be a co-regent, at least in the eastern part of the Empire.[33] Closer analysis of the alleged cartouches of Germanicus revealed, however, that none of them actually belongs to him[34] and the demotic document which was once believed to contain the date of "regnal year 1 under Germanicus"[35] not only does not name Germanicus but also does not bear a date at all.[36]

All the aforementioned sources seem to indicate that Germanicus was eager to demonstrate his loyalty to Tiberius whenever possible, be it out of political calculation or natural modesty. So why do we read in Tacitus' and in Suetonius' accounts that the princeps was dissatisfied with his adoptive son's journey to Alexandria? Perhaps it was not the voyage itself but the unfortunate circumstances of it, which coincided with the famine in Alexandria, which could not have been predicted when Germanicus set out from Rome. Although he does not seem to have intentionally transgressed his rights in anything he did in Egypt, what he actually did is one thing, and how it was later related to Tiberius (not necessarily by people well-disposed to Germanicus) is quite another story.[37]

But if the handling of the problems encountered by Germanicus in Alexandria was only a pretext to get there, then what was the actual motive of his journey to the ancient land of the pharaohs? As it is the account of Tacitus which is our main source for Germanicus' Egyptian voyage, it seems necessary to quote the relevant passages from his *Annals in extenso*:

> *M. Silano L. Norbano consulibus Germanicus Aegyptum proficiscitur cognoscendae antiqui-*
> *tatis. sed cura provinciae praetendebatur, levavitque apertis horreis pretia frugum multaque in*

---

result from the fact that these sons must have already belonged to the imperial college to some extent. I am much indebted to Nicola Barbagli for a discussion on this point as well as for having provided me with the bibliographical references cited in this footnote.

33   For Roman co-regencies and the ways they are reflected in Egyptian material, see Murnane (1977), 105–109.

34   Dils (1994), 347–350 rightly pointed out that the alleged cartouches of Germanicus belonged to other personages, as the epithet *Germanicus* formed part of the official titulary of Caligula, Claudius, Nero, Domitian, and Trajan. Cf. Grenier (1989), 23–35, 40–45, 47–56; von Beckerath (1999), 252–259.

35   Wildung (1990), 220.

36   Vleeming (2011), 630–632. I owe this reference to Joachim Friedrich Quack.

37   Arnaud (1994), 232–236 suggests that Tiberius' dissatisfaction was caused by Germanicus' overuse of his authority as imperial envoy, having entered Alexandria (and not the province of Egypt as such to which he was perfectly authorised) without the emperor's explicit consent. On the other hand, Woods (2021), 5–9, being interested more in Germanicus' Egyptian voyage as a literary device than in what actually happened, argues that Tacitus used the episode as the final reason for Tiberius to order the death of his adoptive son.

vulgus grata usurpavit: sine milite incedere, pedibus intectis et pari cum Graecis amictu, P. Scip-
ionis aemulatione, quem eadem factitavisse apud Siciliam quamvis flagrante adhuc Poenorum
bello accepimus. Tiberius cultu habituque eius lenibus verbis perstricto acerrime increpuit, quod
contra instituta Augusti non sponte principis Alexandriam introisset. nam Augustus inter alia
dominationis arcana, vetitis nisi permissu ingredi senatoribus aut equitibus Romanis inlustri-
bus, seposuit Aegyptum, ne fame urgeret Italiam, quisquis eam provinciam claustraque terrae ac
maris quamvis levi praesidio adversum ingentes exercitus insedisset.

Sed Germanicus, nondum comperto profectionem eam incursari, Nilo subvehebatur, orsus oppi-
do a Canopo, condidere id Spartani ob sepultum illic rectorem navis Canopum, qua tempestate
Menelaus Graeciam repetens diversum ad mare terramque Libyam deiectus. inde proximum
amnis os dicatum Herculi, quem indigenae ortum apud se et antiquissimum perhibent eosque,
qui postea pari virtute fuerint, in cognomentum eius adscitos; mox visit veterum Thebarum
magna vestigia. et manebant structis molibus litterae Aegyptiae, priorem opulentiam complex-
ae; iussusque e senioribus sacerdotum patrium sermonem interpretari referebat habitasse exerci-
tu regem Rhamsen Libya Aethiopia Medisque et Persis et Bactriano ac Scytha potitum quasque
terras Suri Armeniique et contingui Cappadoces colunt, inde Bithynum, hinc Lyc<i>um ad
mare imperio tenuisse. legebantur et indicta gentibus tributa, pondus argenti et auri, numerus
armorum equorumque et dona templis ebur atque odores, quasque copias frumenti et omnium
utensilium quaeque natio penderet, haud minus magnifica quam nunc vi Parthorum aut poten-
tia Romana iubentur.

Ceterum Germanicus aliis quoque miraculis intendit animum, quorum praecipua fuere Mem-
nonis saxea effigies, ubi radiis solis iacta est, vocalem sonum reddens, disiectasque inter et vix
pervias arenas instar montium eductae pyramides certamine et opibus regum, lacusque effossa
humo, superfluentis Nili receptacula; atque alibi angustiae et profunda altitudo, nullis inquiren-
tium spatiis penetrabilis. exin ventum Elephantinen ac Syenen, claustra olim Romani imperii,
quod nunc rubrum ad mare patescit[38].

In the consulship of Marcus Silanus and Lucius Nurbanus, Germanicus set out to Egypt
in order to explore antiquity. But his pretext was care for the province and he reduced
the prices of the crops by opening the granaries, and adopted many habits pleasing to the
crowd: walking around without soldiers, with uncovered feet,[39] and in clothing identical
to that of the Greeks, emulating Publius Scipio who, as we are told, did the same in Sicily,
even though the war with the Punics was still flaming. Tiberius, having expressed his disapproval of his comportment and clothing in mild words, reproached him in the fiercest
manner that contrary to the arrangements of Augustus, he entered Alexandria without the
princeps' consent. For Augustus, among other secrets of his rule, having prohibited senators or the illustrious Roman equites to enter it without permission, singled out Egypt,

---

38   Tac. *Ann.* 2.59–61. For a detailed commentary on this passage, see Goodyear (1981), 372–393.
39   I. e. he wore sandals (*crepidae*) instead of boots (*calcei*), the habit being associated with Greeks
     rather than Romans; Goodyear (1981), 377.

so that no-one who would have kept this province and the keys to the land and the sea, even with small protective force against a great army, could threaten Italy with famine. But Germanicus, not knowing yet that this journey was criticised, sailed up the Nile, starting from the town of Canopus. The Spartans founded it because Canopus, the helmsman of the ship, was buried at that place, when Menelaus, while coming back to Greece, was thrown by a storm to the opposite sea and the land of Libya. Thence, he went to the nearest mouth of the river dedicated to Hercules who, as the natives testify, was born among them and is the most ancient Hercules, and those who later were of the same valour, adapted his cognomen; next, he visited the great remains of the old Thebes. And there remained Egyptian characters on the massive structures, which summarised its former splendour: one of the senior priests, who was told to interpret the speech of his forefathers, related that once there were seven hundred thousand men of military age living in Thebes and that with this army king Rhamses gained control over Libya, Ethiopia as well as over the Medes, Persians, Bactrians, and Scythians, and held under his sway those lands which are inhabited by the Syrians and Armenians as well as by their neighbours, the Cappadocians, up to the Bithynian sea on the one side and to the Lyc<i>an sea on the other. One could also read of the tributes imposed on these peoples, the weight of silver and gold, the number of weapons and horses, and gifts of ivory and aromatic products for the temples as well as of the abundance of the grain and all provisions fetched by every nation, which were not less magnificent than those that are now decreed by the force of the Parthians or by Roman power.

Moreover, Germanicus directed his attention also to other marvels, the most significant of these being the stone image of Memnon, giving back vocal sounds after it has been smitten by the sunrays, and the pyramids scattered through hardly accessible areas in a manner of mountains, raised by the rivalry and wealth of the kings, and the lakes dug in the ground as cisterns for the inundating Nile; elsewhere also canals and depths of such dimension that no measurements of the investigators can penetrate them. Then, he went to Elephantine and Syene, which used to be the border of the Roman empire, which now extends to the Red Sea.

There are some details in Tacitean account which seem indeed striking. Most importantly, Tacitus gives a rather detailed description of Germanicus' travel to Egypt, although it does not seem to have any direct impact on the events recounted later in Book 2. Equally well Tacitus might have included the relation of Germanicus' stay in Egypt in a single paragraph (according to our standards), yet he dedicated as many as three to describe it.[40] And yet Tacitus' account is far from being accurate. Although the historian explicitly states that Germanicus' main aim was to explore antiquity (*cognoscendae antiquitatis*), he lists the actual places visited by Germanicus out of their geo-

---

40   Woods (2021), 2 f.

graphical order.[41] Moreover, in some places, Tacitus indicates nothing but the name of the site where Germanicus stopped, without specifying the actual purpose of the visit. Most strikingly, Tacitus does not relate Germanicus' visit to the tomb of Alexander the Great (which surely must have taken place during his stay in Alexandria[42]) or any impression it must have made on him (as he does for example while relating Germanicus' visit to the site of Actium in *Ann.* 2.53[43]). Moreover, Tacitus completely omits Germanicus' stay in Memphis and his consultation of the oracle of Apis, which is attested by Pliny the Elder.[44] On the other hand, other details within Tacitean account clearly demonstrate that he must have had access to Germanicus' travel journal or a similar source, which enumerated the monuments actually seen by Tiberius' adoptive son,[45] instead of simply mentioning some more or less famous Egyptian monuments which he might or might not have seen on the way.

In order to explain the discrepancies of Tacitus' account scholarly attention shifted from examining the historical reality of Germanicus' Egyptian journey to the study of how it is portrayed by Tacitus. Various interpretations have been put forward in which Tacitus was believed to model his portrayal of Germanicus after the figure of Alexander the Great,[46] to use the Egyptian episode as a complicated meditation on the rise and fall of tyranny and transience of human earthly achievements,[47] to show Germanicus as a tragic hero following the model set by Silius Italicus' presentation of the figure of Hannibal,[48] or to portray his travel to Egypt as a useless waste of time chasing after monuments from an ancient past which had no real bearing on the

---

41 Contra Gissel (2001), 295. The actual order of sites visited by Germanicus is as follows: Alexandria, Canopus, Giza and Memphis, Fayum, Thebes, and Aswan. Although we do not know whether Germanicus visited all of them while proceeding to the southernmost limit of Egypt and then simply returned to Alexandria without any stop, or rather visited some of them while going south and others while returning to the north, Tacitus' account, if followed literally as it stands, would imply that Germanicus shuttled alternately southwards and northwards which is both highly unlikely and impractical.

42 Foertmeyer (1989), 113 rightly points out that in pOxy. 25 2435, rt., 18–22 we can read the following words: "I have already believed that it [i. e. Alexandria] con[stitutes] the most [r]adiant sight, first because o[f] its [he]ro and fou[nd]er, to whom there is a kind of common d[e]b[t] of [tho]se who adhere to the[m], but also through the bene[fac]tions of my grandfather Augustus" (ἤδη δὲ ἡγησάμενος αὐτὴν εἶν[αι] [λ]αμπρότατον θέαμα, τὸ μὲν πρῶτον διὰ τ[ὸν] [ἥ]ρωμα καὶ κτ[ίσ]την, πρὸς ὃν κοινῇ τί ἐστιν ὁ[φ]εί[λημα] [το]ῖς τῶν αὐτ[ῶν] ἀντεχομένοις, ἔπειτα διὰ τὰς εὐε[ργε]σίας τοῦ ἐμοῦ πάππου Σεβαστοῦ·; Greek text after Weingärtner (1969), 73 f. These suggest that Germanicus was eager to see the final resting place of Alexander, despite the opinion of Gissel (2001), 300, who assumes that Tacitus would have mentioned Germanicus' visit to Alexander's tomb, had he made one.

43 Tacitus asserts that the visit at Actium inspired in Germanicus the feelings of both sadness and joy (*tristium laetorumque*) as he was associated with both sides of the conflict, being related to both Octavian and Antony.

44 Plin. *NH* 8.185. Cf. also Solin. 32.19; Amm. 22.14.8.

45 Weingärtner (1969), 15–21; Kelly (2010), 225.

46 Gissel (2001), 278–301.

47 Kelly (2010), 221–237.

48 Manolaraki/Augoustakis (2012), 386–402.

present events.[49] Although each of these interpretations constitutes quite ingenious approach which leads their authors to some interesting and thought-provoking observations, their common weakness is the fact that the supposed allusions allegedly present in Tacitean account are so subtle that they are very difficult to grasp even for a careful historian well versed in classical literature, let alone for ancient Romans, whose level of education is often difficult to define. Of course, Tacitus does connect Germanicus with Alexander the Great, but only at the very end of his account, when he describes the funeral of Tiberius' adoptive son.[50] And even in this case Tacitus presents it in such a way that it is impossible to determine if he shares the view comparing Germanicus to Alexander or just relates how Germanicus was perceived in his own lifetime and upon his death.[51] But had Tacitus wished to compare Germanicus to Alexander, he would have had plenty of occasions to do it in his account and yet he never does.

In order to understand the Tacitean account of Germanicus' travel we have to go back for a moment to what might have really happened. Tacitus explicitly states that Germanicus' care for the province of Egypt was no more than a pretext, while the real motive of his journey was the will to explore antiquity (*cognoscendae antiquitatis*). It has been rightly observed that such an assertion is quite surprising: we would rather expect to find the wish to explore antiquity as a pretext and political reason as the real motive of Germanicus' Egyptian voyage.[52] It is consistent, however, with what Tacitus recounts earlier in Book 2 of his *Annals* concerning Germanicus' visits to historically important places[53] including Actium and Athens (*Ann.* 2.53) as well as Troy (*Ann.* 2.54). Even earlier in Book 1 we are told that while advancing against rebelling tribes in Germania, Germanicus made a detour in order to see the infamous site of the Teutoburg Forest disaster (*Ann.* 1.61–62). In Book 2 Tacitus relates also Germanicus' consultation to the oracle of the Clarian Apollo, which supposedly predicted Germanicus' death in ambiguous words (*per ambages*; *Ann.* 2.54).[54] There is also one point which seems to be underappreciated or even neglected by scholars, namely Tacitus' assertion that Germanicus on his way back from the Propontic cities (which the historian refers to as *veteres locos et fama celebratos*) attempted to behold the mysteries at Samothrace but was driven out from the island by the northern winds encountered on the way (*illum in regressu sacra Samothracum visere nitentem obvii aquilones depulere*; *Ann.* 2.54).

---

49 Ferenczi (2018), 269–276.
50 Tac. *Ann.* 2.73.
51 For a detailed analysis of this passage, see Gissel (2001), 287–290.
52 Capponi (2020), 126.
53 Goodyear (1981), 352 rightly observes that Germanicus did not hurry to reach Syria and Armenia, but made numerous stops on the way in order to visit historical sites and win popularity among the Greeks as a potential future successor of Tiberius.
54 For the oracle of Apollo at Claros, see Goodyear (1981), 358 f.

It seems that it was precisely this same quest for ancient secrets that made Germanicus travel to Egypt. It is noteworthy that Germanicus' Egyptian voyage was in no way related to any of the strategic goals which he was supposed to achieve during his Eastern mission.[55] In theory it is possible that while being in the eastern part of the Empire, Germanicus was informed of the tense economic situation in Alexandria and decided to intervene, using the opportunity to visit one of the most spectacular provinces, but such a scenario is extremely unlikely. It is tempting to suggest that the Egyptian journey must have been planned from the very beginning as a part of Germanicus' quest for ancient and hidden knowledge. It should be stressed, however, that the following lines are not supposed to present an indisputably certain reconstruction of the events, but rather they should be treated as an attempt to revisit the question from a different perspective.

Seeing Germanicus' Egyptian voyage as a quest for hidden knowledge seems to be corroborated by the analysis of Germanicus' itinerary while staying in Egypt. According to Tacitus, Germanicus first arrived at Alexandria and then proceeded to the city of Canopus, whence he went to the south of Egypt. From his account we may infer that he visited the pyramids at Giza[56] (as well as the city of Memphis as attested by the testimony of Pliny the Elder and other sources[57]) and Lake Moeris.[58] Next, he went on to visit the glorious city of Thebes, where he saw the Colossi of Memnon as well as an ancient monument of king Rhamses – as he was assured by one of the elder priests who interpreted the inscriptions for him.

It should be stressed that Germanicus' journey was something far more important than mere sightseeing: it was a true quest for knowledge. Visiting Egypt from its northern- to southernmost borders must have taken at least a couple of weeks or even months.[59] This stands in neat contrast with the actions of Germanicus' direct "predecessors", namely Julius Caesar and Augustus, who limited their stay in Egypt to the city of Alexandria or its immediate vicinity[60] (Augustus is even said to have explicitly declined a proposal to visit the ancient capital of Memphis and to consult the ora-

---

55 Goodyear (1981), 372.
56 Tacitus recounts Germanicus' visit to the pyramids right after the Colossi of Memnon, but nevertheless he must have meant the pyramids at Giza: Weingärtner (1969), 146–149, rather than small pyramids scattered throughout the Theban necropolis. For the latter, see Lehner (1997), 192.
57 Plin. NH, 8.185; Solin. 32.19; Amm. 22.14.8; Weingärtner (1969), 141–146.
58 Germanicus' visit to Lake Moeris can be inferred from the description in Tac. Ann. 2.61, although it should be emphasised that the historian does not explicitly mention the name of this site; Milne (1916), 78; Weingärtner (1969), 149–152.
59 For the exact dates of Germanicus' Egyptian voyage, see Weingärtner (1969), 64–67; Capponi (2020), 123–126. For the realities of the travel by Nile in the preindustrial era, see especially Cooper (2014).
60 According to Suet. Iul. 52.1 Caesar would have visited Egypt almost as far as the border of Ethiopia together with Cleopatra, had not his soldiers refused to follow him.

cle of Apis[61]). Even Alexander the Great did not manage to see all the places visited by Germanicus, as the Macedonian conqueror journeyed exclusively throughout the sites of Lower Egypt.[62] We may suggest that in visiting ancient Egyptian monuments Germanicus realised the wishes of his "predecessors", who were unable to fulfil them for themselves, due to the limited period of time, which they spent in Egypt (and, not unimportantly, in a time of war, which considerably limited the opportunities of Alexander, Caesar, and Octavian for visiting ancient monuments)[63].

One of the most important points of Germanicus' stay in the city of Alexandria must have been a visit to the tomb of Alexander the Great (previously visited also by Caesar and Augustus; the latter is even said to have accidentally broken off Alexander's nose[64]), even if Tacitus does not mention it at all. Perhaps Germanicus visited also other monuments in the city, especially the Library and the lighthouse at Pharos. It would be most interesting to know if Germanicus visited also the tomb of Mark Antony, but unfortunately there is no way to have any certainty in this respect.

Some scholars expressed their surprise at seeing the town of Canopus on the itinerary of an educated Roman such as Germanicus due to the general bad reputation of the city,[65] although the mention of Menelaus' helmsman might hint at the importance of the town for someone interested in the past and any reader of Homer. Nevertheless, the immediate mention of the most ancient of Herculeses[66] by Tacitus suggests that it is precisely the wish to honour the nearby sanctuary of this god at Thonis-Hera-

---

61   Suet. *Aug.* 93.4; Cass. Dio 51.16.4–5. Although Suetonius' account suggests that Augustus did visit some other sites beside Alexandria (*at contra non modo in peregranda Aegypto paulo deflectere ad visendum Apin supersedit* – "However, in traveling over Egypt he not only refrained from slightly changing the route in order to see Apis"), his exact itinerary is impossible to determine. For the travels of important Greek and Roman personages in Egypt, see Foertmeyer (1989), 104–158.

62   According to Curt. 4.7–8, Alexander first visited Pelusium, then proceeded to Memphis, thence he went to the unspecified interior of Egypt, then to the oracle of Amun at Siwa, then to the Lake Mareotis, and then to Memphis for the second time. Arr. *Exped. Alex.* 3.1–5, states that after having arrived at Pelusium, Alexander sent his fleet to Memphis, while he marched with his army to Heliopolis, from whence he eventually got to Memphis. Then he went northwards, to the site of the future Alexandria. Later he visited the oracle of Amun at Siwa to finally come back to Memphis. Plut. *Alex.* 26–27 in turn describes only the founding of Alexandria and visit to the oracle of Amun in the oasis of Siwa. See also Foertmyer (1989), 109; Kelly (2001), 295.

63   It should be added, however, that Germanicus was not the first Roman to visit the southern part of Egypt as there is evidence for Roman visitors on the island of Philae as early as 116 BC; Hillard/ Beness (2001), 22–33; Hillard/Beness (2003), 203–207.

64   Caesar: Lucan *Phars.* 10.14–53; Augustus: Cass. Dio 51.16 4–5.

65   For the negative reputation of Canopus, see Milne (1916), 78; Rivière (2016), 329–331.

66   This motif appears in Hdt. 2.43, cf. Lloyd (1994), 200–205; Heracles/Hercules was identified with Khonsu, one of the Egyptian lunar deities, cf. Brunner (1975), cols 960–963. On the tradition associating Heracles with king Osorcho of the 23rd dynasty (Manetho, fr. 62–63b; cf. *FGrHist* 609 F 19) whom scholars identify with Osorkon IV of Bubastis and Tanis, see von Beckerath (1994), 7 f., Payraudeau (2014), 102 rather than with Osorkon III as previously suggested by Redford (1978–1979), 33–36.

cleion,[67] as the deity was to some extent associated with Alexander the Great,[68] which made Germanicus visit the infamous town of Canopus.[69]

It is quite obvious that in proceeding to the south, Germanicus stopped to visit the pyramids at Giza which even today remain one of the most widely known symbols of ancient Egypt. We often tend to neglect the fact that for the Romans the pyramids were a witness of a long-forgotten past, as the timespan separating Germanicus from the pyramids is actually longer than the one separating our own time from Germanicus'. Unfortunately, Tacitus does not state what Germanicus' (or, for that matter, his own) feelings with respect to the pyramids were, which is a true pity, given the fact that Graeco-Roman opinions on these ancient tombs varied from sublime admiration to complete condemnation.[70]

While in the Memphite area, Germanicus decided to visit the ancient capital of Memphis itself, where he consulted the oracle of Apis. The episode is omitted by Tacitus, but is described by other sources in the following terms:

> *delubra ei gemina, quae vocant thalamos, auguria populorum. alterum intrasse laetum est, in altero dira portendit. responsa privatis dat e manu consulentium cibum capiendo. Germanici Caesaris manus adversatus est haud multo postea exstincti.*[71]

There are twin shrines dedicated to it, which are called thalami, where auguries for the people are performed: if the bull entered one of them, the augury is indicated as favourable, but if it entered the other one, it is indicated as unfavourable. It gives answers to individuals by taking food from the hands of those who consult it. It turned away from the hand of Germanicus Caesar and not long afterwards he died.

> *delubra quibus succedit aut incubat mystice thalamos nominant. dato mina manifestantia de futuris: illud maximum, si de consulentis manu cibum capiat. denique aversatus Germanici Caesaris dexteram prodidit ingruentia, nec multo post Caesar extinctus est.*[72]

The shrines, which it enters or rests in, are mystically called thalami. It gives signs revealing the future: the most important one being if it takes food from the hand of the one who

---

67 Weingärtner (1969), 138–140. For more information on the cult at Thonis-Heracleion, see Goddio (2015), 15–54. For the temple of Heracles/Khonsu, see Goddio (2007), 75–100.

68 According to Arr. *Exped. Alex.* 3.3, Alexander went to the oracle of Amun at Siwa imitating the actions of Perseus and Heracles, his mythical ancestors.

69 Perhaps it should not be underestimated that in the Augustan age Canopus became particularly associated with Mark Antony (Cass. Dio 51.27.2; Ov. *Met.* 15.826–828), Germanicus' grandfather. Could the sojourn in Canopus inspired in him a similar sentiments as those earlier ascribed to him by Tacitus while describing his visit to the site of Actium? It is also interesting to note that Rufinus (*Hist. Eccl.* 11.26), mentions a kind of public school of magical arts that was supposed to exist at Canopus under the pretext of teaching the Egyptian priestly script.

70 Lehner (1997), 38 f.; Curl (2005), 39 f.

71 Plin. *NH* 8.185.

72 Solin. 32.19.

consults it. Indeed, by turning away from the right hand of Germanicus Caesar, it foretold things that threatened him, and not long after that Caesar died.

cumque initiante antistitum numero centum inductus in thalamum esse coeperit sacer, coniec-turis apertis signa rerum futurarum dicitur demonstrare et adeuntes quosdam indiciis auerti uidetur obliquis, ut offerentem cibum aliquando Germanicum Caesarem, sicut lectum est, auer-satus portenderat paulo post euentura[73].

And when it has been introduced by a hundred priests and led into the thalamus-shrine, it begins to be sacred and it is said to demonstrate the signs of future events with clear prophecies and it seems that it turns away from some of those who approach it as, having turned away from Germanicus Caesar, who once offered it food, as it can be read, it indicated what was soon to happen.

In consulting the oracle of Apis, Germanicus followed the example of Alexander the Great, who visited Memphis twice during his stay in Egypt before proceeding to the East for his final confrontation with the Persians.[74] Alexander is also said to have made an offering to Apis,[75] in contrast to Augustus who, according to Suetonius and Cassius Dio, was disinterested in seeing the sacred animal,[76] displaying typically Roman disapproval for Egyptian cults and symbolic role the animals played in them.[77]

Having left Memphis, Germanicus made another stop in the fertile region of Fayum as can be inferred from Tacitus' account, even though the historian does not explicitly evoke the ancient name of the region.[78] Nevertheless, it must have been an important place for Germanicus to visit. Lake Moeris was a natural water basin transformed into a huge reservoir by the rulers of the 12th dynasty,[79] constituting therefore an extant proof of the power of human mind and engineering skills of the Egyptians. Moreover, the site of Hawara, located in the vicinity of Lake Moeris, was renowned for the burial complex of king Amenemhat III. The most impressive part of it was the so-called Labyrinth[80] which was believed to be the seat of hidden knowledge accessible only to the ones who had been initiated in ancient mysteries.[81] It is very likely therefore that

---

73 Amm. 22.14.8.
74 Two visits of Alexander in Memphis are mentioned by Curt. 4.7–8 and Arr. *Exped. Alex.* 3.1–5.
75 Arr. *Exped. Alex.* 3.1.
76 Suet. *Aug.* 93.4; Cass. Dio 51.16.5.
77 Cf. the same feeling of contempt with respect to Egyptian cults expressed in Iuv. 15.1–8; Lucian *Deor. conc.* 10–11. See also Smelik/Hemelrijk (1984), 1852–2000, 2337–2357 Girdvainytė (2015), 91–93.
78 Tac. *Ann.* 2.61; Milne (1916), 78; Weingärtner (1969), 149–152; Ferenczi (2018), 281.
79 Butzer (1976), 36–38.
80 On the Labyrinth, see Lloyd (1970), 81–100; Arnold (1979), 1–9.
81 Hdt. 2.148 claims that the Egyptians refused to show him the subterranean chambers of the Labyrinth where the kings and sacred crocodiles were allegedly buried. This episode seems to be the basis of the later tradition about the mysteries celebrated in the subterranean parts of Egyptian temples and tombs, for which see Assmann (2014), 95–106. It is not without significance that the

40   FILIP TATERKA

Germanicus, who some time earlier wished to behold the mysteries of Samothrace,[82] would have liked to have seen the secrets of the Labyrinth as well.

The next stop on Germanicus' way was the great city of Thebes.[83] Tacitus informs us here that Germanicus visited one of the monuments covered with inscriptions from distant past, which were deciphered for him by one of the elder priests as coming from the reign of king Rhamses. The relevance of this point should not be underestimated: normally we would expect to find here the name of the renowned king Sesostris, who stands as a model for great pharaohs of the past,[84] but instead we find here the name of Rhamses, which indicates that Germanicus must have indeed seen a monument dating from the Ramesside period.[85] This demonstrates that the Tacitean account is a genuine relating of what actually happened while Germanicus was in Thebes, most likely based on Germanicus' travel journal or a similar source.[86] Additionally it testifies to the actual interest of Germanicus in Egyptian antiquities and especially in the texts inscribed on the temple walls which in the opinion of his contemporaries must have borne hidden and mysterious knowledge. Unfortunately, we are unable to say which exact monument Germanicus actually saw or even if Tacitus' account refers to a single monument or rather to a mixture of several edifices. The overall description points to the Ramesseum of Ramesses II of the 19th dynasty and/or temple of Ramesses III of the 20th dynasty at Medinet Habu (both located on the West Bank of the Nile) as the most likely candidates for the monument of king Rhamses as described by Tacitus, although the temple of Karnak (located on the East Bank) has also been suggested

---

Fayum region was an important place of cult of the god Sobek which had flourished there since pharaonic times. Cf. Zecchi (2010). In the Roman Period there were several oracles of various manifestations of Sobek active in the Fayum region. See Frankfurter (1998), 153–161.

82   Goodyear (1981), 357 suggests that Germanicus sought initiation into the mysteries of the Cabiri. For the importance of the Samothracian mysteries and the influence of Samothracian architecture in Rome, see Popkin (2015), 343–373 (I owe this reference to Adam Ziółkowski). For the association of Samothrace with Alexander the Great, which might be important in the context of Germanicus' voyage, see Plut. *Alex.* 2.2 who writes that Philip II allegedly fell in love with Olympias after having been initiated into the Samothracian mysteries at the same time as her.

83   For Germanicus' visit to Thebes, see Kákosy (1989), 129–136.

84   For the figure of Sesostris (based on the historical figures of Senwosret I and Senwosret III of the 12th dynasty) in the Graeco-Roman sources, see especially Obsomer (1989).

85   For the image of Ramesside kings in the classical literature, see Blasius (2003), 305–352 (for the Tacitean account, particularly 338–341). It should be added that it is also an important testimony that in Germanicus' time there were still some priests in Thebes who could actually read hieroglyphic texts from the pharaonic period; contra Canfora (1990), 171, who believes that Germanicus' Egyptian guide used the name of king Rhamses to give a flavour of authenticity to his account. It does not seem likely, however, that Tacitus while writing his *Annals* had a literal translation of the Egyptian text before his eyes as once believed by Jean-François Champollion (1836), xxi.

86   Ferenczi (2018), 271. Contra O'Gorman (2000), 112–114; Kelly (2010), 226 f.; Girdvainytė (2015), 89 f., who interpret the episode as an allusion to the future end of the Roman Empire, which will meet a similar fate as the formerly glorious empire of king Rhamses.

by some scholars.[87] It should be stressed, however, that Tacitus' monument of king Rhamses may in fact be a combination of several monuments which merged into one in the historian's account.

While in Western Thebes, Germanicus also visited the Colossi of Memnon or the extant remnants of the temple of millions of years of Amenhotep III of the 18th dynasty, which was destroyed by an earthquake which occurred already in the pharaonic period.[88] Unfortunately, none of the numerous visitors' graffiti left on the surfaces of the Colossi can be associated with Germanicus' visit.[89] Nevertheless, it seems that by visiting the Colossi of Memnon Germanicus realised an unfulfilled wish of Alexander the Great to see the Palace of Memnon,[90] although it is uncertain if the Macedonian conqueror intended to visit the spot where the Colossi were erected in Western Thebes[91] or rather the site of Abydos also associated with Memnon[92]. It is also interesting to note that Germanicus' visit to Thebes, the most important cult centre of Amun, the same deity who proclaimed Alexander the Great to be a god incarnate and the rightful heir of the pharaohs through his oracle at the oasis of Siwa,[93] can be interpreted as a homage to one of the most important Egyptian deities, identified with Zeus by the Greeks and with Jupiter by the Romans.[94] That way Germanicus would once again be following in the footsteps of Alexander the Great[95], and to a certain extent surpassing his achievements, since while Alexander managed to see only the oracle of the god, Germanicus actually visited his sacred domain and veritable seat on earth.

---

87 Montet (1947) 47–79, attempted to show the exactitude of the Tacitean account, but his interpretation does not seem to be accurate as the Roman historian confuses the actual description of the inscription's contents, which he must have encountered in one of his sources, with some more or less standardised motifs known from other classical sources (i. e. the number of 700.000 soldiers in Rhamses' army – the exact same number is given by Herodotus while describing the army of the Persian king Darius; Hdt. 4.87; Kelly (2010), 227). In fact, it is the general description of the monument which conforms to Egyptian historical reliefs and inscriptions as known from Thebes; cf. Redford (2003) rather than the exact details as given by Tacitus.

88 Stadelmann (2014), 5–22. It should be noted that it was actually the northern Colossus which "sang" at dawn due to some damage caused by another earthquake which occurred at 27 BC, whence its identification with Memnon; Letronne (1833); cf. also Capponi (2020), 133.

89 A. Bernand, É. Bernand (1960). Germanicus' visit to Thebes is, however, otherwise attested by oLouvre 9004 concerning the requisitions made on account of his travel: Wilcken (1963), 490 f., no. 413; Weingärtner (1969), 122 f.

90 Curt. 4.8.3.

91 For the identification of the Palace of Memnon in Thebes as described by the classical authors with the temple of millions of years of Ramesses III at Medinet Habu, see Łukaszewicz (1995), 57–73; Łukaszewicz (2010), 256.

92 For the Palace of Memnon at Abydos, see Kelly (2010), 225 (n24). For Abydos as the seat of hidden knowledge, cf. Iamb. *Myst.* 6.248.

93 On the oracle of Amun at Siwa, see Struffolino (2012).

94 Cf. Plut. *Is.* 9, 354 C–D; Curt. 4.7.5.

95 Hausmann (1995), 327 suggests that Germanicus visited also the temple of Luxor with the Adyton of Alexander the Great; for the latter, see Abd el-Raziq (1984).

From Thebes Germanicus proceeded to visit the island of Elephantine, which once again seems to be highly significant. The Egyptians believed that it was near Elephantine island, the cult centre of the ram-headed god Khnum, that the mythical sources of the Nile should be located.[96] According to Lucan it was the wish of Julius Caesar to explore the sources of the Nile,[97] a wish which he ultimately failed to fulfil (although such traditions, when transmitted in poetry, must be treated with extreme caution). Once again, Germanicus not only followed in the footsteps of his "predecessors",[98] but also, in a way, surpassed their achievements.[99] It is also noteworthy that by reaching the southern borders of Egypt Germanicus emulated the models created by the pharaohs and followed by the Hellenistic monarchs, in which the ruler is supposed to visit his domain from one end to the other.[100] Even if, as we saw, Germanicus did not wish to challenge Tiberius' rule in any way, it is possible that, as a potential successor of the princeps,[101] he felt obliged to fulfil the duties of the ruler, be that in his own or his adoptive father's name.

From the preceding discussion, we should conclude that Germanicus' journey was carefully planned. Germanicus chose to visit the sites which in his opinion might help him in his quest for hidden knowledge. At the same time he seems to have deliberately followed in the footsteps of his actual and spiritual predecessors trying to realise their unfulfilled wishes to see the places which they had not managed to visit and so, in a way, surpassing their achievements whenever possible. Yet, Germanicus did not neglect his duties as a Roman administrator as can be deduced from both Tacitus' account and the edicts issued by him while in Egypt.

The relative length of Tacitean account concerning Germanicus' visit to Egypt seems to indicate that the historian was aware that this journey was an important part of his Eastern mission. Yet, the nature of the presentation of Germanicus' stay in Egypt in the *Annals* indicates that Tacitus failed to understand its importance and

---

96   E.g. Sethy I's (19th dynasty) inscription from the temple at Kanais states that "Then, this place was constructed in the great name of (Men-Ma'at-Ra)| [i.e. Sethy I] and it was very greatly inundated with water like the cavern of the two sources of the Nile at Abu [i.e. Elephantine]" (translation after the hieroglyphic text in Kitchen (1975), 66, 11–12). See also Wainwright (1953), 104–107; Laskowska-Kusztal (2015), 75–89.

97   Lucan *Phars.* 10.189–193. In 10.194–331, Lucan describes how other famous rulers (Sesostris, Cambyses, and Alexander the Great) also failed to discover the sources of the Nile; see Kelly (2010), 230 f.

98   Woods (2021), 5 rightly points out an allusion to king Psammetichus' failed attempt to define the depth of the sources of the Nile (as described in Hdt. 2.28) in Tac. *Ann.* 2.61. This might add one more "predecessor" for Germanicus to emulate in his quest for hidden knowledge.

99   Of course, only in a metaphorical sense, as reaching only to Elephantine, Germanicus could not have seen the actual sources of the Nile. The latter continued to incite curiosity in the Romans, as illustrated by an expedition dispatched later by Nero in order to discover the true sources of the great river. Sen. *Q. Nat.* 6.8.3–5.

100   Hennig (1972), 365; Foertmeyer (1989), 105–107.

101   For Germanicus as one of Tiberius' successors, see Sawiński (2018), 111–142.

consequences.[102] Although scholars have suggested that Tacitus deliberately portrayed Germanicus as a new Alexander the Great,[103] there is nothing in the account itself that suggests it; in fact the only person to whom Germanicus is explicitly compared in the account concerning his stay in Egypt is Scipio Africanus[104] (in the context of his behaviour rather than his achievements) and not Alexander the Great.[105] It seems that it is rather Germanicus who imitates Alexander the Great,[106] and that Tacitus fails to recognise the true meaning of his actions. Moreover, Tacitus presents a disinterest in the actual course of events,[107] which is most clearly expressed by listing the sites visited by Germanicus out of their geographical order, in some instances without properly identifying them. I cannot agree that Tacitus chose to relate only those episodes which enabled him to liken Germanicus to Alexander – this might explain omitting some episodes, but it certainly does not explain why the remaining ones are presented out of their chronological order. Even less likely is the interpretation that Tacitus presents Germanicus as a symbol of hope in an episode constituting a complicated meditation on the rise and fall of tyranny and transience of human earthly achievements.[108] Such an interpretation might have been accurate if Tacitus had composed his work in Germanicus' lifetime. But it does not seem probable that Tacitus could have presented Germanicus as the only hope for the corrupted Principate being fully aware that this hope was long lost with Germanicus' demise.[109]

---

102 Woods (2021), 1–14 rightly observes that Tacitus seems to stress that Germanicus was genuinely interested in historical monuments. The scholar suggests, however, that Tacitus described Germanicus' stay in Egypt in such great detail for a twofold reason: he needed this event as the final factor that persuaded Tiberius to eliminate Germanicus, and at the same time to complete his portrayal of Germanicus as a man of particular *comitas*. The author emphasises, however, that he is not interested in what actually happened, but exclusively in the way the events are presented in Tacitus' account.

103 Gissel (2001), 278–301.

104 Tac. *Ann.* 2.59; Weingärtner (1969), 99–108.

105 For a critique of Gissel's view, see Kelly (2010), 222–226. Yet the author's own interpretation seems to be equally unconvincing (see below).

106 Henning (1972), 364 f.; Foertmeyer (1989), 113 f. For the phenomenon of *imitatio Alexandri*, see Bohm (1989); Kühnen (2008).

107 Ferenczi (2018), 269–274, although I cannot agree with the author that Tacitus is deliberately portraying Germanicus as uselessly wasting time by visiting ancient monuments in Egypt (see below).

108 Kelly (2010), 221–237.

109 It is important to note that the assumption that Tacitus regards Egyptian monuments as symbols of useless waste of time or of a contemptible tyranny seems to be unfounded, see Capponi (2020), 133 f., as the historian never expresses what he actually thinks of these monuments, in contrast to Pliny the Elder who assesses the pyramids as an idle and foolish display of richness by the kings: *regum pecuniae otiosa ac stulta ostentatio* – "the useless and foolish exhibition of riches by kings"; Plin. *NH* 36.75; cf. Goodyear (1981), 385. I find also some difficulty in accepting interpretations such as that proposed by Manolaraki/Augoustakis (2012), 386–402, who argue that the Tacitean portrayal of Germanicus is based on Silius Italicus' presentation of Hannibal. Although such interpretations may lead to interesting observations, they are ultimately impossible to prove without being able to demonstrate that one author actually knew of the other if he never explicitly refers to

Why did then Tacitus choose to eliminate some episodes from his account on Germanicus' stay in Egypt? Two of them should be mentioned here: a visit to the tomb of Alexander the Great and the consultation to the oracle of Apis at Memphis. The first case seems easier to explain. Perhaps a visit to the tomb of Alexander was so natural for everyone arriving at Alexandria that there was no need to explicitly mention it.[110] There is, however, another possibility: Cassius Dio informs us that while Octavian was visiting the tomb of Alexander he declined to see the remains of the Ptolemies, stating that he wanted to see a king and not just some dead bodies.[111] We might easily understand Octavian's feelings with respect to the Ptolemies (if, of course, the story is true); after all it was the last member of the Ptolemaic dynasty who, in his opinion at least, induced one of the most respected Roman generals to renounce his legacy which led to a devastating civil war. But perhaps many years later history repeated itself and now it was Germanicus who was presented with the very same offer, but this time he gave a totally different answer, led by his quest for knowledge and his general interest in antiquity. After all, the Ptolemaic rulers descended from one of Alexander the Great's generals so visiting their tombs might have been interpreted as paying homage to the Macedonian conqueror.[112]

A similar explanation may likewise be presented in the case of the Memphite episode. In this instance, we are once again informed that during his stay in Egypt Octavian was invited to visit the city of Memphis and consult the oracle of Apis which he once again declined, declaring that he preferred to worship gods rather than cattle.[113] And yet Germanicus once again defied Augustus' memory and decided to consult the oracle,[114] which foretold him an imminent death, which eventually proved to be right.[115] Why did Tacitus decide not to mention this episode if in *Ann.* 2.54 he related

---

his work. Moreover, scholars seem to underappreciate the fact that the use of similar imagery by classical authors proves primarily that they shared a common worldview and historical tradition rather than that they were necessarily dependent on one another. For a similar critique, see Woods (2021), 4.

110 Cf. Milne (1916), 77.

111 Cass. Dio 51.16.4–5.

112 It is also important that in *Ann.* 2.43 and 53 Tacitus emphasises Germanicus' relation to both Augustus and Antony. This may suggest that Germanicus did not feel any need to act as if he was ill-disposed to Mark Antony out of respect for the first princeps who eventually defeated him.

113 Suet., *Aug.* 93.4; Cass. Dio 51.16.5.

114 According to Foertmeyer (1989), 114 f., Germanicus wished to demonstrate that he was not like his adoptive grandfather Octavian. Perhaps it is not unimportant that pOxy. 25 2435 contains the minutes of Germanicus' encounter with the Alexandrians on the recto, and the minutes of the encounter of Augustus with an Alexandrian embassy on the verso, see Harker (2008), 69 f. Unfortunately, we are unable to say if Germanicus' actions were deliberately undertaken to distinguish himself from Augustus or rather resulted from the difference of characters of both figures.

115 Interestingly Cass. Dio 51.17.5 recalls another instance of Apis' accurate prophecies, when he describes the bull's lamentations upon the Roman conquest of Egypt, interpreted as an unfavourable sign for the Egyptians who remained resistant to the new conqueror.

a similar event in which it was the oracle of the Clarian Apollo that had foretold Germanicus' death? We cannot suppose that this episode was not described in the source, which Tacitus used while composing his *Annals*.[116] It seems that Tacitus decided to eliminate the episode because it might potentially have cast a negative light on Augustus: if Germanicus visited the oracle and the oracle was right foretelling his death, then Augustus was wrong dishonouring and disrespecting it. It does not mean that Tacitus was an admirer of Augustus, but perhaps for some unknown reason he thought it was safer not to express his critique so openly (this may explain also why Tacitus decided to start his *Annals* with the reign of Tiberius rather than with the one of Augustus). Perhaps the same intention lay behind omitting the description of the visit of Germanicus in Alexander's tomb – it was safer to eliminate the episode altogether instead of casting potentially negative light on Augustus who declined to visit the tombs of the Ptolemies. At the same time it enabled Tacitus to present Germanicus in a more positive manner, as defying Augustus' memory did not conform to the overall portrayal of Tiberius' adoptive son in Tacitus' *Annals*.[117] It is true that Tacitus included a mention of Tiberius criticising Germanicus for breaking Augustus' prohibition against entering Egypt without the princeps' consent, but the way Tacitus portrays this episode (which might have some historical accuracy if we take into account Suetonius' testimony) is rather supposed to emphasise the alleged disagreement between Tiberius and Germanicus in the Tacitean account and Tiberius' accusations against his adoptive son.

To sum up we may say that our sources indicate that Germanicus decided to visit Egypt as a "scholar" rather than as a Roman general.[118] His expedition must have been

---

116   Kelly (2010), 225 points out that Tacitus knew the work of Pliny, so he must have also known the Memphite episode of Germanicus. Another hypothesis was suggested by Capponi (2020), 134–136 that both Pliny and Tacitus used the work of Apion of Alexandria who, as Capponi further suggests, accompanied Germanicus on his travels in Egypt and later on included an account of it in his work on Egyptian history in order to exonerate Germanicus from the accusations of transgressing his competencies by presenting him as a great general, respectful for the culture of Greece and for the history of Egypt.

117   This might also explain why Tacitus passes over in silence Germanicus' speeches to the people of Alexandria, which are otherwise recorded in pOxy. 25 2435, rt. It has been noted that Germanicus' attitude towards the people of Alexandria stands in neat contrast to the one presented some decades earlier by Octavian; Foertmeyer (1989), 114–115, see, however, Barbagli (2019), 43–91 for Augustus' benefactions for the Alexandrians. A totally different interpretation was put forward by Girdvainytė (2015), 91–95, who suggests that both episodes were omitted due to the negative opinions of the Roman authors about the cities of Alexandria and Memphis, and more particularly on animal cults. Similarly, Capponi (2020), 135 suggests that Tacitus omitted this episode in his account, because he did not want to present his hero as worshiping animals, as he despised Egyptian zoolatry. For Tacitus' attitude towards the peoples of the East, see Mellor (2010), 54–60. On the other hand, Goodyear (1981), 382 suggests that the Apis episode was omitted simply due to the fact that in such a brief presentation of events as the Tacitean account of Germanicus' Egyptian voyage many things had necessarily to be passed over in silence.

118   Germanicus' scientific interests are revealed also by the testimony of Solin. 20.9, who, based on Plin. *NH*, 37.42, recounts how Germanicus examined the shores of Germania in order to define

carefully planned from the very beginning and this plan must have been approved by Tiberius, despite any later circumstances which might have changed the princeps' opinion on Germanicus' behaviour in Egypt. The princeps' adoptive son had planned to visit historically important places, just as he did at the earlier stages of his Eastern mission. The sources indicate that he expressed not only great interest in hidden and mysterious knowledge, but also deep respect for ancient culture, be it Greek or Egyptian.[119] At the same time, he did not fail to fulfil his duties as a Roman official and administrator. While in Egypt, Germanicus apparently intended to follow in the footsteps of his actual and spiritual predecessors, particularly Alexander the Great, whom he occasionally wished to surpass in exploring Egyptian mysteries. It seems that the true nature of his Egyptian voyage was not fully understood by Tacitus who appears to undermine its true significance.[120] In contrast to Germanicus the author of the *Annals* presents ostentatious disinterest in Egyptian antiquities at the same time carefully eliminating from his account all episodes which might have cast negative light on the respected figure of Augustus.

These conclusions might seem to be rather speculative, but it is important to emphasise that they should be treated rather as an invitation to revisit Germanicus' travel to Egypt from a different perspective which might bring some new insights, and not as undisputable truths. The scarcity of our sources precludes us from having all the answers, but it is certain that not all problems concerning Germanicus' stay in Egypt have been solved to date, despite two thousand years that separate us from the day when Germanicus first set foot on Egyptian soil.

Bibliography

Abd el-Raziq, Mahmud (1984): Die Darstellungen und Texte des Sanktuars Alexanders des Großen im Tempel von Luxor. Archäologische Veröffentlichungen 16. Mainz am Rhein: Philipp von Zabern.

Arnaud, Pascal (1994): "Transmarinae provinciae. Réflexions sur les limites géographiques et sur la nature des pouvoirs en Orients des "corégents" sous les règnes d'Auguste et de Tibère". In: Cahiers du Centre Gustave Glotz 5, 221–253.

Arnold, Dieter (1979): "Das Labyrinth und seine Vorbilder". In: Mitteilungen des Deutschen Archäologischen Instituts Abteilung Kairo 35, 1–9.

---

the nature of amber. For Germanicus as a scholar, see Mellor (2010), 29. See also Mathieu (1987), 153–167; Assmann (2014), 87 f., 99, 105 for Egypt as the traditional place of education of famous Greek philosophers.

119   For this, see Woods (2021), 9–13.

120   I do not agree with Capponi (2020), 133 f. that Tacitus admired Egypt just as much as Germanicus. The fact that Egyptian monuments are referred to as *miracula* in his account is not enough to indicate that Tacitus indeed shared Germanicus' interest in Egyptian antiquity.

Ash, Rhiannon (2009): "Fission and fusion. Shifting Roman identities in the Histories". In: Woodman Anthony J. (ed.): The Cambridge Companion to Tacitus. Cambridge: Cambridge University Press, 85–99.

Assmann, Jan (2014): From Akhenaten to Moses. Ancient Egypt and Religious Change. Cairo, New York: The American University in Cairo Press.

Baar, Manfred (1990): Das Bild des Kaisers Tiberius bei Tacitus, Sueton und Cassius Dio. Stuttgart: B. G. Teubner.

Barbagli, Nicola (2019): "Il perdono degli Alessandrini. Fortuna di un episodio di clemenza imperiale". In: Cecconi, Giovanni A. et al. (eds.): The Past as Present. Essays on Roman History in Honour of Guido Clemente. Studi e testi tardoantichi. Profane and Christian Culture in Late Antiquity 17. Turnhout: Brepols, 43–91.

von Beckerath, Jürgen (1994): "Osorkon IV. = Herakles". In: Göttingen Miszellen 139, 7–8.

von Beckerath, Jürgen (1999): Handbuch der ägyptischen Königsnamen. Münchner Ägyptologische Studien 49, Mainz: Verlag Philip von Zabern.

Blasius, Andreas (2003): "Das Königtum der Ramessiden im Spiegel der griechisch-römischen Überlieferung". In: Gundlach, Rolf / Rößler-Köhler, Ursula (eds.), Das Königtum der Ramessidenzeit. Voraussetzungen – Verwirklichung – Vermächtnis. Akten des 3. Symposiums zur ägyptischen Königsideologie in Bonn 7.–9.6.2001. Ägypten und Altes Testament 36,3. Wiesbaden: Harrassowitz Verlag, 305–352.

Bohm, Claudia (1989): Imitatio Alexandri im Hellenismus. Untersuchungen zum politischen Nachwirken Alexanders des Großen in hoch- und späthellenistischen Monarchien. München: Tuduv.

Bernand, André, Bernand, Étienne (1960): Les inscriptions grecques et latines du Colosse de Memnon. Bibliothèque d'étude 31. Le Caire: Institut Français d'Archéologie Orientale.

Brunner, Hellmut (1975): "Chons". In: Helck, Wolfgang et. al (eds.): Lexikon der Ägyptologie I. Wiesbaden: Harrassowitz Verlag, cols 960–963.

Butzer, Karl W. (1976): Early Hydraulic Civilization in Egypt. A Study in Cultural Ecology. Chicago: The University of Chicago Press.

Canfora, Luciano (1990): The Vanished Library. A Wonder of the Ancient World, transl. M. Ryle. Berkeley/Los Angeles: University of California Press.

Capponi, Livia (2020): "Germanico in Egitto tra stroria e memoria". In: Cristofoli, Roberto et al. (eds.), Germanico. Nel contesto politico di età Giulio Claudia. La figura, il carisma, la memoria. Perugia, 21–22 Novembre 2019. Roma/Bristol: L'Erma di Bretschneider, 123–139.

Champollion, Jean-François (1836): Grammaire égyptienne, ou principes généraux de l'écriture sacrée égyptienne appliquée à la représentation de la langue parlée. Paris: Firmin Didot.

Cichorius, Conrad (1922): Römische Studien. Historisches, epigraphisches, literargeschichtliches aus vier Jahrhunderts Roms. Leipzig/Berlin: B. G. Teubner.

Cooper, John P. (2014): The Medieval Nile. Route, Navigation, and Landscape in Islamic Egypt. Cairo/New York: The American University in Cairo Press.

Curl, James S. (2005): The Egyptian Revival. Ancient Egypt as the Inspiration for Design Motifs in the West. London/New York: Routledge.

Dils, Peter (1994): "On Several Cartouches Supposedly of C. Iulius Caesar Germanicus". In: Zeitschrift für Papyrologie und Epigraphik 100, 347–350.

Ferenczi, Attila (2018): "Germanicus in Egypt". In: Bács, Tamás A. et al. (eds.), Across the Mediterranean – Along the Nile. Studies in Egyptology, Nubiology and Late Antiquity Dedicated to Lászlo Török on the Occasion of His 75th Birthday I. Budapest: Institute of Archaeology / Research Centre for the Humanities; Hungarian Academy of Sciences / Museum of Fine Arts, 269–276.

Foertmeyer, Victoria A. (1989): Tourism in Graeco-Roman Egypt. PhD dissertation. Princeton University.

Frankfurter, David (1998): Religion in Roman Egypt. Assimilation and Resistance. New Jersey: Princeton University Press.

Girdvainytė, Lina (2015): "Egypt in Roman Imperial Literature. Tacitus' Ann. 2.59–61". In: Literatūra 57, 84–97.

Gissel, J. A. (2001): "Germanicus as an Alexander Figure". In: Classica & Mediaevalia 52, 278–301.

Goddio, Franck (2007): The Topography and Excavation of Heracleion-Thonis and East Canopus (1996–2006). Oxford Centre for Maritime Archaeology. Monograph 1, Oxford: Oxford Centre for Maritime Archaeology.

Goddio, Franck (2015): "The Sacred Topography of Thonis-Heracleion'. In: Robinson, Damian / Goddio, Franck (eds.), Thonis-Heracleion in Context. Oxford Centre for Maritime Archaeology. Monograph 8. Oxford: Oxford Centre for Maritime Archaeology, 15–54.

Goodyear, Frank. R. (1981): The Annals of Tacitus II. Annals 1.55–81 and Annals 2. Cambridge: Cambridge University Press.

Grenier, Jean C. (1989): Les titulatures des empereurs romains dans les documents en langue égyptienne. Papyrologica Bruxellensia 22. Bruxelles: Fondation Égyptologique Reine Elisabeth.

Griffiths, John G. (1970): Plutarch's De Iside et Osiride. Edited with Introduction and Commentary. University of Wales: University of Wales Press.

Harker, Andrew (2008): Loyalty and Dissidence in Roman Egypt. The Case of the Acta Alexandrinorum. Cambridge: Cambridge University Press.

Hausmann, Ulrich (1995): "A Portrait Head of Germanicus from Egypt in the University Museum at Tübingen". In: Bonacasa, Nicola et al. (eds.), Alessandria e il mondo ellenistico-romano. I centenario del Museo Greco-Romano. Alessandria, 23–27 Novembre 1992. Atti del II congresso internazionale Italo-Egiziano. Roma: L'Erma di Bretschneider.

Hennig, Dieter (1972): "Zur Ägyptenreise des Germanicus". In: Chiron 2, 349–365.

Hillard, Tom / Beness, Lea (2001): "Romans in Upper Egypt in 116 B. C.". In: The Bulletin of the Australian Centre for Egyptology 12, 22–33.

Hillard, Tom / Beness, Lea (2003): "The First Romans at Philae (CIL I².2.2937a)". In: Zeitschrift für Papyrologie und Epigraphik 144, 203–207.

Hoffmann, Friedhelm (2015): "Königinnen in ägyptischen Quellen der römischen Zeit" In: Eldamaty, Mamdouh et al. (eds.): Ägyptische Königinnen vom Neuen Reich bis in die islamische Zeit. Beiträge zur Konferenz in der Kulturabteilung der Botschaft der Arabischen Republik Ägypten in Berlin am 19.01.2013. Vaterstetten: Patrick Brose, 139–156.

Hunt, Arthur S. / Edgar, Campbell C. (1934): Select Papyri in Five Volumes II: Non-Literary Papyri, Public Documents. The Loeb Classical Library 282. London / Cambridge, MA: William Heinemann / Harvard University Press.

Kákosy, László (1989): "Germanicus in Theben". In: Acta Antiqua Academiae Scientiarum Hungariae 32, 129–136.

Kaplony, Peter (1980): "Königsring". In: Helck, Wolfgang et al. (eds.): Lexikon der Ägyptologie III. Wiesbaden: Harrassowitz Verlag, cols 610–626.

Kelly, Benjamin (2010): "Tacitus, Germanicus and the Kings of Egypt (Tac. Ann. 2.59–61)". In: Classical Quarterly 60, 221–237.

Kitchen, Kenneth A. (1975): Ramesside Inscriptions I. Historical and Biographical. Oxford: B. H. Blackwell.

Koestermann, Erich (1965): Corneli Taciti libri qui supersunt I. Ab excessu divi Augusti, Leipzig: B. G. Teubner.

Kühnen, Angela (2008): Die imitatio Alexandri und römische Politik in republikanischer Zeit. Würzburg/Augsburg: Rhema Verlag.

Laskowska-Kusztal, Ewa (2015): "Aegyptiaca Vespasiani. Notes on Vespasian's presence on Elephantine". In: Études et travaux 28, 75–89.

Lehner, Mark, (1997): The Complete Pyramids. Solving the Ancient Mysteries. London: Thames and Hudson.

Letronne, Antoine-Jean (1833): La statue vocale de Memnon considéré dans ses rapports avec l'Égypte et la Grèce. Étude historique faisant suite aux recherches pour servir à l'histoire de l'Égypte pendant la domination des Grecs et des Romains. Paris: Imprimerie Royale.

Levi, Mario A. (1924): "L'esclusione dei senatori romani dall'Egitto Augusteo". In: Aegyptus 5, 231–235.

Levick, Barbara (1972): "Tiberius' Retirement to Rhodes in 6 B. C.". In: Latomus 31, 779–813.

Lloyd, Alan B. (1970): "The Egyptian Labyrinth". The Journal of Egyptian Archaeology 56, 81–100.

Lloyd, Alan B. (1994): Herodotus Book II. Commentary 1–98. Études préliminaires aux religions orientales dans l'Empire Romain 43. Leiden, Boston, New York: Brill.

Loyrette, Anne M. (1992): "Les monuments du prince Ouadjmès". In: Memnonia 3, 131–140.

Łukaszewicz, Adam (1995): Aegyptiacae quaestiones tres. Warszawa: Warsaw University.

Łukaszewicz, Adam (2010): "Memnon, His Ancient Visitors and Some Related Problems". In: Lembke, Katja et al. (eds.): Tradition and Transformation. Egypt under Roman Rule. Proceedings of the International Conference, Hildesheim, Roemer- and Pelizaeus-Museum, 3–6 July 2008. Culture and History of the Ancient Near East 41. Leiden, Boston: Brill, 255–263.

Manolaraki, Eleni / Augoustakis, Antony (2012): "Silius Italicus and Tacitus on the Tragic Hero. The Case of Germanicus". In: Pagán, Victoria E. (ed.): A Companion to Tacitus. Oxford: Wiley-Blackwell, 386–402.

Mathieu, Bernard (1987): "Le voyage de Platon en Égypte". In: Annales du Service des Antiquités de l'Égypte 71, 153–167.

Mellor, Ronald (2010): Tacitus' Annals. Oxford: Oxford University Press.

Milne, Grafton J. (1916): "Greek and Roman Tourists in Egypt". In: The Journal of Egyptian Archaeology 3, 76–80.

Montet, Pierre (1947): "Germanicus et le vieillard de Thèbes". In: Anonymous (ed.): Mélanges 1945 III: Études historiques. Paris: Les Belles Lettres, 47–79.

Murnane, William J. (1977): Ancient Egyptian Coregencies. Studies in Ancient Oriental Civilization 40. Chicago: The University of Chicago Press.

Obsomer, Claude (1989): Les campagnes de Sésostris dans Hérodote. Essai d'interprétation du texte grec à la lumière des réalités égyptiennes. Connaissance de l'Égypte ancienne 1. Bruxelles: Connaissance de l'Égypte ancienne.

O'Gorman, Ellen (2000): Irony and Misreading in the Annals of Tacitus. Cambridge: Cambridge University Press.

van Ootenghem, Jan (1959): "Germanicus en Égypte". In: Les études classiques 27, 241–251.

Payraudeau, Frédéric (2014): Administration, société et pouvoir à Thèbes sous la XXIIᵉ dynastie bubastite. Bibliothèque d'étude 160. Le Caire: Institut Français d'Archéologie Orientale.

Poethke, Günther (1977): "Germanicus". In: Helck, Wolfgang et al. (eds.), Lexikon der Ägyptologie II. Wiesbaden: Harrassowitz Verlag, col. 553.

Popkin, Maggie L. (2015): "Samothracian Influences at Rome. Cultic and Architectural Exchange in the Second Century B. C. E.". In: American Journal of Archaeology 119, 343–373.

Redford, Donald B. (1978–1979): "Osorkho … called Herakles". In: Journal of the Society for the Study of Egyptian Antiquities 9, 33–36.

Redford Donald B. (2003): The Wars in Syria and Palestine of Thutmose III. Culture and History of the Ancient Near East 16. Leiden/Boston: Brill.

Rivière, Yann (2016): Germanicus. Prince romain 15 av. J.-C.-19 apr. J.-C. Paris: Perrin.

Rutland, Linda W. (1987): "The Tacitean Germanicus. Suggestions for a Re-Evaluation". In: Rheinisches Museum 130, 153–164.

Sánchez-Ostiz Gutiérrez, Álvaro (1999): Tabula Siarensis. Edición, traducción y comentario. Pamplona: Universidad de Navarra.

Sauneron, Serge (1975): Le temple d'Esna VI. Nᵒˢ 473–546. Le Caire: Institut Français d'Archéologie Orientale.

Sauneron, Serge (2009): Le temple d'Esna VII. Nᵒˢ 547–646. Le Caire: Institut Français d'Archéologie Orientale.

Sawiński, Paweł (2018): The Succession of Imperial Power under the Julio-Claudian Dynasty (30 BC–AD 68). Berlin: Peter Lang.

Shuttleworth-Kraus, Christina (2009): "The Tiberian Hexad". In: Woodman, Anthony. J. (ed.): The Cambridge Companion to Tacitus. Cambridge: Cambridge University Press, 100–115.

Shotter, David. C. (1968): "Tacitus, Tiberius and Germanicus". In: Historia 17, 194–214.

Solazzi, Siro (1928): "Di una pretesta legge di Augusto relativa all'Egitto". In: Aegyptus 9, 296–302.

Smelik, Klaas A. / Hemelrijk, Emily (1984): "Who Knows Not What Monsters Demented Egypt Worships?". Opinions on Egyptian Animal Worship in Antiquity as Part of the Ancient Conception of Egypt". In: Haase, Wolfgang (ed.): Aufstieg und Niedergang der römischen Welt. Geschichte und Kultur Roms im Spiegel der aktuellen Forschung II. Principat, siebzehnter Band (4. Teilband). Religion. Heidentum. Römische Götterkulte, orientalische Kulte in der römischen Welt. Berlin/New York: Walter de Gruyter, 1852–2000, 2337–2357.

Stadelmann, Rainer (2014): "The Colossi of Memnon and the Earthquakes at Thebes". In: Capriotti-Vittozzi, Giuseppina (ed.), Egyptian Curses I: Proceedings of the Egyptological Day Held at the National Research Council of Italy (CNR), Rome, 3ʳᵈ December 2012, in the International Conference "Reading Catastrophes. Methodological Approaches and Historical Interpretation. Earthquakes, Floods, Famines, Epidemics between Egypt and Palestine", 3ʳᵈ–1ˢᵗ Millennium BC, Rome 3ʳᵈ–4ᵗʰ December 2012, CNR – Sapienza University of Rome. Roma: CNR Edizioni, 5–22.

Struffolino, Stefano (2012): L'oasi di Ammone. Ruolo politico, economico e culturale di Siwa nell'antichità: Una ricostruzione critica. Roma: ARACNE.

Syme, Ronald (1958): Tacitus. Oxford: Oxford University Press.

Vleeming, Sven P. (2011): Demotic and Greek-Demotic Mummy Labels and Other Short Texts Gathered from Many Publications (Short Texts II 278–1200). Studia Demotica 9. Leuven: Peeters.

Wainwright, Gerald A. (1953): "Herodotus II, 28 on the Sources of the Nile". In: The Journal of Hellenic Studies 73, 104–107.

Weingärtner, Dieter G. (1969): Die Ägyptenreise des Germanicus. Papyrologische Texte und Abhandlungen 11. Bonn: Habelt.

Wilcken, Ulrich (1963): Grundzüge und Chrestomathie der Papyruskunde II. Chrestomathie. Hildesheim; Georg Olms Verlagsbuchhandlung.

Wildung, Dieter (1990): "Geheimnisvolle Gesichter". In: Antike Welt 21, 206–221.

Williams, Kathryn F. (2009): "Tacitus' Germanicus and the Principate". In: Latomus 68, 117–130.

Woods, David (2021): "Tacitus on the Visit of Germanicus to Egypt". In: Mnemosyne 2021, 1–14.

Zanker, Paul (1988): The Power of Images in the Age of Augustus, transl. A. Shapiro. Jerome Lectures 16. Ann Arbor: The University of Michigan Press.

Zecchi, Marco (2010): Sobek of Shedet. The Crocodile God in the Fayum in the Dynastic Period. Studi sull'antico Egitto 2. Todi: Tau.

Rome's Aims in Germania in AD 14:
Tacitus, *Annales* 1.3.6*
An Attempt to Appraise a Queer Statement

ADAM ZIÓŁKOWSKI

Keywords: Tacitus and Roman imperialism, Augustus' testament, keeping the Empire within limits, Rome's withdrawal from Germania

In the introductory section of the first book of *Annales*, in which Tacitus briefly sketches young Caesar's rise to autocracy and the problem of succession to his unprecedented position (1.1–4),[1] there is a sentence on the military commitments of the Empire at the time of the emperor's death:

> *Bellum ea tempestate nullum nisi adversus Germanos supererat, abolendae magis infamiae ob amissum cum Quintilio Varo exercitum quam cupidine proferendi imperii aut dignum ob praemium.*[2]

> There remained no war at that time except that still fought against the Germani, more to wipe out the disgrace caused by the loss of the army of Quinctilius Varus than from a desire to extend the empire or for some worthy reward.[3]

This sentence, an insert in the passage devoted to internal matters, to which the author returns in the subsequent sentence (1.3.7), is not entirely out of place in that it makes a logical whole with the first independent clause of the preceding one:

---

* This paper was written within the scope of the project 2017/25/B/HS3/01299, financed by the Polish National Science Centre.
1 On the introduction to the *Annales*, see esp. E. Koestermann (1961).
2 Tac. *Ann.* 1.3.6.
3 Translations are mine unless otherwise stated.

At hercule Germanicum Druso ortum octo apud Rhenum legionibus inposuit adscirique per adoptionem a Tiberio iussit, quamquam esset in domo Tiberii filius iuvenis, sed quo pluribus munimentis insisteret.[4]

On the other hand, he placed Germanicus, Drusus' son, in command of eight legions and ordered Tiberius to adopt him, though Tiberius had already a grown-up son in his household, so that thereby he might rely upon a greater number of supports.

Germanicus' advancement to the command of eight legions on the Rhine is followed by a mention of the war for which his *imperium* was intended. In view of the prominence of Germanicus' figure, and especially of his campaigns in Germania, in Tacitus' narrative of the first years of Tiberius' principate, there is nothing surprising in this digression as such; still, there are at least two queer points about it. One is the syntax of the first sentence: were it not for other extant ancient reports, we would surely infer that Augustus conferred on Germanicus the Rhenanian command just before or at the same time as he ordered Tiberius to adopt him, whereas in reality the adoption had taken place ca. eight years earlier. Why does Tacitus express himself so misleadingly? The other is the professed purpose of the war, contrary to all the objectives for which the Romans had till then waged their innumerable wars: not conquest or other "worthy reward", only washing away the ignominy of one military disaster. What does this information convey: Augustus' intent, conjectures of the public of the day, a surmise by Tacitus or some other historian?

I do not intend to attempt to answer the first question which really belongs to the domain of textual rather than strictly historical analysis (after all, Tacitus' ancient readers certainly knew the exact dates of the two events at least as well as the moderns do); besides, considering that the quoted fragment belongs to an extremely concise précis of the state of things in Rome at the start of the narrative, not to the narrative *stricto sensu*, the author could permit himself to sacrifice chronological exactness for some literary effect (see below).[5] It is the second question, which bears on one of the turning points of the ancient world's history,[6] that deserves a closer examination.

---

4   Tac. *Ann.* 1.3.5.
5   It is rash to suggest here an error or *suggestio falsi* on Tacitus' part, as does Goodyear (1972), 114 *ad locum*. As he admits himself, "throughout these chapters [1.1–4] comment and interpretation matter more to T. than historical precision". Goodyear (1972), 88. See below.
6   The turning point in question is not the end of the Roman expansion as such – apart from future conquests in Europe (Britannia, Dacia) one should always bear in mind Fergus Millar's concise verdict: "in the Near East at least, the idea that Roman imperialism and expansionism died out after the early Empire is simply false" (Millar [1993], XIII) – but the removal of one of the two pillars on which it had been based. With the pull-out from Germania the Romans for the first time renounced possession of what they had already considered theirs, abandoning the sacred principle of their imperialism to which they had faithfully adhered for four hundred years: the inviolability of the *imperium populi Romani* in the sense of territories subject to Rome's orders. The other pillar,

Unlike the other Tacitean phrase in the same vein, Augustus' alleged *consilium coer-cendi intra terminos imperii* a little further down the narrative (*Ann.* 1.11.4; see below), this one has hardly ever been the subject or a starting point of scholarly inquiry, possibly because of the context in which it is situated. When quoted, it usually serves as a corroboration of a historian's opinion that by the time of Augustus' death the Romans had given up Germania, with its literal meaning taken for granted. A good example is in one of Ronald Syme's papers: "At the death of Augustus the German War was still going on – for honour and prestige, not for conquest or any visible gain (*Ann.* 1.3.6). The motive of revenge for Quinctilius Varus, namely *recepta signa*, was duly advertised in the triumphal arch at Rome (*Ann.* 2.41)".[7] Typical of him, Sir Ronald did not bother to consider the three-year-long gap between the setting of the two references – which he presented as complementary – and everything that happened in the meantime in Tacitus' narrative, starting with the momentous change of the *princeps*. The aim of this paper is precisely to put the Roman objectives in Germania at the time of Augustus' death as presented in Tacitus, *Annales* 1.3.6, under a somewhat closer scrutiny. Needless to say, I neither want nor dare to endeavour something similar to the studies by Dieter Timpe[8] or Reinhard Wolters.[9] My subject matter is one phrase in Tacitus and I shall primarily try to see how it fits with the rest of his narrative and other ancient reports, starting with those closest to the year of Augustus' death.

The first point to be examined is whether a directive to this effect was among the *mandata* Germanicus received from Augustus when, after the consulate, sometime at the turn of A. D. 12 he set out for Gaul. Considering that in *Annales* throughout his western command he acted on his own judgement and with regard to military matters his goal was to resubjugate the rebellious Germanic tribes up to the Elbe (see below), in the light of *Ann.* 1.3.6 the alternative is, seemingly, that either he overstepped his instructions or Tacitus misinformed his readers.

The main argument for the former possibility is the apparent concordance of the quoted sentence with the *consilium coercendi intra terminos imperii* ("advice to keep the empire within [present] limits"), according to Tacitus attached to the first emperor's will (Tac. *Ann.* 1.11.4; see below). This *consilium*, however, though corroborated by Cassius Dio (56.33.5), also raises doubts about its reality or, if real, exact meaning, and so requires a look at the annexes to Augustus' will as recorded by Tacitus, Suetonius and Dio.[10]

---

the *imperium*-holders' right to make war on Rome's neighbours without asking any permission, disappeared together with the free Republic.

7   Syme (1979), 324.
8   Timpe (1968), see Timpe (2012).
9   Wolters (2008).
10 On various problems with annexes to Augustus' will see especially Hohl (1933), 112–114; Hohl (1937); Ober (1982), both very critical of Cassius Dio's report (with good reason, see below).

opes publicae continebantur [*in libello*], *quantum civium sociorumque in armis, quot classes, regna, provinciae, tributa aut vectigalia, et necessitates ac largitiones. quae cuncta sua manu perscripserat Augustus addideratque consilium coercendi intra terminos imperii, incertum metu an per invidiam.*[11]

[*libellus*] contained [the state of] public resources: the number of citizens and allies under arms, fleets, subject kingdoms, provinces, tributes or taxes, financial obligations and doles to be distributed. All that Augustus wrote out with his own hand and added an advice to keep the empire within [present] limits, one does not know whether out of fear or jealousy.

tribus voluminibus, uno mandata de funere suo complexus est, altero indicem rerum a se gestarum, quem vellet incidi in aeneis tabulis, quae ante Mausoleum statuerentur, tertio breviarium totius imperii, quantum militum sub signis ubique esset, quantum pecuniae in aerario et fiscis et vectigaliorum residuis. Adiecit et libertorum servorumque nomina, a quibus ratio exigi posset.[12]

In three volumes he contained: in the first instructions for his funeral; in the second a summary of the deeds he had accomplished, which he willed to be engraved upon bronze tablets that would be fixed at the entrance to the Mausoleum; in the third a short account of [the state of] the whole empire: how many soldiers there were under the standards and where, how much money there was in the public treasury and the imperial coffers, and what revenues were in arrears. He also added the names of freedmen and slaves from whom the official account could be demanded.

[1] ... ἐσεκομίσθη δὲ καὶ βιβλία τέσσαρα· καὶ αὐτὰ ὁ Δροῦσος ἀνέγνω. ἐγέγραπτο δὲ ἐν μὲν τῷ πρώτῳ ὅσα τῆς ταφῆς εἴχετο, ἐν δὲ τῷ δευτέρῳ τὰ ἔργα ἃ ἔπραξε πάντα, ἃ καὶ ἐς χαλκᾶς στήλας πρὸς τῷ ἡρῴῳ αὐτοῦ σταθείσας ἀναγραφῆναι ἐκέλευσε. [2] τὸ τρίτον τά τε τῶν στρατιωτῶν καὶ τὰ τῶν προσόδων τῶν τε ἀναλωμάτων τῶν δημοσίων, τό τε πλῆθος τῶν ἐν τοῖς θησαυροῖς χρημάτων, καὶ ὅσα ἄλλα τοιουτότροπα ἐς τὴν ἡγεμονίαν φέροντα ἦν, εἶχε, [3] καὶ τὸ τέταρτον ἐντολὰς καὶ ἐπικρήψεις τῷ Τιβερίῳ καὶ τῷ κοινῷ, ἄλλας τε καὶ ὅπως μήτ᾽ ἀπελευθερῶσι πολλούς, ἵνα μὴ παντοδαποῦ ὄχλου τὴν πόλιν πληρώσωσι, μήτ᾽ αὖ ἐς τὴν πολιτείαν συχνοὺς ἐσγράφωσιν, ἵνα πολὺ τὸ διάφορον αὐτοῖς πρὸς τοὺς ὑπηκόους ᾖ. [4] τά τε κοινὰ πᾶσι τοῖς δυναμένοις καὶ εἰδέναι καὶ πράττειν ἐπιτρέπειν, καὶ ἐς μηδένα ἕνα ἀναρτᾶν αὐτὰ παρῄνεσέ σφισιν, ὅπος μήτε τυραννίδος τις ἐπιθυμήσῃ, μήτ᾽ αὖ πταίσαντος ἐκείνου τὸ δημόσιον σφαλῇ. [5] γνώμην τε αὐτοῖς ἔδωκε τοῖς τε παροῦσιν ἀρκεσθῆναι καὶ μηδαμῶς ἐπὶ πλεῖον τὴν ἀρχὴν ἐπαυξῆσαι ἐθελῆσαι· δυσφύλακτόν τε γὰρ αὐτὴν ἔσεσθαι, καὶ κινδυνεύσειν ἐκ τούτου καὶ τὰ ὄντα ἀπολέσαι ἔφη. [6] τοῦτο γὰρ καὶ αὐτὸς ὄντως ἀεί ποτε οὐ λόγῳ μόνον ἀλλὰ καὶ ἔργῳ ἐτήρησε· παρὸν γοῦν αὐτῷ πολλὰ ἐκ τοῦ βαρβαρικοῦ προσκτήσασθαι οὐκ ἠθέλησε.[13]

---

11   Tac. *Ann.* 1.11.3–4.
12   Suet. *Aug.* 101.4.
13   Cass. Dio 56.33.1–6.

… Four books were then carried in and Drusus read them. In the first were written down the things that were to be done regarding the funeral; in the second all the deeds that he had performed, which he commanded also to be engraved upon bronze steles to be set at his tomb; the third had [an account of] the armed forces, the public revenues and expenditures, the amount of money in the treasuries, and all other things that concern the running of the empire; and the fourth injunctions and admonitions for Tiberius and the community, one to the effect that they should not free many slaves, in order that the city be not overcrowded with promiscuous mob, and also not enrol many as citizens, in order that there should be a marked difference between themselves and the subject peoples; to entrust all public matters to all those who had the capacity to comprehend and to act, and never allow them to depend on one person, so that no one would desire tyranny, nor would the republic be overthrown because of his fall. He also gave them the advice to be content with what they had and under no circumstances to be willing to increase further the empire. He said that it would be hard for them to guard and by this they would run the risk of losing what was theirs. In fact, he himself always observed that not only with words but also with deeds; at all events, in the past he might have gained a lot of foreign lands but did not wish to do so.

The fact that Tacitus does not mention the first two *volumina*/βιβλία of the other testimonies is irrelevant to the present argument considering the context of his report, the session of the senate after Augustus' funeral,[14] devoted to the most urgent current political issues, starting with the crucial determination of the powers of the new *princeps* (1.11–14). Besides, he has already referred to the matters these *volumina* contained, the dead emperor's instructions for his funeral and the personal record of his achievements (what we know as *Res gestae divi Augusti*): to the first directly in his account of the preceding session of the senate some time in the beginning of September,[15] devoted exclusively to the *suprema Augusti*, and of the funeral itself, and to the second allusively in the antithetical assessments of his rise to power and rule (1.8–10).[16] The really important difference is that whereas he describes the *consilium coercendi intra terminos imperii* as an attachment of sorts to the *libellus* identical with the *tertium volumen*/τρίτον βιβλίον of the other authors, Suetonius does not mention it at all (in his report the annex to the *breviarium totius imperii* contained but the names of freedmen and slaves from whom accounts could be demanded), whereas Cassius Dio includes the same advice (γνώμη) in a τέταρτον βιβλίον along with some directives concerning the internal policy of the empire.

---

14 Usually dated to 17 September on the assumption, based on Tac. *Ann.* 1.10.8–11.1, that the session started with the *senatusconsultum* on divine honours to Augustus, securely dated to that day in *Fasti Amiternini*, *Fasti Antiates Minores* and *Fasti Viae dei Serpenti*; see Degrassi (1963), 510.

15 Variously dated between 3 and 11 September, see Hohl (1937), 326 (n1); Swan (2004), 306 (*ad* Cass. Dio 56.31.2).

16 On possible use by Tacitus of *RGDA*, see Schmidt (1983).

With respect to the discrepancy between Suetonius and Cassius Dio about the number of *volumina*/βιβλία attached to the will, Trajan's *a studiis* and Hadrian's *ab epistulis*, with his habit of combing the archives for exact data, was certainly better informed than a Severan senator.[17] This being agreed on, the easiest way to defend Dio's account is to support it with Tacitus': the τέταρτον βιβλίον would technically have been an appendix to the τρίτον and as such did not deserve to be quoted separately. This, however, can hardly be reconciled with the last part of Suetonius' report which in fact mentions an appendix, but dealing with a different matter: had there been another, we would expect Suetonius to cite it as well. The other trouble with Dio's "fourth book" is that "injunctions and admonitions" concerning the internal policy he specifies are even more suspect. The first two – on manumissions and granting of the Roman citizenship – are unnecessary as they repeat what had always been Augustus' policy; the third – governing the empire by an enlightened collective rather than by a single person, to prevent tyranny or leaving the State without a head – is utter nonsense.[18] It is a fact that Velleius mentions an admonition (written *manu propria*, as in Tacitus) on internal policy which Augustus would have left to Tiberius (*primum principalium eius* [*Tiberii*] *operum fuit ordinatio comitiorum, quam manu sua scriptam Augustus reliquerat*; "the first of his acts as emperor was the regulation of the voting assemblies, which Augustus had left in his own handwriting")[19], the matter of which would appear to be the change of the electoral procedure put into effect by Tiberius at the very beginning of his principate (*Tum primum e campi comitia ad patres translata sunt*; "Then for the first time the voting was transferred from the Campus to the senators")[20]. According to Anthony Woodman this injunction would have been included in Tacitus' *additio* or Dio's τέταρτον βιβλίον.[21] However, in answer to his comment on Velleius' passage, where he brands as "exceptionally perverse" the rejection of the causal link between Augustus' alleged *ordinatio comitiorum* in his account and Tiberius' *translata comitia* in Tacitus,[22] it is worth asking why then the latter does not inform his readers that Tiberius only implemented that momentous change which in reality had been conceived by Augustus himself. Contrary to Velleius (and Tiberius) who had every interest in presenting the new *princeps*' innovation as the fulfilment of an instruction left by his safely dead predecessor, Tacitus had no reason whatsoever to hide its alleged originator. Besides, even if we admit Augustus' authorship of the Tiberian *ordinatio comitiorum*, it does not follow that it was included in any of the additions to his will. The existence of Augustus' "political testament" is thus very suspect, which certainly does not strengthen the

17   See especially Hohl (1937), 328 f.
18   Hohl (1933), 113.
19   Vell. Pat. 2.124.3.
20   Tac. *Ann.* 1.15.1.
21   Woodman (1977), 225–227.
22   Woodman (1977), 225.

case for the historicity of his *consilium*/γνώμη to keep the empire within the present confines.

The argument that Tacitus (apparently) and Dio (certainly) reckoned it as historical – witness the former's biting remark: *incertum metu an per invidiam*, and the latter's approving comment on Augustus' alleged restraint regarding conquests and annexations in 56.33.6[23] – is not very strong either considering that they were written respectively one hundred and two hundred years after the event. On the other hand, whereas the admonitions on internal matters reported by Cassius Dio are nonsensical not only in substance but chiefly in context, there is nothing absurd *in se* in an advice on the future external policy attached this way or another to the summary of the public revenues and the military strength of the empire. It seems therefore that, when trying to establish whether this advice is historical or not, it is better – literally for the sake of argument[24] – to assume the former and test its probability by a confrontation with evidence contemporary with or only slightly later than Germanicus' western *imperium*, starting with the relevant parts of the text whose Augustan authorship is beyond doubt, the *Res gestae*:

> *Omnium provinciarum populi Romani, quibus finitimae fuerunt gentes, quae non parerent imperio nostro, fines auxi. Gallias et Hispanias provincias, item Germaniam, qua includit Oceanus a Gadibus ad ostium Albis fluminis pacavi, Alpes a regione ea, quae proxima est Hadriano mari, ad Tuscum pacari feci? nulli genti bello per iniuriam inlato. Classis mea per Oceanum ab ostio Rheni ad solis orientis regionem usque ad fines Cimbrorum navigavit, quo neque terra neque mari quisquam Romanus ante id tempus adit, Cimbrique et Charydes et Semnones et eiusdem tractus alii Germanorum populi per legatos amicitiam meam et populi Romani petierunt ...; 27: Armeniam maiorem interfecto rege eius Artaxe cum possem facere provinciam, malui maiorum nostrorum exemplo regnum id Tigrani ... tradere; ... 30: Pannoniorum gentes, quas ante me principem populi Romani exercitus nunquam adit, devictas per Ti. Neronem, qui tum erat privignus et legatus meus, imperio populi Romani subieci protulique fines Illyrici ad ripam fluminis Danuvi. Citra quod Dacorum transgressus exercitus meis auspiciis victus profligatusque est, et postea trans Danuvium ductus exercitus meus Dacorum gentes imperia populi Romani perferre coegit.*[25]

---

23 Repeated in very similar words in Dio's rendering of Tiberius' encomium of the deceased emperor at the latter's funeral: τὸ τοῖς ἅπαξ ἀναγκαίως κτηθεῖσιν ἀρκεσθῆναι αὐτὸν καὶ μηδὲν ἕτερον προσκατεργάσασθαι ἐθελῆσαι, ἐξ οὗ πλειόνων ἂν δόξαντες ἄρχειν καὶ τὰ ὄντα ἀπωλέσαμεν; "he was satisfied with what by necessity had been acquired in the past, neither did he wish to make more acquisitions, which, while supposedly enlarging the empire, would have led to losing what we have" (Cass. Dio 56.41.7).

24 Perhaps the most forcefull argument that the *consilium* was a pure invention on Tiberius' part is in Ober (1982), 324–328, who thinks, however, that it was actually delivered verbally at the senate's session on 17 September 14. I am not sure of that seeing what would be happenning on the east bank of the Rhine in the next twenty-four months.

25 *RGDA* 26–27, 30 (Cooley with modifications).

I extended the territory of all those provinces of the Roman people which had neighbouring peoples who were not subject to our authority. I brought under control the Gallic and Hispanic provinces, and similarly Germania, which are bound by Ocean from Gades to the mouth of the river Elbe. I brough the Alps under control from the region which is the nearest to the Adriatic Sea as far as the Tyrrhenian Sea, but attacked no people unjustily. My fleet navigated through Ocean from the mouth of the Rhine to the region of the rising sun as far as the territory of the Cimbri; no Roman before this time has ever approached this area by either land or sea, and the Cimbri and Charydes and Semnones and other Germanic peoples of the same region sent me envoys to request my friendship and that of the Roman people ... Although I could have made Greater Armenia a province on the assassination of Artaxes its king, I preferred, in accordance with the example set by our ancestors, to hand this kingdom over to Tigranes ... The Pannonian peoples had never had an army of the Roman people come near to them before I became leader. I made them subject to the rule of the Roman people through the agency of Tiberius Nero, who at that time was my stepson and legate, and I advanced the boundary of Illyricum to the bank of the river Danube. An army of Dacians which crossed over onto this side of that river was conquered and overwhelmed under my auspices, and afterwards my army was led across the Danube and compelled the Dacians to endure the commands of the Roman people.

As has repeatedly been pointed out, in the text Germania up to the Elbe is an integral part of the empire, on par with the *Galliae et Hispaniae provinciae*;[26] the independent Germanic tribes beyond the Elbe are carefully distinguished from their western brethren as those who sought (and, no doubt, obtained) the status of *amici populi Romani* (*RGDA* 26). What we have, then, is the situation before A. D. 9; Arminius' revolt, the annihilation of the occupation army and the loss of control over a greater part of the province, have not been noted.[27] We find the same attitude with regard to Pannonia: *Pannoniorum gentes* have been conquered by Tiberius as Augustus' stepson and legate; *bellum Pannonicum*, the greatest war of the first principate, which the former brought to a successful conclusion as the latter's adopted son and holder of an independent *imperium proconsulare*, is passed over in silence.[28]

The obvious *trait d'union* between Augustus' alleged testamentary advice not to expand the empire further and *RGDA* is the correspondence between Dio's remark that he could in fact make further conquests in τὸ βαρβαρικόν but declined to do so, and the emperor's boast that he could have turned Armenia into a province but preferred to give it to Tigranes (*RGDA* 27). Another 'barbarian' land which Augustus certainly left in peace in spite of it having been, for obvious historical and geopolitical reasons, at the very top of the list of his potential conquests, was Britain; witness Tacitus': *Agr.* 13.3:

---

26   As stressed with particular insistence by Werner Eck; see Eck (2011), 12; Eck (2018), 129 f., 135 f.
27   See e. g. Scheid (2007), 71, with ample modern bibliography.
28   Scheid (2007), 79.

Mox bella civilia et in rem publicam versa principum arma, ac longa oblivio Britanniae etiam in pace: consilium id divus Augustus vocabat, Tiberius praeceptum[29].

Then came the civil wars and the arms of our leaders were turned against the republic, and then a long oblivion of Britannia even in peace: the divine Augustus called it strategy, Tiberius an instruction.

Less certain, but still probable, is the *regnum Marobodui*: the *amicitia* Tiberius struck with the king of the Marcomanni after the outbreak of the Pannonian insurrection could be construed as desisting from further attempts to conquer his kingdom. Whatever the causes, a certain "restraint" is thus indubitable; but it concerned precisely the lands which had not been regular Roman provinces before (Armenia's provincial status in 34–30 B. C. clearly did not count, having been imposed by M. Antonius; hence, most probably, Augustus' insistence in *RGDA* that he gave the country to Tigranes *maiorum nostrorum exemplo*) and which his armies never occupied. The case of Germania was entirely different: it had been conquered, it had been a province for more than fifteen years and was even now being brought back into obedience, as Illyricum a couple of years before. Judging by *RGDA*, if Augustus really did advise his successors to hold back from further conquests, it is difficult to believe that his advice embraced the rebellious Germania.

Turning to the texts composed after the *Res gestae*, chronologically the next is the *Tabula Siarensis*, closely followed by the historical work of Velleius Paterculus. It seems, however, that we can legitimately put at the head of the list Tacitus' report on Germanicus' triumph, apart from the final, bitterly ironic comment probably an almost verbatim rendering of the inscription on the triumphal arch set up on the occasion *propter aedem Saturni*,[30] and of the entry in an official text similar to the extant *Fasti Triumphales*, both certainly ensuing from the appropriate *acta senatus*.[31] Together with another fragment by Tacitus, the most relevant to my subject (the one on the manner in which the war ended), plus the only mention of Germanicus' campaigns in the extant text of Cassius Dio's *Romaika*, our dossier is as follows:

Fine anni arcus propter aedem Saturni ob recepta signa cum Varo amissa ductu Germanici, auspiciis Tiberii, et aedes Fortis Fortunae ... dicantur. C. Caelio L. Pomponio consulibus Germanicus Caesar a. d. VII. Kal. Iunias triumphavit de Cheruscis Chattisque et Angrivariis quaeque aliae nationes usque ad Albim colunt. vecta spolia, captivi, simulacra montium, fluminum, proeliorum; bellumque, quia conficere prohibitus erat, pro confecto accipiebatur.[32]

---

29   Tac. *Agric.* 13.3; see also Strabo 2.5.8.
30   As suggested by the legend *SIGN(is) RECEPT(is) DEVICTIS GERM(anis)* on the obverse of a *dupondius* commemorating Germanicus' triumph, struck *ex senatus consulto* under his son: *RIC* I² 57 (Caius). See Agata Kluczek' contribution in this volume.
31   On Tacitus' use of the *acta senatus*, see Mommsen (1909), 253–263, especially 261 f.
32   Tac. *Ann.* 2.41.1–2

At the end of the year were dedicated: an arch by the temple of Saturnus for the recovery, under the command of Germanicus and the auspices of Tiberius, of the military standards lost with Varus, and the temple of Fors Fortuna ... In the consulate of C. Caelius and L. Pomponius Germanicus Caesar triumphed on the seventh day before the Kalends of June over the Cherusci, the Chatti, the Angrivarii, and all the other peoples who live right up to the Elbe. Spoils were carried, captives, pictorial representations of mountains, rivers and battles, and the war which he was prohibited to complete, was considered as completed.

... senatum populumque Romanum id monum[entum aeternae dedi]casse memoriae German-ici Caesaris cum i{i}s Germanis bello superatis et [deinceps] a Gallia summotis receptisque signis militaribus et vindicata frau[dulenta clade] exercitus p(opuli) R(omani) ordinato statu Galliarum ...[33]

... the senate and the Roman people had dedicated this monument to the eternal memory of Germanicus Caesar for, after having overcome the Germani in war and next driven them off from Gallia, recovered the military standards and avenged the fraudulent defeat of an army of the Roman people, and regulated the situation in the Galliae ...

123.1: *Quippe Caesar Augustus cum Germanicum nepotem suum reliqua belli patraturum mi-sisset in Germaniam. ... 129.2: Quibus praeceptis instructum Germanicum suum imbutumque rudimentis militiae secum actae domitorem recepit [Tiberius] Germaniae! Quibus iuventam eius exaggeravit honoribus, respondente cultu triumphi rerum, quas gesserat, magnitudini!*[34]

For Caesar Augustus, after he had sent his grandson Germanicus to Germania to put an end to whatever remained of the war ... How well had his [Tiberius'] dear Germanicus been trained under his instructions, having so thoroughly learned the rudiments of military science under him that Tiberius was later to welcome him home as conqueror of Germania. What honours did he heap upon him, young though he was, making the magnificence of his triumph correspond to the greatness of his deeds.

Reductus inde in hiberna miles, laetus animi quod adversa maris expeditione prospera pensavis-set. addidit munificentiam Caesar, quantum quis damni professus erat exsolvendo. nec dubium habebatur labare hostis petendaeque pacis consilia sumere, et si proxima aestas adiceretur, posse bellum patrari. sed crebris epistulis Tiberius monebat rediret ad decretum triumphum: satis iam eventuum, satis casuum. Prospera illi et magna proelia: eorum quoque meminisset, quae venti et fluctus, nulla ducis culpa, gravia tamen et saeva damna intulissent. se novies a divo Augusto in Germaniam missum plura consilio quam vi perfecisse. sic Sugambros in deditionem acceptos, sic Suebos regemque Maroboduum pace obstrictum. posse et Cheruscos ceterasque rebellium gen-tis, quoniam Romanae ultioni consultum esset, internis discordiis relinqui. precante Germanico annum efficiendis coeptis, acrius modestiam eius adgreditur alterum consulatum offerendo cuius

33   *Tabula Siarensis* 1.12–15 (quoted after Sánchez-Gutiérrez (1999), 52, 115–123).
34   Vell. Pat. 2.123.1, 129.2 (Shipley with modifications).

munia praesens obiret. simul adnectebat, si foret adhuc bellandum, relinqueret materiem Drusi fratris gloriae, qui nullo tum alio hoste non nisi apud Germanias adsequi nomen imperatorium et deportare lauream posset. haud cunctatus est ultra Germanicus, quamquam fingi ea seque per invidiam parto iam decori abstrahi intellegeret.[35]

The army returned to winter quarters, rejoicing at having made up for the infelicitous sea expedition with the successful one. Caesar added a bounty recompensing in full whatever loss anybody declared. Nor was there any doubt that the enemy was faltering and taking up counsels about asking for peace, and if the coming summer was added, the war might be brought to completion. But Tiberius in frequent letters admonished him to return for the decreed triumph: there had been already enough successes, enough misfortunes. His battles had been successful and great; all the same, he should also remember that winds and waves had inflicted, through no fault of the commander, grave and severe losses. He himself, sent to Germania nine times by the divine Augustus, had achieved more by sagacity than by force: in this way the Sugambri had been forced to surrender, in this way the Suebi and king Maroboduus had been put within bounds by the peace. Seeing that the Roman revenge had been taken thought of, the Cherusci and other rebellious peoples might be left to their internal dissensions. When Germanicus begged to have one more year to finish what had been begun, he even more strongly assaulted his modesty offering him a second consulate, the duties of which he himself would assume. At the same time he added that if the fighting would still go on, let the occasion for glory be left to his brother Drusus, who, there being at the moment no other enemy, could win the name of *imperator* and return with a laurel wreath nowhere else but in Germania. Germanicus hesitated no longer, though he realised that all that was pretence and that by envy he was being dragged away from the already achieved distinction.

Γερμανικὸς δὲ τῇ ἐπὶ τοὺς Κελτοὺς στρατείᾳ φερόμενος εὖ μέχρι τε τοῦ ὠκεανοῦ προεχώρησε, καὶ τοὺς βαρβάρους κατὰ τὸ καρτερὸν νικήσας τά τε ὀστᾶ τῶν σὺν τῷ Οὐάρῳ πεσόντων συνέλεξέ τε καὶ ἔθαψε, καὶ τὰ σημεῖα τὰ στρατιωτικὰ ἀνεκτήσατο.[36]

Germanicus, said to have waged a successful campaign against the Germani, advanced as far as the Ocean, won a crushing victory over the barbarians, gathered and buried the bones of those who had fallen with Varus, and recovered the military standards.

At the outset, it must be emphasized that the granting of the triumph is of no avail for estimating the objectives of Germanicus' campaigns against the Germani. We know that it was decreed in 15, when the war was going on:

Druso Caesare C. Norbano consulibus decernitur Germanico triumphus manente bello; quod quanquam in estatem summa ope parabat, initio veris et repentino in Chattos excursu precepit ...[37]

---

35   Tac. *Ann.* 2.26.
36   Cass. Dio 57.18.1 (Xiphil. 134.20–32).
37   Tac. *Ann.* 1.55.1.

> During the consulate of Drusus Caesar and C. Norbanus a triumph was decreed for Germanicus with the war still going on. Although he intended to prosecute it with utmost effort in summer, he forestalled it in early spring with a sudden raid against the Chatti.

What is more, judging by Tacitus' narrative, the resolution was passed at the beginning of the year, when the only success Germanicus could boast of was the attack on the Marsi in the autumn of the previous year (*Ann.* 1.49.3–51.4). In other words, the triumph was decreed, so to say, in advance, once the news of the first success that could boost Germanicus' image and restore the public confidence in the legions' invincibility reached Rome. Timpe argues that the decree could be issued only after Germanicus' salutation as *imperator* some time in the summer (*Ann.* 1.58.5) and that it should be linked with that which awarded the *triumphalia insignia* to his legates, evidently after the end of the year's campaign (*Ann.* 1.72.1: *decreta eo anno triumphalia insignia A. Caecinae, L. Apronio, C. Silio ob res cum Germanico gestas*).[38] This possibility is, however, decidedly faint. Apart from assuming a colossal chronological blunder on Tacitus' part, of the two imperatorial salutations Germanicus received, the other, the date of which is unknown, occurred certainly before 15 (in 16, after the victory at Idistaviso, the soldiers saluted Tiberius as *imperator* [*Ann.* 2.18.2; see 2.22.1]), possibly in 14, after the aforementioned attack on the Marsi, i. e. just before the senate's decree. The alternative year 13, for which we have no information on Germania because of a long lacuna in Cassius Dio's narrative, is, in my opinion, less probable, not only for being based on a dubious argument *ex silentio*,[39] but also – considering that Germanicus' *imperium proconsulare*, bestowed by Augustus in 11 (Cass. Dio 56.25.2), clearly ceased after the old emperor's death, since it had to be renewed at the instigation of his successor (*Ann.*,

---

38   "In this year triumphal insignia were decreed for A. Caecina, L. Apronius and C. Silius for deeds accomplished with Germanicus". See Timpe (1968), 45 f.

39   The only support for this *unbekannte Siege* (Wolters' wording, see below in this note) is the posited date of the last, twenty first imperial salutation of Augustus and the contemporary seventh salutation of Tiberius (*RIC* I² *Augustus* 242–243). Syme (1979), 317–320, argued that they must have occurred in 13, the occasion being Germanicus' otherwise unattested campaign east of the Rhine. See now Wolters (2014/2015), 203–207. Syme (1978), 53 f., 63–65, slightly altered in Syme (1979), 319, found an echo of that hypothetical campaign in Ovid. *Pont.* 3.4.88–112, with the corollary that Germanicus went there together with Tiberius, which would explain the poet's addressing the latter, not the former, as the future victor of the Germani. On a less strained reading Ovidius is hoping that, after the Pannonians, the day of reckoning will duly come for the Germani as well. It is worth noting that, as is often the case, Syme's prestige has made some scholars read into the sources what they do not say; see e. g. Swan (2004), 297 (under AD 13): "Campaigning by Tiberius and Germanicus on the Rhine front (Suet. *Cal.* 8.3; cf. Vell. 2.123.1)", though the two authors mention only Germanicus and do not report any fighting. Faoro (2016), argues that the said salutations took place no earlier than 26 June 14, when Augustus and Tiberius assumed *tribunicia potestas* for, respectively, thirty-seventh and seventeenth time, which would rule out Germanicus' posited campaign: in summer 14 he was carrying out the census of the Gallic provinces (*Ann.* 1.31.2, 33.1), the mutiny was helped by the legionaries' long idleness (*Ann.* 1.31.3). See, in this volume, the paper by Paweł Sawiński, whose conclusions, however, are different from mine.

1.14.3)[40] – it is only logical to expect that the success which prompted the senate's triumphal decree reported by Tacitus took place under the auspices of Tiberius (the *signa* were recovered *ductu Germanici, auspiciis Tiberii: Ann.* 2.24.1).[41] Be that as it may, even assuming that Timpe is right, the recovery in the land of the Bructeri of the first of the legionary eagles lost in the Teutoburg Forest (*Ann.* 1.60.3), one of the feats for which Germanicus would celebrate the triumph, took place after he had received the title of *imperator*. Evidently, the achievements for which he was granted the triumph were not exactly those for which he celebrated it two and a half years later.

We learn from the *Tabula Siarensis* and Tacitus' paraphrases that the triumph was celebrated for the following exploits: the victory over the Germans living as far as the Elbe, and so revenge for the "treacherous" Teutoburg disaster, the recovery of the *signa militaria* lost in that battle, epitomized by the finding of the legionary eagles (the second was found in the territory of the Marsi at the end of the campaign of 16 [*Ann.* 2.25.3]; the third would be recovered only ca. 41 in the land of the Chauci [Cass. Dio 60.8.7]) and the warding off of the threat to the Gallic provinces. Assuming that they reflect the aims of the war as they were formulated on the occasion, the next obvious step should be to compare them with Velleius' narrative. At this point a difficulty arises: Velleius' presentation of Germanicus' campaigns is devoid of any substance whatsoever. He first says that Germanicus was sent by Augustus to Germania "to finish off the remains of the war" (*reliqua belli patraturum*). In fact, when we compare the "official" list of Germanicus' achievements with those which Velleius' ascribes to Tiberius in his campaigns of 10 and 11, the war had to all intents and purposes been "won" by the latter (the Germans had repeatedly been defeated,[42] Gallia secured), his successor having apparently been left little more than recover the lost *signa*:

> (120.1–2) *mittitur ad Germaniam, Gallias confirmat, disponit extercitus, praesidia munit et se magnitudine sua, non fiducia hostis metiens, qui Cimbricam Teutonicamque militiam Italiae minabatur, ultro Rhenum cum exercitu transgreditur. Arma infert hosti quem arcuisse pater et patria contenti erant; penetrat interius, aperit limites, vastat agros, urit domos, fundit obvios*

---

40 Thus Mommsen (1887–1888), 2, 1158, rejected by such *lumina* as Peter Brunt (1974), 179 f. and Syme (1979), 320 f., I do not quite see why.

41 The weak point of my proposition is Tacitus' silence on Germanicus' posited imperatorial salutation in his account of the campaign of 14, especially in view of the fact that he duly reports Germanicus' salutation in the following year and Tiberius' in 16 (see Paweł Sawiński's paper in this volume). Still, I think it is easier to assume Tacitus' momentary inattentiveness (or wasn't it that he dispensed with mentioning the stage implied anyhow by the bestowal of the triumph?) rather than a victorious campaign that left no traces in our admittedly lacunose sources and whose very occurrence hardly fits with what we know about the situation in Rome, Gallia and Germania during the first year and a half of Germanicus' sole command.

42 At least in Velleius' narrative. Cassius Dio paints a very different picture of these campaigns: in 10 Tiberius just watched the Germans across the Rhine (56.24.6 = Zon. 10.37 [453.7–10 D]), in 11 he and Germanicus did cross the river, but did not venture far and failed to bring the enemy to battle or subjugate any rebellious tribe (56.25.2–3).

maximaque cum gloria, incolumi omnium, quos transduxerat, numero in hiberna revertitur;
(121.1) Eadem virtus et fortuna subsequenti tempore ingressi Germaniam imperatoris Tiberii
fuit, quae initio fuerat. Qui concussis hostium viribus classicis peditumque expeditionibus ...[43]

Sent to Germania, he reassured the Gallic provinces, arranged the troops, strengthened the forts, and, appraising himself by his own greatness, not by the confidence of the enemy who threatened Italy with an army of Cimbric and Teutonic size, he led the army across the Rhine. He advanced against the enemy whom his father and his country would have been content to be warded off, penetrated deep into the interior, opened up roads, laid waste fields, burned houses, slaughtered those who opposed him and returned in great glory, with the whole army intact, to winter quarters. ... The same valour and good fortune as in the first campaign accompanied Tiberius in his subsequent invasion of Germania. After he had broken the enemy's strength by expeditions on sea and land ...

It turns out, however, that something still remained to be done, considering that upon Germanicus' return Tiberius hailed him as *domitor Germaniae* and granted him a triumph whose magnificence corresponded to the greatness of his exploits. These exploits, however, are not specified (unlike, we may note, those of Tiberius' other collaborators Velleius mentions in the relevant paragraph [2.129] to illustrate the reigning *princeps'* magnanimity); all that we find is that Germanicus had learned *rudimenta militiae* from his adoptive father and that in Germania he followed his *praecepta*, which implies that the son's successes were to a large extent the father's. Whatever the reason of this elusiveness, from the perspective of the present paper the really important point Velleius makes is in the opening sentence of the passage on the disaster in Teutoburg Forest, which he describes as "the most terrible calamity, above which no defeat among foreign peoples had been more dangerous for the Romans since that of Crassus in Parthia" (*atrocissimae calamitatis qua nulla post Crassi in Parthis damnum in externis gentibus gravior Romanis fuit*).[44] For Tiberius' eulogist, writing ca. twelve years after Germanicus' death, the former Roman province of trans-Rhenanian Germania was the land of *externae gentes*, like the Parthian Kingdom.[45] At this moment we are clearly in a world different from that of Augustus' *Res gestae*.

More importantly still, we are in a world different from that of Germanicus' campaigns as well. As has been noticed above, in Tacitus' narrative his aim was to reconquer the province; this is shown not only by the just quoted passage on the end of the campaign of 16, especially on the manner in which he was half persuaded, half ordered to abandon his Germanic enterprise, but also by his strategy throughout the war: incessant devastating incursions into the territories of the rebellious tribes to terrorize

---

43 Vell. Pat. 2.120.1–2, 121.1.
44 Vell. Pat. 2.119.1.
45 I think that this phrase is the best rebuttal of the opinion that Tiberius did not renounce the reconquest of Germania but decided to change methods to achieve it, as in Timpe (1968), *passim*.

them into submission. Of course, one could argue that it was Augustus' death which released his adoptive grandson from constraints imposed by the policy the gist of which Tacitus expressed as *consilium coercendi intra terminos imperii*, and so enabled him to adopt a much more aggressive policy towards the rebels whose conquest had warranted the posthumous bestowal on his natural father of the *agnomen* he inherited. We have seen, however, that the instruments for implementing that policy – eight legions, i. e. one third of the armed forces of the Empire – had been put at Germanicus' disposal already in 13, the same year in which Augustus, in the *Res gestae*, firmly included Germania west of the Elbe among the possessions of the Roman people. Returning to the question asked at the beginning of this paper, it is therefore most improbable that a directive to abstain from trying to recover that province was among the *mandata* Germanicus received from Augustus when, after the consulate, sometime at the turn of 12 he set out for Gaul.

There remains still another faint possibility, namely that the ailing Augustus changed his mind still later, in the last months of his life, and this way or another sent his adoptive grandson new instructions which the latter would overstep upon learning of his death; but is so desperate a speculation worth considering?[46] Our sources on Germanicus' campaigns make up a coherent picture. They were waged in order to reconquer Germania; the decision to abandon the almost achieved (at least according to Tacitus) objective and the corresponding re-formulation of the war's aims to revenge (*ultio*) for the humiliation of the Teutoburg disaster (epitomized by the recovery of the legionary eagles lost in that battle) and the warding off of the threat to the Gallic provinces, was Tiberius' doing, possibly decided as early as in 15 (if we interpret the voting of the triumph as the signal to end the war),[47] whether from jealousy, as Tacitus intimates, or for other reasons, the most probable being easily the disproportionality between the drain of the empire's resources to re-subjugate the rebellious province and benefits it could procure.[48] The only discordant note – as we have seen, Augustus' posthumous *consilium coercendi intra terminos imperii*, if historical, referred to dif-

---

46   The last year of Augustus' life must have been like the last years of Elisabeth I of England, with the monarch doing nothing and all the parties involved waiting impatiently for his/her demise.

47   Thus especially Timpe (1968), 54–58. In his reconstruction this interpretation is linked with the controversial redating of the senate's decree on Germanicus' triumph to the end of the campaign of AD 15 (see above), which would imply that only the campaign of the following year was waged against Tiberius' wish (the one at the end of the campaigning season of the year 14 hardly counts, having been a sort of katharsis of the rebellious legions after their mutiny at the news of Augustus' death). Needless to say, the most legitimate hypothesis that the voting of the triumph was a signal on Tiberius' part to end the war (there is no doubt that in those years, if ever, he could not simply order Germanicus about) does not stand and fall with Timpe's dating. If accepted, it would be another argument against the import of *Ann.* 1.3.6.

48   On Tiberius' other reasons to put an end to the Germanic war, see different propositions in Timpe (2008), 199–236 (geostrategy) and Eck (2011) (dynastic policy, more precisely, fear of Germanicus as potential rival).

ferent lands – is struck by "our" sentence at the beginning of his narrative, *Ann.* 1.3.6. Its incongruity stands out in a particularly striking fashion when set against Tacitus' report on Germanicus' campaigns, it being the only place where he adopts the "Tiberian"/"Velleian" perspective and ascribes to unspecified Roman decision-makers of the time of Augustus' death an objective incompatible with the rest of his description and which elsewhere he expressly presents as a pretext on which two years later the then ruling *princeps* recalled his adoptive son from Germania (*Ann.* 2.26.2 and 2.41.2).

Which Tacitus should be believed: the one from *Ann.* 1.3.6 or from his main account? Or perhaps: why in 1.3.6 he wrote something so utterly at variance with his subsequent narrative? The sentence itself does not suggest that he tried to obtain some dazzling effect, similar to that which, e. g., his favourite historian Sallustius achieved with a blatant absurdity (which, though, not only the naive Plutarch, but many a critical modern historian as well, have accepted as a historical fact) of having "ascertained" that Bocchus long could not make up his mind whether to betray Iugurtha to Sulla or Sulla to Iugurtha:

> Sed ego comperior Bocchum magis Punica fide quam ob ea, quae praedicabat, simul Romanos et Numidam spe pacis attinuisse multumque cum animo suo volvere solitum, Iugurtham Romanis an illi Sullam traderet[49].

> But I have ascertained that Bocchus, with Punic faith rather than for the reasons which he declared, was deluding with the hope of peace both the Romans and the Numidian, and that he long meditated whether to hand over Iugurtha to the Romans or Sulla to him.

It is easiest to see in it a slip of the author's pen; but even this simplistic answer raises the question of what made Tacitus, normally in full control of both his *kalamos* and his subject matter, commit it. A better trail is to look for it in Tacitus' intricate style, often generating – not only when quoted out of context – what appear inconsistencies or even absurdities,[50] which makes recovery of his personal opinions an onerous task.[51] A sign in this direction is the phrase about the lack of *cupido proferendi imperii*, which we also find in a slightly different form in Book Four of *Annales*, in the famous digression

---

49 Sall. *Iug.* 108.3.
50 The most famous of such apparent absurdities is surely: *Maneat, quaeso, duretque gentibus, si non amor nostri, at certe odium sui, quando urgentibus imperii fatis nihil iam praestare fortuna maius potest quam hostium discordiam*, where the crucial *urgentibus imperii fatis*; "Let there continue and endure, I pray, among foreign peoples if not affection for us, at least hatred for one another, since, as the destiny of empire drives us on, fortune can furnish us nothing greater than the discord of the enemy" (Tac. *Germ.* 33, Benario), with *fata* translated as "doom", i. e. destruction, instead of the primary and in this particular case obvious "destiny", i. e. world-rule (especially considering the year in which the work was written, Trajan's first imperial consulate), which rather surprisingly turns Tacitus into a particularly gloomy prophet foretelling the fall of the Empire. See Benario (1968), 37–50; Timpe (1995), 203–228.
51 Luce (1968).

on the unattractiveness of the subject matter of his work compared to the writings of those who wrote on Rome's earlier history:

> *Pleraque eorum quae rettuli quaeque referam parva forsitan et levia memoratu videri non nescius sum: sed nemo annalis nostros cum scriptura eorum contenderit qui veteres populi Romani res composuere. Ingentia illi bella, expugnationes urbium, fusos captosque reges, aut si quando ad interna praeverterent, discordias consulum adversum tribunos, agrarias frumentariasque leges, plebis et optimatium certamina libero egressu memorabant: nobis in arto et inglorius labor; immota quippe aut modice lacessita pax, maestae urbis res et princeps proferendi imperi incuriosus erat.*[52]

I am not unaware that many things which I have related and which I am going to relate may perhaps appear insignificant and not worth remembering; but no one should compare our annals with the writings of those who have written accounts of the past deeds of the Roman people. They wrote, freely digressing, about great wars, stormings of cities, kings chased and captured, or, when they turned to internal matters, about conflicts between consuls and tribunes, agrarian and corn laws, fights between the optimates and the plebeians. Ours is a restricted and inglorious labour: in fact, peace was unshaken or slightly disturbed, the state of affairs in the City dismal, the emperor indifferent to extending the empire.

The situation so described, while set in the middle of Tiberius' reign, might almost just as well have been applied to the *extrema Augusti* with which Tacitus opens his narrative (*Ann.* 1.1–5) as an introduction to the proper subject of his work. In fact, with the first *princeps* worn out by old age and bodily illness (*Ann.* 1.4.2: *provecta iam senectus aegro et corpore fatigabatur*), and dominated by his sinister wife determined to secure the imperial succession for her even more baleful son, two of the main traits that would characterize the rule of his successor – the external peace undisturbed or only slightly infringed, the growing gloominess of the state of affairs in the City – are already there; the third, the ruler's inattentiveness to extending the empire, is sort of presaged by ascribing to the war of reconquest of a rebellious province a motivation which, while out of place at the moment in which it is set, in little more than two years would become the official position of the archetypal *princeps proferendi imperii incuriosus*. A small anachronism, then, negligible compared to the apparent misdating of Germanicus' adoption in the preceding sentence (see above) and – on the foregoing interpretation of its function – quite understandable.

Be that as it may – obviously enough, we shall never know for sure what exactly Tacitus had in mind while writing the sentence under discussion – I think that there is every reason to remove it from our dossier on the turning point of the world's history

---

52   Tac. *Ann.* 4.32.

referred to at the beginning of this paper. In its light the decision to definitely abandon the trans-Rhenanian conquests was made by Augustus some time after the Teutoburg disaster. Now, putting aside the question of its (un)historicity, Tacitus' assertion to this effect is not only at variance with the rest of his narrative, but also placed in the part of the work in which historical accuracy is subordinated to the book's overall design in general, and to preparing the ground for the immediately following principate of Tiberius in particular. In other words, it looks that he himself did not consider his allegation in *Ann.* 1.3.6 literally true: if so, there is no place for it among arguments of those who ascribe the epoch-making decision to abandon what had already been a Roman dependency, and so, in practice, to stop the Roman machine of conquest, to Augustus and not to Tiberius.

Bibliography

Benario, Herbert W. (1968): "Tacitus and the Fall of the Roman Empire". In: Historia 17, 37–50.

Brunt, Peter A. (1974): "C. Fabricius Tuscus and an Augustan Dilectus". In: Zeitschrift für Papyrologie und Epigraphik 13, 161–185.

Degrassi, Atillio (1963): Inscriptiones Italiae XIII: Fasti et elogia. 2: Fasti anni Numani et Iuliani: accedunt Feralia, Menologia rustica, Parapegmata. Roma: Istituto poligrafico dello stato.

Eck, Werner (2011): "Augusto – la Germania – Varo – Tiberio. Il fallimento di una storia romana di successi". In: Rivista Storica Italiana 123, 5–25.

Eck, Werner (2018): "*Consilium coercendi intra terminos imperii*. Motivationswandel in der augusteischen Expansionspolitik?". In: Segenni, Simonetta (ed.): Augusto dopo il bimillenario. Un bilancio. Milano: Le Monnier Università, 128–137.

Faoro, Davide (2016): "Nota sulla cronologia delle acclamazioni imperatorie XV–XXI di Augusto e III–VII di Tiberio Cesare". In: Zeitschrift für Papyrologie und Epigraphik 199, 208–212.

Goodyear, Frank R. D. (1972): The Annals of Tacitus. Volume I (Annals I. 1–54). Cambridge: Cambridge University Press.

Hohl, Ernst (1933): "Wann hat Tiberius das Prinzipat übernommen?". In: Hermes 68, 106–115.

Hohl, Ernst (1937): "Zu den Testamenten des Augustus". In: Klio 30, 323–342.

Koestermann, Erich (1961): "Der Eingang der Annalen des Tacitus". In: Historia 10, 330–355.

Luce, Torrey J. (1968): "Tacitus' Conception of Historical Change. The Problem of Discovering the Historian's Opinions". In: Ash, Rhiannon (ed.): Tacitus. Oxford Readings in Classical Studies. Oxford: Oxford Readings in Classical Studies, 339–356.

Millar, Fergus (1993): The Roman Near East. 30 B. C. – A. D. 337. Cambridge, Mass.–London: Harvard University Press.

Mommsen, Theodor (1887–1888): Römisches Staatsrecht³. Leipzig: S. Herzel.

Mommsen, Theodor (1909): "Das Verhältniss des Tacitus zu den Acten des Senats". In: Gesammelte Schriften 7, 253–263.

Ober, Josiah (1982): "Tiberius and the Political Testament of Augustus". In: Historia 33, 306–328.

Sánchez-Ostiz Gutiérrez, Álvaro (1999): Tabula Siarensis. Edición, Traduccíon y Comentario. Pamplona: Ediciones Universidad de Navarra.

Scheid, John (2007): Res gestae divi Augusti. Hauts Faits du Divin Auguste. Texte établi et traduit par John Scheid. Paris: Les Belles Lettres.

Schmidt, Hatto H. (1983): "Tacitus und die nachgelassenen Schriften des Augustus". In: Heinen, Heinz et al. (eds.): Althistorischen Studien. Hermann Bengtson zum 70. Geburtstag dargebracht von Kollegen und Schülern. Wiesbaden: Franz Steiner Verlag, 178–187.

Swan, Peter M. (2004): The Augustan Succession. An Historical Commentary on Cassius Dio's Roman History. Books 55–56 (9 B. C.–A. D. 14). Oxford: Oxford University Press.

Syme, Ronald (1978): History in Ovid. Oxford: Oxford University Press.

Syme, Ronald (1979): "Some Imperatorial Salutations". In: Phoenix 33, 308–329.

Timpe, Dieter (1968): Der Triumph des Germanicus. Untersuchungen zu den Feldzügen der Jahre 14–16 n. Chr. in Germanien. Bonn: Rudolf Habelt.

Timpe, Dieter (1995): "Die Germanen und die fata imperii". In: Timpe, Dieter (ed.): Romano-Germanica. Gesammelte Studien zur Germania des Tacitus. Berlin-Boston: Walter de Gruyter, 203–228.

Timpe, Dieter (2008): "Römische Geostrategie im Germanien der Okkupationszeit". In: Kühlborn, Johann S. (ed.): Rom auf dem Weg nach Germanien. Geostrategie, Vormarschstrassen und Logistik. Mainz: Philipp von Zabern, 199–236.

Timpe, Dieter (2012): "Die Varusschlacht in Ihren Kontexten. Eine kritische Nachlese zum Bimillennium 2009". In: Historische Zeitschrift 294 (3), 593–652.

Wolters, Reinhard (2008): Die Schlacht im Teutoburger Wald. Arminius, Varus und das römische Germanien. München: C. H. Beck.

Wolters, Reinhard (2014/2015): "Germanicusfeldzüge vor den Germanicusfeldzügen? Annalistische Rekonstruktionen *ante excessu divi Augusti*". In: Palamedes 9/10, 197–209.

Woodman, Anthony J. (1977): Velleius Paterculus. The Tiberian Narrative (2.94–131). Cambridge: Cambridge University Press.

Ad spes Germanici coercendas
Germanicus and Piso
in the Second Book of Tacitus' Annals

JAKUB PIGOŃ

Keywords: Germanicus, Tacitus, Gnaeus Calpurnius Piso, narrative technique, rumours in historical narrative

In his Göttingen speech of 1896, which he delivered to mark the 37th birthday of the German emperor Wilhelm II, Friedrich Leo highlighted the literary aspect of Tacitus' historical work; he emphasised, among other things, the Roman historian's ability to control his audience's perception and to put forward, by means of subtle innuendo, some pieces of information which he himself never actually presented as confirmed facts. To illustrate this phenomenon, Leo cites as his example the narrative segment relating to the death of Germanicus:

> Even today most readers of Tacitus will believe that it was in his work that they read that Tiberius had ordered Piso to poison Germanicus. Yet Tacitus himself says that this part of the charges against Piso proved groundless; moreover, nowhere does he put the blame for Germanicus' death on Tiberius or Livia. However, the aim of his narrative is to make the reader ready to believe the worst – and he succeeds in this.[1]

---

*   Final work on this chapter was carried out during my stay in Oxford in July/August 2022. I am grateful to the Lanckoroński de Brzezie Foundation for granting me a scholarship which made this stay possible.

1   "Noch heute werden die meisten Leser des Tacitus meinen, bei ihm gelesen zu haben, daß Tiberius den Germanicus habe durch Piso vergiften lassen; und doch sagt Tacitus selbst, dieser Teil der Anklage sei als grundlos nachgewiesen worden; auch gibt er nirgends dem Tiberius, wie wohl der Livia, geradezu die Schuld. Wohl aber geht die Absicht seiner Erzählung darauf, den Leser das Schlimmste glauben zu machen; und er erreicht sie"; Leo (1960), 272. Cf. Walker (1952), 117; Hausmann (2009), 139 f. Since Leo, Tacitus' "art of innuendo" has been the subject of many studies; the classic paper is Ryberg (1942).

74   JAKUB PIGOŃ

In what follows I would like to undertake a closer inspection of some narrative devices used by the historian in his account of the last period of Germanicus' life – from his German triumph celebrated in Rome in May 17 to his death in Daphne near Antioch in Syria in October 19 (*Ann.* 2.41–72). I will leave out, however, the presentation of the aftermath of his death and, in particular, the narrative of the trial of Piso – which, since the late nineties of the last century (when the *Senatus Consultum de Cn. Pisone Patre* was published), has been the subject of lively scholarly debate.[2]

Taking Germanicus' triumph (an event which might be seen to constitute a symbolical climax of his achievements hitherto) as the starting point of the present discussion requires some explanation. Tacitus strongly underlines this episode, most significantly by placing it at the beginning of the narrative of the year 17, despite the fact that the triumph was not celebrated until 26th May – and the historian, interestingly, gives its exact date (day and month), thus departing from his regular practice of not dating historical events.[3] It transpires that the description of the triumph serves to introduce some ideas which will play an important role in the subsequent narrative of Book Two, culminating in the scene of Germanicus' death. Thus the triumph, paradoxically (and in Tacitus such paradoxes occur quite frequently), forebodes the impending catastrophe. The first sentence of the passage relating to the festivities (2.41.2)[4] recalls the language of the official Roman calendar:

> C. Caelio L. Pomponio consulibus Germanicus Caesar a. d. VII. Kal. Iunias triumphavit de Cheruscis Chattisque et Angrivariis quaeque aliae nationes usque ad Albim colunt.

> With C. Caelius and L. Pomponius as consuls, on the seventh day before the Kalends of June, Germanicus Caesar triumphed over Cherusci, Chatti, Angrivarii, and the other nations who live as far as the Albis.[5]

There then follows a short description of the *pompa triumphalis* (*vecta spolia, captivi, simulacra montium fluminum proeliorum*; "carried in the procession were spoils, cap-

---

2   See e.g. Barnes (1998); Talbert (1999); Eck (2000). For the *editio princeps* of the Piso decree, see Eck et al. (1996). The Latin text, with an English translation and commentary, is conveniently accessible in Lott (2012), 125–157, 255–311.

3   See Ginsburg (1981), 22 for the significance of the dating of Germanicus' triumph in Tacitus.

4   If no author and title are given, references in this chapter are to Tacitus' *Annals*.

5   The Latin text of the *Annals* is quoted throughout after the edition by Heinz Heubner (Stuttgart 1983, Bibliotheca Teubneriana) and all English translations from this work are by A.J. Woodman; see Woodman (2004). For Tacitus' phrasing, cf. the entry on Germanicus' triumph in the *Fasti Ostienses*: [*VII kal. Iun. Germ]anic(us) Caes[a]r [triumphavi]t ex German(ia)* ("on the seventh day before the Kalends of June, Germanicus Caesar triumphed over Germania"). The naming of the prince at 2.41.2 as "Germanicus Caesar" seems to recall the official language; apart from this passage, Tacitus uses the double name only twice (1.14.3; 1.31.1), in both cases not without reason. On the other hand, in such official documents as the *Tabula Siarensis* or the *Senatus Consultum de Cn. Pisone Patre* (*SCPP*) this is the standard form.

tives, and representations of mountains, rivers, and battles")[6] – but this objective account is unexpectedly supplemented by an ironical comment: *bellumque, quia conficere prohibitus erat, pro confecto accipiebatur* ("and the war, because he had been prevented from concluding it, was accepted as concluded", 2.41.2). The use of the passive voice at the end of this sentence (*accipiebatur*, "was accepted") leaves the question open as to who actually regarded the war in such a way.[7] Two possibilities may be considered: either *accipiebatur* refers to Tiberius (thus the emperor would lurk behind two passive verbs in this sentence, *prohibitus erat*, "had been prevented", and *accipiebatur*), or to the inhabitants of Rome who witnessed these events. In the latter case the phrase *pro confecto accipiebatur* would be bitterly ironic – not only the historian, who views the scene from a much later perspective, but also contemporary Romans were aware of the unfairness with which Germanicus was treated; he was granted the triumph only for the purpose of covering up the fact that he had been deprived of "his" legions and ordered to return to Rome. In my opinion, it is this second possibility, making the people of Rome the implied subject of the passive *accipiebatur*, which has to be preferred, because later in this chapter it becomes clear that we watch the triumph of Germanicus from the perspective of the inhabitants of Rome (*augebat **intuentium** visus*, "the sight of the onlookers was intensified") – and that, importantly, Tacitus moves swiftly from what was displayed before their eyes to what was present in their minds (*sed suberat occulta formido, **reputantibus** ...*, "but there was an undercurrent of hidden alarm, as they reflected ...").[8] And the Romans' thoughts were focused on some disturbing parallels from the past (2.41.3):

6   Cf. Strabo 7.1.4, who gives a detailed catalogue of German captives who were led in the triumph, including the wife of Arminius, Germanicus' Cheruscan adversary. The captives are, in fact, the only element in his (probably eye-witness) account of the triumphal pomp. See Östenberg (2009), 138 f.

7   For similar formulations, cf. *Hist.* 4.40.1 (*ignotis adhuc moribus crebra oris confusio pro modestia accipiebatur*, "as his character was still unknown, repeated blushes were taken as proof of modesty"; all translations from the *Histories* in this chapter are by K. Wellesley); *Ann.* 6.8.5 (*libertis quoque ac ianitoribus eius notescere pro magnifico accipiebatur*, "becoming known even to his freedmen and doorkeepers was interpreted as magnificent"); 6.13.2 (*silentium eius non civile [...] sed in superbiam accipiebatur*, "his own silence was interpreted not [...] as citizenlike but in terms of haughtiness"); 12.43.1 (*frugum quoque egestas et orta ex eo fames in prodigium accipiebatur*, "a scarcity of crops too and the famine arising from it were interpreted as prodigies"). So we have in these passages a community (consisting of senators or Romans) who interpret or evaluate certain facts – and this interpretation may go in direction other than the right (*Hist.* 4.40.1) or expected one (*Ann.* 6.13.2).

8   Note the contrast between what is evident (*eximia ipsius species*, "the exceptional scene of the man himself") and what remains hidden (*occulta formido*, "hidden alarm"). On this passage, see O'Gorman (2000), 55 f. and Waddell (2020), 149 f. (who draws attention to an abrupt shift in Tacitus' account of the triumph "from a vivid description of one of the greatest spectacles in the Roman world to the dark foreboding by which the onlookers, much like Tacitus' reader, are suddenly overwhelmed").

... reputantibus haud prosperum in Druso patre eius favorem vulgi, avunculum eiusdem Marcellum flagrantibus plebis studiis intra iuventam ereptum, breves et infaustos populi Romani amores.

... as they reflected that the goodwill of the public had been disadvantageous in the case of Drusus, his father, that his uncle Marcellus had been snatched away in mid-youth from the burning devotion of the plebs, and that brief and unpropitious were the loves of the Roman people.

Words and phrases used in this passage refer both to the preceding and to the subsequent narrative. Before the chapter under discussion, the term *favor* ("goodwill") appears three times, always in reference to Germanicus (1.7.6; 1.33.2; 1.52.2). The second occurrence (1.33.2) is the most important from our perspective, because of the juxtaposition of Germanicus and his father:

*Quippe **Drusi** magna apud **populum Romanum** memoria credebaturque, si rerum potitus foret, libertatem redditurus; unde in Germanicum **favor** et spes eadem.*

The memory of Drusus among the Roman people was considerable, and it was believed that, if he had been in charge of affairs, he would have given them back their freedom. Hence goodwill toward Germanicus, and the same hope.

This is, obviously, an instance of the idea of *hereditas gloriae* (inheritance of honour), a crucial element of the Romans' culture of memory. Germanicus is perceived by the Roman people along the same lines as his father was; he also inherited the benevolence (*favor*) of the citizens of Rome from Drusus.[9] And immediately following this passage, there is a character sketch of Germanicus in which emphasis is placed on precisely those features which make him so unlike Tiberius.[10] The combination *favor et spes* ("goodwill [...] and hope") is also worth noticing; the motif of the hopes inspired by Germanicus, and also his own hopes, plays an important role in the first two books of the *Annals*; we will return to this point later.

The inhabitants of Rome who were watching the triumphal procession of Germanicus on 26th May 17 could not have helped entertaining sombre thoughts when they noticed a peculiar connection between the friendly attitude of the masses (*favorem vulgi*, "the goodwill of the public"; *flagrantibus plebis studiis*, "the burning devotion

---

9 See also Suet. *Calig.* 4: *sic vulgo favorabilis, ut ...* ("he was so popular with the masses that ..."). All translations from Suetonius in this chapter are by J. C. Rolfe (Loeb).

10 *Nam iuveni civile ingenium, mira comitas et diversa a Tiberii sermone vultu, adrogantibus et obscuris* ("for the young man had the instinct of an ordinary citizen and a remarkable affability quite different from Tiberius' conversation and look, arrogant and dark as they were"). On such contrasting juxtapositions in Tacitean character portrayals, see Römer (1999).

of the plebs") and the tragic fate of Drusus[11] and Marcellus.[12] This is, undoubtedly, a subtle foreshadowing of Germanicus' death, but also a suggestion that this death was brought about by the intrigues of people for whom Germanicus' *favor* was unacceptable. We should pay attention to the phrase *intra iuventam ereptum* ("had been snatched away in mid-youth"), used in reference to Marcellus. Tacitus employs a very similar phrase once again – and puts it in the mouth of Germanicus when he delivers his farewell speech on his death bed. He says that if he were dying from natural causes – and not, as he adds later, as a result of the criminal machinations of Piso and Plancina – he might justifiably bear a grudge even against the gods for forcing him to die in the bloom of his youth (*quod me parentibus liberis patriae **intra iuventam** praematuro exitu **raperent**,* 2.71.1). It is highly probable that the historian expects his readers to associate these two passages (2.41.3 and 2.71.1); thus it becomes clear that the fate of Germanicus is, in a sense, a repetition of that of Marcellus.[13] The verbal parallelism makes the reader inattentive to a rather important difference: in the case of Marcellus *intra iuventam* meant that he was 19 years old, whereas in the case of Germanicus, that he was 33.

Immediately after the words *breves et infaustos populi Romani amores* ("brief and unpropitious were the loves of the Roman people"), Tacitus says that the Roman *plebs* received a *congiarium* from Tiberius, distributed in the name of his nephew, and that Germanicus was nominated to the consulship for the next year, together with the emperor. These decisions were intended to persuade the Romans that Tiberius harboured friendly feelings towards his nephew. However, this aim was thwarted (2.42.1):

---

11 For allegations that Drusus (Tiberius' younger brother) was killed by Augustus, see Suet. *Claud.* 1.4: ... *nec dissimulasse umquam pristinum se rei p. statum, quandoque posset, restituturum. Unde existimo nonnullos tradere ausos suspectum eum Augusto revocatumque provincia et, quia cunctaretur, interceptum veneno* ("and he made no secret of his intention of restoring the old-time form of government, wherever he should have the power. It is because of this, I think, that some have made bold to write that he was an object of suspicion to Augustus; that the emperor recalled him from his province, and when he did not obey at once, took him off by poison") – but Suetonius strongly disbelieves this story. At 2.82.2, after the news about Germanicus' illness reached the capital, Tacitus makes the citizens of Rome recall the fate of Drusus and associate it with that of his son: *vera prorsus de Druso seniores locutos: displicere regnantibus civilia filiorum ingenia, neque ob aliud interceptos, quam quia populum Romanum aequo iure complecti reddita libertate agitaverint* ("their elders had spoken altogether truly about Drusus: rulers were prone to be displeased with citizenlike instincts in their sons, and they had been cut off only because they had aspired to incorporate the Roman people under equal rights, with freedom restored"). So this passage may also be linked with 2.42.3 (and with 1.33.2). And note the use of the verb *intercipio* ("cut off") with reference to Germanicus' (or Drusus') alleged killing at 2.71.1 (Germanicus' speech), 2.82.2 and 3.12.4 (and in the Suetonian passage quoted above); see De Vivo (2003), 92f.

12 See Cass. Dio 53.33.4 for rumours that Claudius Marcellus' death in 23 BC was caused by Livia.

13 And Tacitus invites his audience to suppose that this parallelism extends as far as the (alleged) poisoning of the two men (see previous note).

Nec ideo sincerae caritatis fidem adsecutus[14] amoliri iuvenem specie honoris statuit struxitque causas aut forte oblatas arripuit.

Yet he did not thereby gain credibility for the soundness of his affection and, determined to dislodge the young man by a display of honour, he manufactured reasons or seized on those offered by chance.

There follows a retrospective account of the events in the East – Cappadocia is treated in greater detail,[15] while remarks on Commagene, Cilicia, Syria and Judaea are brief. All this serves to explain how to understand the words (which initially seem rather enigmatic) about the causes which the emperor either created himself (*struxit*) or made use of when they occurred (*forte oblatas arripuit*). In this way Tacitus skilfully passes from the triumph of Germanicus to his being granted special powers for his Eastern mission; in the next chapter (2.43) the historian summarises Tiberius' senatorial speech and the senate's decree relating to the mission.[16]

But it would be advisable to take a closer look at the sentence quoted above, because it provides us with a good example of this peculiar art that the Roman author employs to convey a message to his readers which has not been explicitly expressed in words. Words have specific literal meaning, but what is implied by them is more important than what is spelled out. *Amoliri* means, literally, 'to remove'. When applied to people, this verb is used twice by Tacitus, apart from our passage, and in both cases it refers to Nero, who wants to "remove" his wife Octavia. The historian fails to specify whether divorce or physical elimination is meant.[17] Tacitus is deliberately unspecific; his audience well knows that soon after the divorce Octavia was accused and tried, banished

---

14   Cf. 1.72.2, also about Tiberius: *non tamen ideo faciebat fidem civilis animi; nam legem maiestatis reduxerat* ("yet he did not thereby engender belief that he was citizenlike in spirit: he had brought back the law of treason"). The same idea, albeit differently expressed, appears at 15.39.3, in reference to Nero's actions during the Great Fire of Rome.

15   Tacitus gives a detailed description of the situation in Cappadocia (which in that year was transformed from an "independent" kingdom into a Roman province) because it enables him to paint a gloomy picture of Tiberius, harbouring an inveterate rancour against the Cappadocian king Archelaus. Deceitfully induced by Tiberius to come to Rome, the monarch was put on trial and soon met his end; Tacitus characteristically expresses uncertainty about the cause of his death (*finem vitae sponte an fato implevit*, "he consummated, whether of his own accord or naturally, the end of his life"). It seems that the historian's intention is to suggest a parallel between Tiberius' treatment of Archelaus and that of Germanicus; the difference is that Archelaus was summoned from the East to Rome whereas Germanicus will be despatched from Rome to the East.

16   2.43.1: *tunc decreto patrum permissae Germanico provinciae, quae mari dividuntur, maiusque imperium, quoquo adisset, quam iis qui sorte aut missu principis obtinerent* ("then by a decree of the fathers Germanicus was entrusted with the provinces that are separated by the sea, and, wherever he went, with a greater command that entrusted to those who held them by lot or on dispatch from the princeps").

17   *Hist.* 1.13.3: *eoque Poppaeam Sabinam [...] deposuerat, donec Octaviam uxorem amoliretur*, "this was why the emperor, until such times as he could get rid of his wife Octavia, had planted his mistress Poppaea Sabina on Otho"; *Ann.* 14.59.3: *nuptias Poppaeae [...] maturare parat Octaviamque*

to the island of Pandateria and finally executed. The author is deliberately unspecific, too, when he speaks about Tiberius' plans concerning Germanicus. Readers may construe his *amoliri* in one way or another; the historian does not assume responsibility for their interpretations.[18] Also the phrase *specie honoris* ("by a display of honour", as rendered by Woodman) deserves a comment. The noun *species* in the meaning of 'sham, pretext'[19] (cf. the English adjective 'specious') is one of Tacitus' key-words, used frequently in reference to Tiberius, whose most characteristic feature was, according to the historian, hypocrisy (*simulatio*).[20] Here, the emperor decides to "remove" his adoptive son under the pretence of an honourable distinction; in a rather similar way the historian writes about Otho, whom Nero "banished" to Lusitania as the imperial legate of this province: *in provinciam Lusitaniam **specie legationis** seposuit* ("packed him off to the province of Lusitania in the guise of its governor", *Hist.* 1.13.4). And, finally, let us look at the word *struxit*. Literally speaking, Tiberius "built the causes" – which means that he took the (in actual fact) only apparent troubles in the East as a convenient pretext to "remove" Germanicus. Connotations evoked by the verb *struere* may be ominous. Tacitus uses it in reference to an ambush, a ruse, groundless accusations or a treacherous assassination.[21] To take one example: his digression about the *capaces imperii*, a few aristocrats reputedly named by Augustus on his death bed as capable or

---

    coniugem amoliri ("he prepared to hasten his wedding to Poppaea [...], and also to dislodge his spouse, Octavia").

18   See Ryberg (1942), 392. She quotes the sentence we are discussing and adds: "This is less than an actual charge [of killing Germanicus, directed against Tiberius] only because of the somewhat vague meaning of 'amoliri'".

19   *Species* also has other meanings in Tacitus, e. g. 'view', 'form' or 'spectre'. In the meaning of 'sham, pretext' in reference to Tiberius e. g. 2.36.4 (*favorabili in speciem oratione vim imperii tenuit*, "the speech being apparently aimed at winning goodwill, he retained the essence of his command"); 4.57.1 (*tandem Caesar in Campaniam, specie dedicandi templa ...*, "Caesar at last withdrew into Campania, in a show of dedicating temples ..."); 6.1.1 (*speciem venturi simulans*, "simulating a scene of impending arrival"). For a full discussion, see Percy, Jr. (1973); Valenti Pagnini (1987). A very close parallel to the *specie honoris* of our passage (2.42.1) is found at 2.5.1 (in chapters 2.1–4 Tacitus gives a retrospective account of the situation in the East): *ceterum Tiberio haud ingratum accidit turbari res Orientis, ut **ea specie** Germanicum suetis legionibus abstraheret novisque provinciis impositum dolo simul et casibus obiectaret* ("as for Tiberius, the disruption of affairs in the East was a not unwelcome development, since with that pretext he could drag Germanicus away from his familiar legions and install him in new provinces, exposing him to guile and hazard"). See De Vivo (2003), 85.

20   Another term used in this context is *dissimulatio* (the concealment of one's true thoughts and intentions; *simulatio*, on the other hand, refers to pretending something which one does not really possess). See esp. 6.50.1: *iam Tiberium corpus, iam vires, nondum dissimulatio deserebat* ("it was now that Tiberius' body and strength were letting him down; but not yet his dissembling"). The famous obituary of Tiberius (6.51) gives a succinct story of the man who, during the major part of his life, disguised his real self. It needs to be emphasised that this view of Tiberius originated in historical tradition prior to Tacitus; the merit of our historian was to bring it into higher relief. See Giua (1975).

21   E. g. 2.65.4; 4.10.3; 4.68.2; 11.12.1. Cf. Walker (1952), 159.

80 JAKUB PIGOŃ

willing (or both) to hold imperial power, ends with the following sentence: *omnesque* *[…] variis mox criminibus* **struente Tiberio** *circumventi sunt* ("and indeed all of them […] were trapped by various subsequent charges set up by Tiberius", 1.13.2). Thus we get a picture of an emperor who engages in intrigues, fabricates charges and is ready to commit a crime in order to attain his political aims. *Struxit* in the sentence under discussion here is closely related to *specie honoris* – and all this should be associated with Tiberius' *simulatio*.

We now pass to the next chapter (43) and it soon becomes obvious that it plays a pivotal role in Tacitus' narrative strategy, the aim of which is to arouse suspicions about Tiberius and to create the impression that he had some hidden intentions concerning his adoptive son. Having stated the conferment of special powers on Germanicus by the senate for his Eastern mission (see note 16 above), Tacitus mentions a change in the office of the legate of Syria (and this is presented retrospectively, as evidenced by two verbs in the pluperfect tense):[22] Creticus Silanus, a senator connected by betrothal with the family of Germanicus, was replaced in this post by Gnaeus Piso. There follows a character sketch of Piso as a violent and disobedient man (*ingenio violentum et obsequii ignarum*, "temperamentally violent and a stranger to compliance") and Tacitus underlines that his recalcitrance (*ferocia*) was inherited from his father, who had taken part in the African campaign against Julius Caesar and had joined Brutus and Cassius afterwards.[23] Also Plancina, Piso's wife, is said to have stimulated his attitude; as a result Piso was only with difficulty inclined to yield to Tiberius and showed no respect to his sons.[24] The following three sentences deserve to be quoted in full (2.43.4):

> **Nec dubium** habebat se delectum, qui Syriae imponeretur ad spes Germanici coercendas. **Crededidere quidam** data et a Tiberio occulta mandata; et Plancinam **haud dubie** Augusta monuit aemulatione muliebri Agrippinam insectandi.

---

22   See Drogula (2015), 128.
23   … insita ferocia a patre Pisone, qui civili bello resurgentes in Africa partes acerrimo ministerio adversus Caesarem iuvit, mox Brutum et Cassium secutus concesso reditu petitione honorum abstinuit, donec ultro ambiretur delatum ab Augusto consulatum accipere ("with the innate defiance of his father Piso (who in the civil war helped the resurgence of the party in Africa with the keenest of service against Caesar and then, after following Brutus and Cassius, was allowed to return but refrained from seeking office until he was spontaneously solicited to accept a consulship tendered by Augustus)", 2.43.2; consulate in 23 BC, together with the emperor). On *ferocia* as something inherited from one's father, see 1.12.4 (on Asinius Gallus): *Pollionisque Asinii patris ferociam retineret* ("retained the defiance of Pollio Asinius, his father"; cf. Cass. Dio 57.2.5, where Gallus' paternal παρρησία or outspokenness is mentioned). See Traub (1953). It is worth pointing out that the two future antagonists, Piso and Germanicus, are characterised by Tacitus as sons inheriting an important feature of their disposition from their respective fathers (for Germanicus and Drusus, see 1.33.2).
24   … vix Tiberio concedere, liberos eius ut multum infra despectare ("he scarcely yielded to Tiberius and looked down on the man's children as greatly beneath him", 2.43.3). In this way Tacitus indicates that Piso, when sent to the East, will not be inclined to obey Germanicus.

Nor did he have any doubt that he had been selected for installation in Syria to curb Germanicus' hopes. (Certain people believed that secret instructions had been given to him by Tiberius; and without doubt Augusta warned Plancina in womanly rivalry to assail Agrippina.)

There are several points which are worth discussing here.[25] Firstly, the statement about the curbing of Germanicus' hopes (*spes*) as the real reason of Piso's nomination. What hopes are being referred to here? Occasionally, Tacitus uses *spes* while speaking about someone's excessive ambitions or even attempts at political upheaval, for example in reference to Sejanus (3.29.4; 4.68.4) or Agrippina the Younger (12.57.2).[26] Here, however, such connotations of *spes* are out of the question (but see below, note 29). It is worth pointing out, on the other hand, that *spes* appears three times in the preceding narrative in reference to Germanicus – and what is meant there are not his own hopes, but, rather, the expectations which he aroused among the Romans in general or among the rebelling legionaries.[27] The Romans believed that Germanicus, like his father several years earlier, would be willing to restore freedom, that is, the republican form of government (1.33.2: *credebaturque, si rerum potitus foret, libertatem redditurus; unde in Germanicum favor et **spes** eadem*, "and it was believed that, if he had been in charge of affairs, he would have given them back their freedom. Hence goodwill toward Germanicus, and the same hope"). The soldiers assumed that Tiberius' nephew would not acquiesce to his uncle's coming to the throne, but, rather, would make a bid for power himself, with the help of his legions (1.31.1: … ***magna spe** fore ut Germanicus Caesar imperium alterius pati nequiret daretque se legionibus vi sua cuncta tracturis*, "with high hopes that Germanicus Caesar would be unable to suffer the command of another and would entrust himself to the legions, who would handle everything by their own force"). However, it quickly became apparent that Germanicus remained steadfastly loyal to the new emperor: *sed Germanicus quanto **summae spei** propior, tanto impensius pro Tiberio niti* ("yet, the closer Germanicus now was to that highest of all hopes, the more emphatically did he strive on Tiberius' behalf", 1.34.1). It appears, therefore, that the phrase *ad spes Germanici coercendas* ("to curb Germanicus' hopes") should be interpreted in the light of those previous passages and that, in spite of the literal sense,[28]

---

25 For 2.43.4 as "ein Musterbeispiel der taciteischen Insinuationskunst", see Hausmann (2009), 119.

26 See esp. 4.68.3: *audentius iam onerat Seianum, saevitiam superbiam spes eius* ("the other, more boldly now, loaded accusations upon Sejanus and his savagery, haughtiness, and hopes"; the strong alliteration, partly preserved by Woodman, underscores Sejanus' endeavours).

27 For these expectations, and Germanicus' failure to respond to them, see Damtoft-Poulsen (2020), 160–175, who rightly emphasises "the immensity and the vagueness of the hopes attached to Germanicus" (163) and notes that "Germanicus' own aspirations remain an enigma even after his death" (165, cf. 2.71.2).

28 I take *spes Germanici* as (on the literal level of meaning at least) hopes harboured by Germanicus (the subjective genitive). Latin usage allows such collocations as *spes salutis, victoriae*, etc. (a

82 JAKUB PIGOŃ

what is meant here are rather hopes placed on Germanicus by those who supposed that he might be considered a welcome alternative to his unpopular uncle.[29]

Secondly, it is worth considering those *occulta mandata*, or secret orders (in writing?), allegedly received by Piso from the emperor. In the subsequent narrative, Tacitus refers to them three more times, but, importantly, he never does so in his own name; they are mentioned in a statement by a character in the story or as an object of a rumour. Neither does he specify the content of those orders. The reader has reason to suppose that they were somehow connected with Germanicus and his Eastern mission – and that they definitely did not concern assistance or support which the senior politician might lend to the emperor's nephew. On his death bed Germanicus himself mentions people who falsely invoke "nefarious orders" (2.71.4: *fingentibus scelesta mandata aut non credent homines aut non ignoscent*, "those fabricating criminal instructions will either not be believed by men or not forgiven").[30] However, since *occulta mandata* are frequently discussed in scholarship relating to Tacitus' treatment of the last period of Germanicus' life, I will not deal with them in detail.[31]

On the other hand, it would be advisable to dwell for a while on three phrases used by Tacitus to introduce new pieces of information. Thus we have, firstly, *nec dubium*

---

hope for/of sth., the objective genitive), but in this case this possibility has to be ruled out (*pace* Damtoft-Poulsen (2020), 163); there seems to be no instance of *spes* + the genitive of a noun relating to a person used in the latter meaning.

29 Cf. 3.4.1 (the people of Rome on the day when Germanicus' ashes were deposited in the Mausoleum of Augustus): *concidisse rem publicam, nihil spei reliquum clamitabant* ("kept shouting that the state had collapsed and no vestige of hope remained"). In reference to Germanicus, *spes* is also used at 2.49.2 (the consecration of the temple of the Goddess of Hope; this episode most probably should be taken symbolically), 2.71.1 (*Caesar paulisper ad spem erectus*, "Caesar was roused briefly to hope" – shortly before his death) and 2.71.2 (the prince refers to *spes meae* or "my hopes" in his final speech to arouse pity). See, apart from Damtoft-Poulsen (2020) (cf. note 27 above), Delpeyroux (2009), 489–497 (who writes, apropos 1.31.1: "Dans ce passage, ce sont donc les sentiments et les espoirs des légions qui sont décrits, et non ceux de Germanicus", 492). But it is also possible to treat *ad spes Germanici coercendas* as mirroring Piso's own thoughts; in that case *spes* may refer to Germanicus' (alleged, not real) political ambitions vis-à-vis Tiberius. If we follow this interpretation, the passage under discussion may be regarded as an instance of 'embedded focalisation'; for this term, see de Jong (2014), 50–56.

30 It is on this high note that Germanicus ends his speech. Technically speaking, these are his *ultima verba* or "last words" (on this concept, see Schmidt (1914); Ronconi (1966)), although in the next chapter Tacitus also recounts (in reported discourse) what the dying prince told his wife.

31 For other references to *mandata*, see 2.77.1 (a statement by Domitius Celer which Tacitus gives in reported speech); 3.16.1 (a rumour recalled by the historian according to which during his trial Piso held in his hand a document, allegedly – so his friends maintained – containing *litteras Tiberii et mandata in Germanicum*, "a letter from Tiberius and instructions against Germanicus"; he wanted to disclose the document in the senate, but Sejanus persuaded him not to do this). The second passage may be cited in support of the view that the alleged *mandata* were given to Piso in writing. On the *occulta mandata* (which are also mentioned in Suet. *Tib.* 52.3), see e.g. Ryberg (1942), 394; Shatzman (1974), 564; De Vivo (2003), 97f. According to Koestermann (1958), 338, there is no reason to doubt this story: "An der Existenz der *occulta mandata* ist trotz der vorsichtigen Zurückhaltung des Tacitus Ann. 2, 43, 4 nicht zu zweifeln, da sie in der Natur der Sache liegen".

habebat ("nor did he have any doubt"). Consequently, what follows these words is presented as the subjective view of Piso: it was Piso himself who had no doubts that he had been nominated to the governorship of Syria *ad spes Germanici coercendas*. The second phrase is *credidere quidam*, "certain people believed"; here, a piece of information relating to secret orders received by Piso rests on the conviction of some people who are not further specified. It is likely that in this case Tacitus has no written historical sources in mind; if he had wanted to cite such sources, the historian would have written *tradidere quidam* ("some have transmitted"; thus 2.29.2; 6.23.2; 15.45.3).[32] It is better to understand the phrase as follows: some contemporary Romans believed – or even were convinced – that Piso had been given such orders. Of course, we are not told on what grounds they held this belief and on what evidence Tacitus bases his claim. But such statements are frequently found in his works.[33] It may even be maintained that Tacitus' aim in resorting to such statements is not only to suggest a certain version of historical events for which he does not want to claim responsibility, but also to paint an atmosphere of uncertainty, secrecy and the strictly controlled circulation of information which, not only in Tacitus' view, was something highly characteristic of the principate as a political system – in contrast to the republic.[34] And now we come to the third phrase – *haud dubie* ("without doubt"). In this case we have every reason to think that Tacitus passes from subjective convictions or opinions (those of Piso himself or those of contemporary Romans) to hard facts; according to him, there is no doubt that Livia advised Plancina to assume a defiant attitude towards Agrippina.[35] We are not informed what the historian's sources are for the content of the conversation between

---

32 Or e. g. *tradunt* ("transmit", *Hist.* 1.41.1; *Ann.* 1.29.4; 13.17.2); *apud auctores reperio* ("in the authors of affairs I discover", 3.3.1). As is well known, Tacitus does not cite his sources regularly and even when he cares to do so, he refers to them in a general way. There are few exceptions to this rule, most of them in *Ann.* 13–15. See e. g. Martin (1981), 199–213.

33 E. g. *Hist.* 1.14.1 (why did Galba choose Piso as his successor); 5.22.3 (why did Petilius Cerialis stay overnight outside the military camp); *Ann.* 15.52.3 (why did Piso, the leader of the plot against Nero, fail to get in touch with the consul Vestinus). The most interesting statement of this kind is found at *Agr.* 40.2 (a freedman of Domitian was allegedly sent to Agricola to induce him to leave his British province; note Tacitus' comment: *sive verum istud, sive ex ingenio principis fictum ac compositum est*, "the story may be true, or it may be a fiction invented to suit the emperor's character"; all translations from the *Agricola* in this chapter are by A. R. Birley).

34 This view is particularly strongly expressed by Cassius Dio (53.19), who in this respect seems to follow an anonymous historian from the early principate; cf. Flach (1973), 58–60.

35 See De Vivo (2003), 86: "le trame di Livia Augusta con Plancina al fine di perseguitare Agrippina sono riferite, invece [*scil.* in contrast to the two pieces of information which precede], come un dato di fatto". The theme of Livia's secret conference(s) with Plancina reappears at 2.82.2, where Tacitus reports complaints voiced by the inhabitants of Rome after the news about Germanicus' illness reached Rome (*ideo nimirum in extremas terras relegatum, ideo Pisoni permissam provinciam; hoc egisse secretos Augustae cum Plancina sermones*, "that, of course, was the reason for his relegation to the farthest lands, that the reason for Piso's being entrusted with the province! This was what Augusta's secret conversations with Plancina had done!"). But, in that passage, we are on the level of *rumores*, not established facts.

84

JAKUB PIGOŃ

the two ladies, a meeting to which, most probably, there were no witnesses. We are prone to suppose that the subject matter of this conversation – or even the very fact of its having taken place – is also based only on what contemporary Romans believed (or surmised) – but Tacitus formulates this sentence differently[36] and, by doing so, he suggests to his readers that *haud dubie* lends credibility to *credidere quidam* (because *monuit* ("warned") is, in a sense, a continuation of *occulta mandata*).[37]

What seems rather puzzling in the passage under discussion (2.43.4) is Tacitus' emphasis on subjective opinions and sentiments – even if they are, to a certain extent, corroborated by the author by means of the last segment, in which *haud dubie* appears. The historian might have connected the senatorial decree conferring special powers on Germanicus with Tiberius' decision to send Piso to Syria in a quite different way, adducing hard facts and drawing from official documents. But, strangely, it is only *ex post*, from the speech delivered by Tiberius in the senate at the beginning of the trial of Piso, that we learn that he was sent to Syria as a helper (*adiutor*) for Germanicus – which means that the missions of Germanicus and Piso were strongly related to each other. The emperor's words, given by Tacitus in reported discourse, are as follows (3.12.1):

> *Patris sui legatum atque amicum Pisonem fuisse adiutoremque Germanico datum a se auctore senatu rebus apud Orientem administrandis.*

> Piso had been his father's legate and friend and had been given by himself, on the senate's authority, to Germanicus as his helper in the administration of affairs in the East.

Apart from this passage, the word *adiutor* only appears once in Tacitus, in reference to Sejanus, but not in the official context (4.7.1).[38] However, what needs to be stressed

---

36 So the historian does not write: *credidere quidam data et a Tiberio occulta mandata; et Plancinam ab Augusta monitam esse* … (to paraphrase Woodman, "certain people believed that secret instructions had been given to him by Tiberius; and that Augusta had warned Plancina in womanly rivalry to assail Agrippina").

37 In a somewhat similar manner, Tacitus passes from a rumour to something which he presents as a fact in *Hist.* 4.86.1: *unde* **creditur** *Domitianus occultis ad Cerialem nuntiis fidem eius temptavisse, an praesenti sibi exercitum imperiumque traditurus foret.* **Qua cogitatione** *bellum adversus patrem agitaverit an opes viresque adversus fratrem, in incerto fuit* … ("from this town it is believed that Domitian sent secret messengers to seduce Cerialis from his allegiance and see if he would hand over the army and supreme command to himself when they met. He may have been toying with the idea of fighting his father, or it may have been a manoeuvre to gain support and vantage against his brother. No one could tell …"). In the second sentence, only the motives of Domitian's intended action are a matter of dispute (*in incerto fuit*); the action itself (*qua cogitatione*) is treated, in contrast with the previous sentence, as something real and confirmed. The difference is that in *Ann.* 2.43.4 we have two separate (alleged) events.

38 While complaining about Sejanus' influence with Tiberius, Drusus says that *incolumi filio adiutorem imperii alium vocari* ("with a son alive and well, someone else was being called 'assistant in command'"). For this term in connection with Sejanus, see also Vell. 2.127.3: *singularem principalium onerum adiutorem* ("incomparable associate in all the burdens of the principate", transl. by F. W. Shipley). See Woodman (2018), 71 f.

here is that precisely the same word, relating to the same situation, is found in the senatorial decree about Piso (*SCPP*). We read there that Piso, having arrived in Syria, initiated actions which were at variance with what was intended by Germanicus "although he should have kept in mind that he was assigned as an Assistant to Germanicus Caesar, who had been dispatched by our Princeps with the authority of this House to put overseas affairs in order" (*SCPP* 29–31).[39] This coincidence does not seem incidental, especially if we take into account that Tacitus normally avoids using official or quasi-official terminology relating to Roman politics and administration. It is highly probable, in my view, that both the historian who records Tiberius' speech and the senators who deal with the case of Piso in December 20 are referring to the content of the senatorial decree from 17 concerning special powers for Germanicus.[40] And it is also highly likely that in that decree Piso was mentioned as a man who would offer assistance to the prince in the East in his capacity as Germanicus' *adiutor*[41] – whatever this somewhat enigmatic term might have meant in this context.[42]

Thus it appears that in 2.43 Tacitus might have connected Germanicus' mission and Piso's nomination by directly referring to the senatorial decree from 17, a document which he (in all probability) knows, since he paraphrases a portion of it.[43] And in this chapter he might have invoked the description of Piso as Germanicus' helper – making

39 ... *cum deberet meminisse* **adiutorem** *se* **datum** *esse Germanico Caesari, qui* **a principe** *nostro* **ex auctoritate huius ordinis** *ad rerum transmarinarum statum componendum missus esset* ... The translation by Griffin which I quote (Griffin (1997), 251) is more accurate than that by Lott (2012), 143, who wrongly takes the *cum* clause as causal rather than concessive.

40 Or the law (*lex de imperio Germanici Caesaris*) which must subsequently have been passed and which, most probably, closely followed both the content and the form of the *senatus consultum*.

41 See Eck et al. (1996), 157: "Doch ist es durchaus denkbar, daß Tiberius im Zusammenhang der Erörterung, wie die Probleme in den östlichen Provinzen geregelt werden sollten, dem Senat auch Mitteilung darüber machte, Piso solle als *adiutor* dem Germanicus beigegeben werden. Dies könnte dann auch in die Meinungsäußerung des Senats, d. h. in ein *senatus consultum* aufgenommen worden sein, weshalb Tacitus es wohl auch in den *acta senatus* gefunden hatte".

42 We should bear in mind that Tiberius made Piso his legate in Syria before he requested the senate to vote on special powers for Germanicus. For a different view about the appearance of the term *adiutor* in both Tacitus and the *SCPP*, see Drogula (2015), 137 f.: "Syme's emphasis on the description of Piso as *adiutor* to the prince seems to make too much of the term. If anything, the word was probably invoked by Tacitus and the *SCPP* to intensify the appearance of Piso's guilt" (the reference is to Syme (1986), 373). However, if this is so, it would be difficult to explain the agreement between Tacitus and the *SCPP*. Syme wrote before the *SCPP* was discovered; its discovery seems to have strengthened his position.

43 Compare 2.43.1 (quoted in note 16 above) with *SCPP* 33–35: *de quo* [*scil. Germanico*] *lex ad populum lata esset, ut in quamcumq(ue) provinciam venisset, maius ei imperium quam ei, qui eam provinciam proco(n)s(ule) optineret, esset* ... ("about whom a law has been presented to the people that into whatever province he should go he should have greater authority than the proconsul governing that province", transl. by J. B. Lott). See Eck et al. (1996), 158–162; they note, among other things, that there is no discrepancy between Tacitus (who speaks about both proconsuls and imperial legates) and the document (which mentions proconsuls only). For a discussion of Tacitus' and the *SCPP*'s respective passages concerning the nomination of Piso and his position *vis-à-vis* Germanicus, see Damon (1999), 146–151.

the best of the ironical associations of the term *adiutor* in the context of the dramatic events of the two ensuing years. The historian readily employs such irony elsewhere. To give just one example (a particularly apposite one, in view of the present discussion): when he mentions Sejanus for the first time early in his narrative, he makes use of the ironical connotations of the word *rector* ("guide"), also a quasi-official title, akin to *adiutor*.[44] When in September 14 Tiberius' son Drusus was despatched to the rebelling legions of Pannonia, Sejanus played an important role in his retinue. Tacitus succinctly presents the praetorian prefect as *rector iuveni et ceteris periculorum praemiorumque ostentator* ("a mentor for the young man and, for the others, a living demonstration of perils and prizes", 1.24.2). Both parts of this chiastically arranged phrase should be taken as relevant not only to the present situation, but also to the future. So *periculorum praemiorumque ostentator* ("a living demonstration of perils and prizes") foreshadows the prefect's role in the later part of Tiberius' principate, especially after the emperor's departure from Rome (see e. g. 4.74). And *rector iuveni* ("a mentor for the young man") takes on an extra meaning in the light of Sejanus' plot – described at length in the opening chapters of Book 4 (4.7–11) – to poison the *iuvenis* whose "guide" he had been nine years earlier.[45] So Tacitus might have chosen to take the same path of foreshadowing and dramatic irony when speaking about Germanicus and Piso in 2.43. He preferred, instead, to take another route. As a result, what dominates in this chapter is not irony but innuendo and an emphasis on unconfirmed, subjective opinions and sentiments.

My discussion of just three chapters from the middle of Book 2 (2.41–43) has been so extensive because they set the tone for the ensuing narrative; Tacitus expects his readers to proceed along the lines drawn in this powerful introduction to the Germanicus and Piso story. Thus, in dealing with the rest of his account, it will be unnecessary to dwell on every detail. Instead, we shall concentrate on some selected items.

Tacitus' account of Germanicus and Piso in the East is divided into two annalistic years, 18 (chs. 53–58) and 19 (chs. 59–88; here chs. 73–88 deal with events occurring after Germanicus' death, among them Piso's abortive military action to regain Syria and the reaction in Rome to the dramatic news coming from the East;[46] and chs. 63–68

---

44 See Drogula (2015), 137 for some differences between *rectores* and *adiutores*.

45 Most modern historians reject the story (which, apart from Tacitus, is told by Suetonius and Cassius Dio) that Drusus was murdered.

46 In chapters 84–88, other events from the year 19 that have no direct reference to the Germanicus story are recounted. But the book's last chapter (88), with its obituary of Germanicus' Cheruscan adversary Arminius, is in fact highly relevant to the Roman prince. Compare, e. g., *petitusque armis cum varia fortuna certaret, dolo propinquorum cecidit* ("while his struggle with them was meeting with variable fortune, he fell to the cunning of his kinsmen", 2.88.2) with *quorundam florentem et tot bellorum superstitem muliebri fraude cecidisse* ("a once flourishing survivor of so many wars has fallen to womanly foul play", 2.71.2) from Germanicus' death-bed speech; also the story of the poison which Tiberius reportedly refused to deliver to Arminius' German enemies is important. For the nexus of associations, see Pelling (2012), 306–309.

Ad spes Germanici coercendas 87

describe affairs in Germany, Thrace and Cilicia, unconnected, at least *prima facie*, with either Germanicus or Piso).[47] The narrative of the year 18 is unique in the *Annals* in that it is entirely devoted to external affairs. The obvious reason for this is Tacitus' desire to focus his audience's attention on Germanicus (and Piso) alone; "[n]o events at Rome [...] are allowed to distract us from Germanicus as his path crosses with that of Piso and dissension between them begins".[48] The historian moves from Germanicus (chs. 53–54) to Piso (ch. 55) to Germanicus once again (chs. 56–58); in the last section Piso also appears, because the two men meet at Cyrrus in Syria (and they depart "in open hatred", 2.57.3). In the first Germanicus unit an account is given of the prince's journey from Nicopolis in Epirus to Colophon in Lydia with stops at Actium, Athens, Ilium (Troy) and some other places. Tacitus underlines the importance of the past[49] – both that which is quite recent (the battle of Actium) and, especially, the distant past, notably that connected with the origins of Rome (2.54.2: *adito Ilio quaeque ibi varietate fortunae et nostri origine veneranda*, "after going to Ilium and the venerable places there which have experienced such variation in fortune and from which our own origins derive"). Another important element in this section is the theme of the mutability of fortune (see the passage on Troy quoted in the previous sentence) and of the intertwining of things happy and sad. This is evidenced by what is said about the prince's visit at Actium – the place of Octavian's victory also evokes memories of Mark Antony in Germanicus; they both are among his ancestors, so *magnaque illic imago tristium laetorumque* ("and vivid was the vision there of sadness and delight", 2.53.2).

But, despite this section's strong focus on the past, the future is perhaps even more underscored here. Firstly, the historian notes that Germanicus stopped at Lesbos, *ubi*

47 But, once again (see notes 15 and 46 above), the story of the Thracian rulers Rhescuporis and Cotys (uncle and nephew, cf. Tiberius and Germanicus), told in chapters 64–67, should be read as Tacitus' indirect commentary on the events around Germanicus. See Mc Culloch, Jr. (1984), 91–99; Devillers (2014).

48 Thus Ginsburg (1981), 77. Occasionally, we have annalistic units in the *Annals* in which only internal affairs are recorded; such is the case with years 23, 32 and 33 in the Tiberian books. Ginsburg (1981), 54.

49 The glorious past of the places which he visited appealed to Germanicus (2.53.3: *hinc ventum Athenas, foederique sociae et **vetustae** urbis datum, ut uno lictore uteretur*, "from here the journey was to Athens, and his concession to our treaty with this allied and olden city was that he used only one lictor"; 2.54.1: *tum extrema Asiae [...] intrat, cupidine **veteres** locos et fama celebratos noscendi*, "than it was the edge of Asia [...] [that] he entered [...], in his desire to become acquainted with old places celebrated by fame"); his journey to Egypt the next year, undertaken in the first place on account of its antiquities (2.59.1: *Germanicus Aegyptum proficiscitur cognoscendae **antiquitatis**. Sed cura provinciae praetendebatur ...*, "Germanicus departed for Egypt to become acquainted with antiquity. But his pretext was concern for the province ..."), illustrates this attitude of his most clearly. This should be connected with the fact that, as Pelling (2012), 297–300 notes, the Tacitean Germanicus is, in a sense, a figure of the past, rather badly suited to the realities of Tiberian Rome. On Tacitus' treatment of Germanicus' eastern journey, discussed in the light of material evidence relating to it, see Damon/Palazzolo 2019. On the material evidence itself, see Blonce/Gangloff 2013.

Agrippina novissimo partu Iuliam edidit ("where Agrippina in her latest childbirth produced Julia", 2.54.1). *Novissimo* ("latest") is foreboding: no other children from this marriage will be born. Secondly, and emphatically placed at the end of this section, there is an account of Germanicus' visit at the oracle of Apollo Clarius in Colophon. Tacitus describes in some detail (44 words) the local method of predicting the future and then adds, briefly (11 words), as though it were an afterthought: *et ferebatur Germanico per ambages, ut mos oraculis, maturum exitum*[50] *cecinisse* ("and it was said that he prophesied for Germanicus – in ambiguities, as is the custom with oracles – a timely departure", 2.54.4).[51]

The Piso unit which immediately follows begins thus: *At Cn. Piso, quo properantius destinata inciperet, civitatem Atheniensium turbido incessu exterritam oratione saeva increpat* ... ("as for Cn. Piso, to hasten the start of his designs he berated the community of the Athenians – already terrified by his turbulent entrance – in a savage speech ...", 2.55.1). The conjunction *at* is regularly used by Tacitus to mark the transition to a new segment of the narrative (with other people as protagonists and, frequently, the action happening in another place). It should be emphasised that the historian likes to juxtapose two narrative units in such a way as to create an inner tension between them, with episodes from one section shedding light on those from another (or casting a shadow of dramatic irony on them).[52] And Tacitus expects his readers to make con-

---

50 Here I depart from Heubner, who prints *exitium*, the reading of the Medicean manuscript. *Exitum*, on the other hand, is an emendation proposed by Karl Heraeus; he cites in support of his conjecture the words from Germanicus' death-bed speech: *praematuro exitu raperent* ("for snatching me [...] by a premature departure", 2.71.1). This emendation is accepted by, e. g., Koestermann and Goodyear (who notes, however, that there is no clear-cut distinction between *exitus* 'ending, demise, death' and *exitium* 'destruction, ruin, catastrophe': "the dividing line is sometimes a little blurred", Goodyear (1981), 360). If *exitum* were the correct reading, we would have a fine ring composition in the Germanicus section: *sed eum honorem Germanicus iniit* ("but Germanicus entered upon his office", 2.53.1) at the beginning and *maturum exitum cecinisse* ("prophesied [...] a timely departure", 2.54.4) at the end. More importantly, we would have a truly oracular ambiguity of the prophecy, since *exitum* may mean either 'departure' (*OLD* 1) or 'death' (*OLD* 4) and *maturum* either 'occurring at the proper time' (*OLD* 7) or 'occurring before the proper time' (*OLD* 9). See Woodman (2004), 67 (n92); Seider (2022), 37 f.

51 Of course, the motif of the mutability of fortune also contributes to the foreshadowing of the impending catastrophe. The fall of Troy played an important role in the Roman symbolic imagination.

52 To pick two examples at random: in *Hist.* 1.12–50, Tacitus alternates between the narrative of Galba and that of Otho (who forms a plot to overthrow the old emperor and eventually kills him); decisive steps taken by the conspirators are recounted in 1.27.2–28 and in chapter 29 we come back to Galba, whom we left two chapters earlier when he was making a sacrifice to the gods. Tacitus says now: *ignarus interim Galba et sacris intentus fatigabat alieni iam imperii deos* ("meanwhile, Galba was unaware of what was afoot. Preoccupied with the sacrifice, he continued to offer his importunities to the gods of an empire no longer his", 1.29.1). My second example comes from *Ann.* 11 and it concerns the tension between the narrative of Claudius (especially in his capacity as censor) and that of Messalina and her adulteries; in chapter 12 Tacitus speaks about the beginning of her new affair and in the following chapter he shifts to Claudius: *at Claudius matrimonii sui ignarus et munia*

nections themselves; if a telling juxtaposition is made, there is no need for an explicit commentary. Moreover, the very transition from one segment to another may contain a hidden message. Such is the case, I believe, here: the last item in the first unit is the oracle about the prince's *maturus exitus* while the next unit begins with the name of Piso and the stress is laid on the speed with which he wants to put his plans (*destinata*) into action. We are thus invited to link Germanicus' approaching death with the legate of Syria;[53] to treat *properantius* (lit. 'more swiftly') as a counterpart to *maturum*; and to ask ourselves about the true meaning of those *destinata* – is there a connection between them and the *occulta mandata* ("secret instructions") of chapter 43?

An interesting parallel to this technique may be found in Tacitus' account of the Great Fire of Rome in *Annals* 15. It begins in chapter 38 with the famous alternative: *sequitur clades, forte an dolo principis incertum (nam utrumque auctores prodidere)* ("there followed a disaster – whether by chance or by the princeps' cunning being uncertain (authors have transmitted each alternative)", 15.38.1).[54] Tacitus proceeds, without mentioning Nero, and vividly describing the first stage of the calamity. Towards the end of this chapter he notes that some people forbade extinguishing the fire and some others even threw torches and shouted that they were authorised to act in this way; there follows another "loaded alternative"[55] (so they frame this narrative unit), this time to put forward possible motives behind these actions: *sive ut raptus licentius exercerent seu iussu* ("whether to conduct their looting more licentiously or by order", 15.38.7). And precisely at this point the historian shifts his narrative from Rome to Antium and says: *eo in tempore Nero Anti agens …* ("at the same time Nero was at Antium …", 15.39.1). No word is explicitly spoken about this, but the reader is invited to connect *iussu* ("by order") with *Nero*: if there were orders to help to spread the fire, the emperor was responsible for them. And, moreover, the transition to Nero makes the second possibility more plausible, at least on the intuitive level.[56]

Of course (to come back to 2.55), Tacitus not only implicitly suggests a connection between Germanicus' *maturus exitus* and Piso, but also explicitly mentions in the "Pi-

---

censoria usurpans, theatralem populi lasciviam severis edictis increpuit … ("but Claudius, ignorant of his own marriage and exercising his censorial responsibilities, in stern edicts berated the people's recklessness at the theatre", 11.13.1).

53 See De Vivo (2003), 89: "Tacito ha scandito i tempi narrativi così da porre in successione la profezia di morte [di Germanico] e l'apparizione del presunto assassino …". He also thinks that the term *destinata* "non può non richiamare, in qualche modo, gli *occulta mandata*". See also Hausmann (2009), 121; Waddell (2020), 150.

54 Other literary sources (Pliny the Elder, the *Octavia Praetexta*, Suetonius and Cassius Dio) make the emperor responsible for the Great Fire. For the alternative at 15.38.1, see Yavetz (1975).

55 See Whitehead (1979).

56 Whitehead (1979), 492 lists both 15.38.1 and 15.38.7 in his third category: "Emphasis probably or certainly on second (or last) alternative" (487). But see Ash (2018), 184 (on 15.38.7): "T. avoids deciding between his two alternative explanations", but the choice of vocabulary "accentuates the first motive". Cf. Cass. Dio 62.17.1 where the desire to plunder is stated as an uncontested fact.

sonian" section the legate's actions which stemmed from his enmity to Germanicus. In fact, the very first item put forward by the historian, Piso's hostile speech to the Athenians, becomes a veiled attack on the prince.[57] The phrase *quo properantius destinata inciperet* ("to hasten the start of his designs") may thus be taken (apart from the implied connection with Germanicus' death, as suggested above) as referring to Piso's intentions to undermine the position of Germanicus in every possible way;[58] we should add that these two interpretations are not mutually exclusive.

It has been pointed out by many scholars that Tacitus himself never states explicitly that Germanicus' death was caused by poison. This was Germanicus' own conviction, mentioned by the historian for the first time in chapter 69[59] and repeatedly put forward afterwards, firstly in the prince's soliloquy (2.70), then in his death-bed speech (2.71).[60] But, conversely, nowhere does he assert that Germanicus died of natural causes. So, it would seem, the verdict of the historian is: *non liquet*.[61] But, crucially, he never

57   2.55.1: ... *oblique Germanicum perstringens, quod contra decus Romani nominis non Athenienses tot cladibus exstinctos, sed conluviem illam nationum comitate nimia coluisset* ("delivering a glancing blow at Germanicus on the grounds that, contrary to the dignity of the Roman name, he had, with excessive affability, paid court not to Athenians, who after so many disasters were extinct, but to that famous cesspit of nations"). For *comitas* or affability as one of the most distinct characteristics of Germanicus, see 1.33.2; 1.71.3; 2.13.1; 2.72.2. Piso alone finds fault with Germanicus' *comitas*. Interestingly, Tacitus uses the same verb *perstringo* at 2.59.1 when he speaks about Tiberius' criticism of Germanicus' behaviour during his stay in Egypt; this suggests an affinity between the emperor and his legate in their respective attitudes towards Germanicus.

58   See Goodyear (1981), 360 (on *destinata*): "His purpose, then, T. implies, was to undermine and counteract whatever Germanicus might do". Given the emphasis on Piso's haste in chapter 55 (*navigatione celeri*, "by a fast voyage"; *vix diei moram perpessus*, "scarcely enduring a day's delay") one might think that his aim (*destinata*) was to reach the Syrian province as quickly as possible; this impression is wrong, however, since he stops for quite a while at Athens – evidently in order to give vent to his hostility to Germanicus.

59   2.69.3: *saevam vim morbi augebat persuasio veneni a Pisone accepti* ("the savage violence of the disease was increased by his conviction that he had been given poison by Piso"). There is an interesting parallel at *Agr.* 43.2: *et augebat miserationem constans rumor veneno interceptum*, "the sympathy that was felt was increased by the persistent rumour that he had been poisoned" (observe the use of the verb *intercipio*; see note 11 above). Scholars have noted numerous similarities between Tacitus' presentation of Germanicus and that of Agricola; they are also found in the accounts of their deaths and include allegations of poisoning; see De Vivo (2003), 90–94.

60   And, significantly, it is as Germanicus' assertion that Piso's responsibility for his death is mentioned (only once) in the *SCPP* (27 f.: ... *morientem Germanicum Caesarem, cuius mortis fuisse c[aussam Cn.] Pisonem patrem ipse testatus sit ...*, "Germanicus Caesar, as he lay dying (and he himself testified that Cnaeus Piso was cause of his death) ...", transl. by J. B. Lott).

61   Tacitus is aware of how one's presuppositions influence one's perception of reality. Note what he says about the cremation of Germanicus' corpse at Antioch: *corpus antequam cremaretur nudatum in foro Antiochensium, qui locus sepulturae destinabatur, praetuleritne veneficii signa, parum constitit: nam ut quis misericordia in Germanicum et praesumpta suspicione, aut favore in Pisonem pronior, diversi interpretabantur* ("before his body was cremated, it was stripped in the forum of Antiochians, the place which was marked out for burial; but there was no general agreement whether it presented the signs of poisoning: interpretations differed according to whether one was more inclined toward Germanicus through pity and the presumption of suspicion, or toward Piso through

says even this;[62] and, moreover, his treatment of the trial of Piso clearly shows that he knows on what weak foundations the charge of poisoning was based (3.14).[63]

We should also note that throughout the narrative relating to Germanicus and Piso in the East (2.53–61; 69–83) much attention is paid to reports, opinions, hearsay and also to how other people perceived, or reacted to, a protagonist's words or deeds. Even the content of the oracle received by Germanicus at Colophon is presented as a report rather than an established fact (*ferebatur*, "it was said", 2.54.4). When Tacitus says that many good soldiers in Syria were ready to obey Piso, in spite of the highly reproachable actions he had undertaken, he explains this by their belief (based on a rumour) that Tiberius himself approved of them (*quod haud invito imperatore ea fieri occultus rumor incedebat*, "because there had spread a concealed rumour that such developments were not contrary to the Commander's will", 2.55.6).[64] And Piso's reproachful comment made during a banquet held by the king of Nabataea is introduced by the historian as follows: *vox quoque eius audita est* ("his voice was heard saying", 2.57.4), the implication being that what was heard by others was more important than what Piso actually said.[65]

---

goodwill", 2.73.4; according to Cassius Dio 57.18.9, on the other hand, the inspection of his body before the cremation unambiguously proved that he had been poisoned). Significantly, the historian omits the story of Germanicus' heart which (allegedly) was not consumed by fire; we know from Pliny the Elder (*HN* 11.187) and Suetonius (*Calig.* 1.2) that during Piso's trial this was used as evidence that Germanicus had been poisoned (because, as Suetonius explains, *cuius ea natura existimatur, ut tinctum veneno igne confici nequeat*, "and it is supposed to be a characteristic of that organ that when steeped in poison it cannot be destroyed by fire").

62   In contrast to what he says about Agricola: *nobis nihil comperti adfirmare ausim* ("I would not venture to assert that we have any definite evidence", *Agr.* 43.2). This sentence, most probably corrupted by manuscript transmission, immediately follows that which I quoted in note 59 above).

63   But even here he hides his own views behind such phrases as *solum veneni crimen **visum est** diluisse* ("only the charge of poisoning did they [*scil.* the defence] seem to have wiped out") and *quippe absurdum **videbatur*** ("it seemed not to ring true", *scil.* to administer the poison during a banquet, before the eyes of so many guests). The pivotal sentence in this chapter is this: *sed iudices per diversa implacabiles erant, Caesar ob bellum provinciae inlatum, senatus numquam satis **credito** sine fraude Germanicum interisse* ("but the judges were variously implacable, Caesar on account of the war inflicted on the province, the senate never really believing that Germanicus' demise had been without foul play", 3.14.3). Even after the charge of poisoning was overthrown, the senators still believed that this was not a natural death. Note also Tacitus' epilogue to the trial of Piso at 3.19.2. For his narrative of the trial as a whole, see Woodman/Martin (1996), 110–118.

64   For the idea of rumours as causes of events in Tacitus, see Gibson (1998). The passage quoted above is adduced at p. 119.

65   And also: what the friends of Germanicus made of Piso was more important than what he actually was. Here, the crucial passage is 2.57.2: *sed amici accendendis offensionibus callidi intendere vera, adgerere falsa ipsumque et Plancinam et filios variis modis criminari* ("but his friends, astute in inflaming his sense of offence, let fly with the truth, heaped up falsehoods, and in various ways incriminated Piso, Plancina, and their sons"). Intriguingly, the imagery of kindling fire has previously been used in reference to Piso (2.43.3: *sed praeter paternos spiritus uxoris quoque Plancinae nobilitate et opibus accendebatur*, "but besides his father's spirit he was fired by the nobility and wealth of his wife too, Plancina"); and, out of six attestations of *callidus* ("astute") in *Annals* 1–6, three are used to describe Tiberius (1.80.2; 2.30.3; 6.24.3; cf. 11.3.2).

Certainly, quite a number of things relating to the mutual relations between Germanicus and Piso are stated by Tacitus as facts, not as reports or rumours. Thus we learn that Germanicus granted a request from the Parthian king and removed Vonones from Syria to Cilicia partially because he wanted to offend Piso (2.58.2);[66] that Piso reacted in a hostile manner to the people of Antioch showing their happiness when Germanicus had recovered from his (first) illness (2.69.2); that the prince, already mortally ill, wrote a letter to Piso in which he renounced his friendship (2.70.2).[67] Some items are, however, less straightforward. Such is the case with the following sentence: *tum Seleuciam degreditur [scil. Piso], opperiens aegritudinem, quae rursum Germanico acciderat* ("then he departed for Seleucia, waiting upon the illness which again had befallen Germanicus", 2.69.2). The (uncontested) fact was that Piso retired to Seleucia. But what about *opperiens aegritudinem* ("waiting upon the illness")? Was his reason for remaining there really that he wanted to wait for the termination of Germanicus' illness (one way or the other)? This seems plausible, given the short distance from Seleucia to Antioch (16 miles). But we have an impression that Tacitus implies a sinister message here: Piso stayed at Seleucia in order to wait for the death of his enemy. A narrow line dividing fact and allegation (veiled as fact) has been, so it seems, crossed.[68]

On the other hand, pieces of information directly bearing on the story of Germanicus' illness and death as a result of a conspiracy are not adduced as established facts. There is one exception: Tacitus says that in Germanicus' residence in Syria human bones, magic spells and tablets with his name on them, half-burnt ashes and other such objects were found; objects, he explains, by means of which human souls are believed to be devoted to the underworld.[69] I suppose that the rather unspecific way in which this piece of information is presented (the passive *reperiebantur*, "were discov-

---

66 *Datum id non modo precibus Artabani, sed contumeliae Pisonis, cui gratissimus erat [scil. Vonones] ob plurima officia et dona, quibus Plancinam devinxerat* ("this was not only a concession to the plea of Artabanus but an insult for Piso, by whom he [*scil.* Vonones] was extremely favoured on account of the very many duties and gifts with which he had bound Plancina to himself"). The word *contumelia* ("insult") also appears at 2.55.6 (where it refers to Plancina throwing insults at Agrippina and Germanicus) and at 2.69.1 (where it refers to Germanicus insulting Piso, who repaid in kind). So both sides of the conflict behaved similarly (at least to a degree).

67 *Componit epistulas, quis amicitiam ei renuntiabat* ("he composed a letter in which he renounced their friendship"), a fact also recorded in *SCPP* 28 f. But here Tacitus adds: *addunt plerique iussum provincia decedere* ("many people add that he was ordered to withdraw from the province"). So this piece of information does not rest on as firm a basis as the previous one. It is remarkable how the historian differentiates (if he cares to do so) between various levels of reliability of his material.

68 This makes us ponder whether the first example from those given above, concerning Vonones' removal to Cilicia (2.58.2), does not belong to the same category. What evidence can Tacitus cite to substantiate what he says about Germanicus' motives for removing Vonones?

69 2.69.3: *et reperiebantur solo et parietibus erutae humanorum corporum reliquiae, carmina et devotiones et nomen Germanici plumbeis tabulis insculptum, semusti cineres ac tabo obliti aliaque malefica, quis creditur animas numinibus infernis sacrari* ("and in fact there were discovered, unearthed from the ground and walls, remains of human bodies, spells and curses and the name 'Germanicus' etched on lead tablets, half-burned ashes smeared with putrid matter, and other malefic devices by which

Ad spes Germanici coercendas 93

ered", without any details allowing us to say by whom, when or in what circumstances) makes it more akin to those items in the narrative which rest on hearsay or subjective opinions than to those which are given as hard facts. Three points may be made in connection with this passage. Firstly, there is no *explicit* indication that Piso (or Plancina) was involved. However, it is enough to look at the preceding sentence (*saevam vim morbi augebat persuasio veneni a Pisone accepti; et reperiebantur* …, "the savage violence of the disease was increased by his conviction that he had been given poison by Piso; and in fact there were discovered …") as well as the following one (*simul missi a Pisone incusabantur ut valitudinis adversa rimantes,* "at the same time envoys from Piso were censured for probing the adverse state of his health")[70] to come to the conclusion that Piso's presence is also implied in what is put in the middle. Secondly, the magic actions referred to at 2.69.3 may seem unrelated to Tacitus' main object in these chapters, namely to create an impression (without saying so explicitly in his own name) that Germanicus might have been killed by poison. But, of course, to assert that these two (magic and poison) are unrelated would be to ignore the Romans' conviction about the strong association between magic practices, witchcraft and poisoning (and women).[71] This is also evident from what Suetonius says in the same context: *Pisoni […] non prius suscensere in animum induxerit [scil. Germanicus], quam* **veneficiis** *quoque et* **devotionibus** *impugnari se comperisset* ("he could not make up his mind to break with him, until he found himself assailed also by potions and spells", *Calig.* 3.3).[72] And, thirdly, the way in which Tacitus introduces the magic spells theme (*et reperiebantur*

---

it is believed that souls are consecrated to the infernal divinities"). This is also mentioned by Suetonius (*Calig.* 3.3) and Cassius Dio (57.18.9). See Lund (2009).

70 We are expected to connect this sentence with that about Piso's retirement to Seleucia, discussed above. For a parallel passage in the *Agricola*, see *Agr.* 43.2: *ceterum per omnem valetudinem eius crebrius quam ex more principatus per nuntios visentis et libertorum primi et medicorum intimi venere, sive cura illud sive inquisitio erat* ("all the same, all through his last illness there were more visits from leading freedmen and court physicians than is usual with emperors who pay their visits by proxy, whether that meant anxiety or espionage"). See note 59 above for similarities between the death of Germanicus and that of Agricola.

71 For this association (as applied to Tacitus' *Annals*, but with many examples taken from other writers), see Santoro-L'hoir (2006), 158–198. The passage about Domitius Afer's accusation against Claudia Pulchra may be cited as illustrating the nexus of themes in question: *crimen impudicitiae, adulterum Furnium, veneficia in principem et devotiones obiectabat* ("he flung at her a charge of immorality, involving Furnius as her adulterer, and poisoning and curses aimed at the princeps", 4.52.1). The role of Plancina becomes important here (even if, in her case, no *adulterium* is attested); and Tacitus also mentions another woman, Martina (2.74.2: *infamem veneficiis ea in provincia et Plancinae percaram,* "a woman infamous for poisoning in the province and particularly dear to Plancina"; she was brought to Italy for the trial of Piso by Germanicus' friends, but died in suspicious circumstances before reaching Rome: 3.7.1). Note also *muliebri fraude cecidisse* ("has fallen to womanly foul play") in Germanicus' death-bed speech (2.71.2); here, *muliebris fraus* may mean both 'treachery perpetrated by a (or, rather, the) woman' and 'treachery worthy of a woman' (or 'woman-like').

72 And see 3.13.2 (Piso's accusers recite charges against him in the senate): *postremo ipsum devotionibus et veneno peremisse* ("finally he had annihilated the man himself by curses and poison").

immediately following the sentence about the *persuasio veneni*) strongly suggests that what he says here should be viewed, first and foremost, from the perspective of Germanicus' own perception (cf. *comperisset*, "he found", in the quotation from Suetonius): that such items have been found in his residence only adds to his conviction that he has been poisoned.[73] Thus we come back to the observation made at the beginning of this paragraph – that the *et reperiebantur* sentence is the only one in which Tacitus mentions something relating to the alleged killing of the prince and presents it as an established fact. From the formal point of view this is certainly right; but if we consider the whole context and Tacitus' presentation of the story, we have to admit that Germanicus' subjective opinions are, even here, more important than the (objective) fact that the magic items have been discovered.[74]

The most explicit condemnation of Piso (and Plancina) as Germanicus' killers comes, undoubtedly, in his dying speech (2.71). There is no need to discuss it here. Suffice it to say that what Germanicus says on his death bed has been meticulously prepared by the historian in the preceding narrative. We have been able to observe how by means of various literary devices (choice of vocabulary, arrangement of material, meaningful juxtaposition, imagery, etc.) he manages to *recreate* the atmosphere of uncertainty, doubts and suspicions which must have surrounded the events of the year 19. As he says on another occasion: *atrociore semper fama erga dominantium exitus* ("report being always more frightful in relation to one's departed masters", 4.11.2). This is probably one of the main reasons why he has decided to bring hearsay, unconfirmed reports and opinions so much into the foreground in the narrative of Germanicus' last three years.

Bibliography

Ash, Rhiannon (2018): Tacitus, Annals, Book XV. Cambridge: Cambrigde University Press.
Barnes, Timothy D. (1998): "Tacitus and the *Senatus Consultum de Cn. Pisone Patre*". In: Phoenix 52, 125–148.
Blonce, Caroline / Gangloff, Anne (2013): "Mémoire du voyage de Germanicus en Orient". In: Cahiers du Centre Gustave Glotz 24, 113–134.

---

73 The same applies to the next sentence (*simul missi a Pisone incusabantur ut valitudinis adversa rimantes*, "at the same time envoys from Piso were censured for probing the adverse state of his health"): whether these accusations were made by Germanicus himself or his friends, the important thing is that they had an impact on Germanicus' conviction of his being poisoned.

74 A few words of comment may be added about the sentence *saevam vim morbi augebat persuasio veneni a Pisone accepti* ("the savage violence of the disease was increased by his conviction that he had been given poison by Piso"). The consequence of what is presented as Germanicus' subjective opinion was that his illness became (on the objective level) more severe. So the two spheres (the subjective and the objective) may influence each other. Cf. note 64 above on rumours as causes of events.

Damon, Cynthia (1999): "The Trial of Cn. Piso in Tacitus' *Annals* and the *Senatus Consultum de Cn. Pisone Patre*. New Light on Narrative Technique". In: American Journal of Philology 120, 143–162.

Damon, Cynthia / Palazzolo, Elizabeth (2019): "Defining Home, Defining Rome: Germanicus' Eastern Tour". In: Biggs, Thomas / Blum, Jessica (eds.): The Epic Journey in Greek and Roman Literature. Cambridge: Cambridge University Press, 194–210.

Damtoft-Poulsen, Aske (2020): "Teleology with a Human Face. 'Sideshadowing' and its Effects in Tacitus' Treatment of Germanicus (*Annals* 1–2)". In: Turner, Aaron (ed.): Reconciling Ancient and Modern Philosophies of History. Berlin/New York: de Gruyter, 149–182.

de Jong, Irene J. (2014): Narratology and Classics. A Practical Guide. Oxford: Oxford University Press.

De Vivo, Arturo (2003): "Le parole ambigue della storia. La morte di Germanico negli *Annales* di Tacito". In: Viparelli, Valeria (ed.): Tra strategie retoriche e generi letterari. Dieci studi di letteratura latina. Napoli: Liguori, 69–102.

Delpeyroux, Marie F. (2009): "Pouvoir de la parole, pouvour des armes. Les relations entre Tibère et Germanicus dans les *Annales*". In: Devillers, Olivier / Meyers, Jean (eds.): Pouvoirs des hommes, pouvoir des mots, des Gracques à Trajan. Hommages au Professeur Paul Marius Martin. Louvain: Peeters, 485–505.

Devillers, Olivier (2014): "Rhescuporis, Cotys, Tibère et Germanicus (Tacite, *Annales*, 2.64–67)". In: Revue Africaine des Études Latines 1, 15–24.

Drogula, Fred K. (2015): "Who Was Watching Whom? A Reassessment of the Conflict Between Germanicus and Piso". In: American Journal of Philology 136, 121–153.

Eck, Werner et al. (1996): Das Senatus consultum de Cn. Pisone patre. München: C. H. Beck.

Eck, Werner (2000): "Die Täuschung der Öffentlichkeit oder die 'Unparteilichkeit' des Historikers Tacitus". In: Antike und Abendland 46, 190–206.

Flach, Dieter (1973): Tacitus in der Tradition der antiken Geschichtsschreibung. Göttingen: Vandenhoeck & Ruprecht.

Gibson, Bruce J. (1998): "Rumours as Causes of Events in Tacitus". In: Materiali e Discussioni per l'Analisi dei Testi Classici 40, 111–129.

Ginsburg, Judith (1981): Tradition and Theme in the *Annals* of Tacitus. New York: Arno Press.

Giua, Maria A. (1975): "Tiberio simulatore nella tradizione storica pretacitiana". In: Athenaeum 53, 352–363.

Goodyear, Frank R. (1981): The Annals of Tacitus. Books 1–6. Vol. II: Annals 1.55–81 and Annals 2. Cambridge: Cambrigde University Press.

Griffin, Miriam (1997): "The Senate's Story". In: Journal of Roman Studies 87, 249–263.

Hausmann, Michael (2009): Die Leserlenkung durch Tacitus in den Tiberius- und Claudiusbüchern der "Annalen". Berlin/New York: de Gruyter.

Koestermann, Erich (1958): "Die Mission des Germanicus im Orient". In: Historia 7, 331–375.

Leo, Friedrich (1960): "Tacitus" (originally published in 1896). In: Id.: Ausgewählte kleine Schriften. 2 Vols. (ed.) Fraenkel, Eduard. Roma: Edizioni di Storia e Letteratura, Vol. 2, 263–276.

Lott, J. Bert (2012): Death and Dynasty in Early Imperial Rome. Key Sources with Text, Translation, and Commentary. Cambridge: Cambrigde University Press.

Lund, Allan A. (2009): "Zur Vergiftung des Germanicus (Tac. *Ann.* 2,69)". In: Philologus 153, 173–180.

Martin, Ronald H. (1981): Tacitus. London: Batsford.

Mc Culloch, Jr., Harold Y. (1984): Narrative Cause in the Annals of Tacitus. Königstein im Taunus: Verlag Anton Hain.

O'Gorman, Ellen (2000): Irony and Misreading in the *Annals* of Tacitus. Cambridge: Cambrigde University Press.

Östenberg, Ida (2009): Staging the World. Spoils, Captives, and Representations in the Roman Triumphal Procession. Oxford: Oxford University Press.

Percy, Jr., Lee T. (1973): Tacitus' Use of *Species, Imago, Effigies*, and *Simulacrum*. PhD diss. Bryn Mawr College. https://repository.brynmawr.edu/cgi/viewcontent.cgi?article=1116&context=dissertations, Access Date 20.01.2021.

Pelling, Christopher (2012): "Tacitus and Germanicus" (originally published in 1993). In: Ash, Rhiannon (ed.): Tacitus. Oxford Readings in Classical Studies. Oxford: Oxford University Press, 281–313.

Römer, Franz (1999): "Kontrastfiguren in den Annalen des Tacitus". In: Acta Antiqua Academiae Scientiarum Hungaricae 39, 297–312.

Ronconi, Antonio (1966): "*Exitus illustrium virorum*". In: Reallexikon für Antike und Christentum. Vol. 6, 1258–1268.

Ryberg, Inez S. (1942): "Tacitus' Art of Innuendo". In: Transactions and Proceedings of the American Philological Association 73, 383–404.

Santoro-L'hoir, Francesca (2006): Tragedy, Rhetoric, and the Historiography of Tacitus' *Annales*. Ann Arbor: University of Michigan Press.

Schmidt, Willibald (1914): De ultimis morientium verbis (PhD diss. Marburg). Marpurgi Cattorum: C. Schaaf.

Seider, Aaron (2022): "Remembering the Future in Tacitus' *Annals*. Germanicus' Death and Contests for Commemoration". In: Popkin, Maggie L. / Ng, Diana Y. (eds.): Future Thinking in Roman Culture. New Approaches to History, Memory, and Cognition. London: Routledge, 37–53.

Shatzman, Israel (1974): "Tacitean Rumours". In: Latomus 33, 549–578.

Syme, Ronald (1986): The Augustan Aristocracy, Oxford: Clarendon Press.

Talbert, Richard J. A. (1999): "Tacitus and the *Senatus Consultum de Cn. Pisone Patre*". In: American Journal of Philology 120, 89–97.

Traub, Henry W. (1953): "Tacitus' Use of *Ferocia*". In: Transactions and Proceedings of the American Philological Association 84, 250–261.

Valenti-Pagnini, Rossana (1987): Il potere e la sua immagine. Semantica di *species* in Tacito, Napoli: Società Editrice Napoletana.

Waddell, Philip (2020): Tacitean Visual Narrative. London: Bloomsbury.

Walker, Bessie (1952): The Annals of Tacitus. A Study in the Writing of History, Manchester: Manchester University Press.

Whitehead, David (1979): "Tacitus and the Loaded Alternative". In: Latomus 38, 474–495.

Woodman, Anthony J. (2004): Tacitus, The Annals. Translated, with Introduction and Notes. Indianapolis/Cambridge: Hackett.

Woodman, Anthony J. (2018): The Annals of Tacitus, Book 4. Cambridge: Cambridge University Press.

Woodman, Anthony J. / Martin, Ronald H. (1996): The Annals of Tacitus, Book 3. Cambridge: Cambridge University Press.

Yavetz, Zvi (1975): "*Forte an Dolo Principis* (Tac. *Ann.* 15.38)". In: Levick, Barbara (ed.): The Ancient Historian and His Material. Essays in Honour of C. E. Stevens on His Seventieth Birthday. Westmead: Farnborough, 181–197.

Roman Military Discipline
and Germanicus' Political Position*
A Note on D. 49.16.4.13

MICHAŁ NORBERT FASZCZA

Keywords: Germanicus' political and military power, Roman military discipline, Roman military law, succession of imperial power

Arrius Menander, the Roman jurist from the turn of the second and third centuries AD,[1] mentions the legislative activity of Germanicus regarding military matters:

Edicta Germanici Caesaris militem desertorem faciebant, qui diu afuisset, [sed postea constitutum est, si animum revertendi aliquando habuisset] ut is inter emansores haberetur. Sed sive redeat quis et offerat se, sive deprehensus offeratur, poenam desertionis evitat: nec intetest, cui se offerat vel a quo deprehendatur.[2]

The edicts of Germanicus Caesar counted a soldier who had been absent for a long time as a deserter, but it was subsequently laid down that if he had at any time had the intention of returning, he should be counted among those absent without leave. But whether [such a soldier] returns and gives himself up or whether he is arrested and handed over, he avoids

---

*   I would like to express my gratitude to the Lanckoroński Foundation for the award of a scholarship to support my research in Rome in 2021. I am also indebted to Professor Adam Ziółkowski for his comments, as well as for his linguistic corrections.

1   On the career and works of Arrius Menander see Kunkel (1952), 233 f.; Giuffrè (1974a); Giuffrè (1974b), 73–87.

2   D. 49.16.4.13. The Latin text was based on the classic edition prepared by Theodor Mommsen. The emendation he introduced to the version from *Codex Berolinensis olim Rosnyanus* (R) comes from *Liber Florentinus* (F); Mommsen (1889), 837.

the punishment for desertion; nor does it matter to whom he gives himself up or by whom he is arrested (transl. Alan Watson).[3]

Arrius Menander does not explain when or in what circumstances Germanicus issued the edicts, which opens an interesting field for research. First, our understanding of the content of Germanicus' regulations largely depends on one's placing the quoted passage in the chronological context, mainly based on information contained in narrative sources. Harsh treatment of soldiers guilty of absence without leave had to be related to a specific event requiring decisive action. Our admittedly limited information about details of Germanicus' career makes it possible to distinguish two such events which, however, took place in entirely different circumstances; our understanding of motive, or motives, which induced him to issue these edicts will thus depend on dating them.

The second point is to put Germanicus' edicts in a broader context of the evolution of the Roman military discipline during the reign of the first two Julio-Claudian emperors. It is clear that his conduct had to stay within the framework of the newly created political and military order, but just as the Imperial army was evolving, so – one expects – did the Roman military law, which makes it indispensable to define at least general changes taking place in that sphere during the first generations of the Principate. Were Augustus' solutions different from those adopted by Tiberius? Do our sources contain analogies to Germanicus' disciplinary edicts?

The final point is the question of the basis on which Germanicus was able to issue military edicts. His role within the dynasty may have been of greater importance than that formally exercised command on behalf of the emperor, but the lack of precise information about basic mechanisms of Augustan disciplinary system naturally limits the scope of enquiry. As a result, some questions must remain unanswered, but the passage in the *Digesta* seems to be too important in the study of both Germanicus and the Roman *ius militiae* to just quote it without broader comment.

Dating the edicts

During the Republic, issuing edicts was a part of the powers of the magistrates, including those holding *imperium militiae*, whether consuls, praetors or proconsuls.[4] Although none of the ancient authors states that the *ius edicendi* was exercised in the same way during the reign of Augustus, the reasons for the law-making activity

---

3   Compare Clarence E. Brand's translation: *The edicts of Germanicus Caesar used to classify as a deserter a person who had been so long absent that he was considered absent without leave; but [now] whether he voluntarily returns and surrenders himself, or is apprehended and brought back, he escapes punishment for desertion; and it makes no difference to whom he surrenders, or by whom he is apprehended.*

4   Berger (1953), 448.

of Germanicus should be sought in his formal military functions; otherwise it would be nothing more than usurpation of competences. He might have received the legal and military power allowing him to issue the edicts twice: when he was in command against the Germanic tribes in AD 13–16[5] or later, holding the *imperium proconsulare maius* in AD 17–19.[6] The tasks entrusted to Germanicus in the East were less of military and more of diplomatic nature,[7] which on the face of it makes his getting involved in the problem of desertions in that capacity decidedly less likely. It is therefore more probable that his regulations concerning military discipline were a part of his efforts to restore obedience after the mutiny initiated by the legions stationed in Germania Inferior (Lower Germany) after the death of emperor Augustus in AD 14,[8] but neither should his mission in the East be dismissed out of hand. In fact, he encountered disciplinary problems among the military in both cases, even if their essence was not of the same nature.

Judging by Arrius Menander's report, Germanicus apparently treated absence without leave (*emansio*) as desertion (*desertio*). In the Roman Republic there was no such military offense as *emansio*, and the absence without leave could be considered as desertion *tout court*.[9] During the reign of Augustus *emansio* was most likely also treated in the same way, since – judging by extant legal sources – it seems to have not been considered a separate category of offence until the third century AD.[10] Why then did Germanicus issue edicts on a matter which did not raise legal doubts? On the other hand, it is worth mentioning Cicero's opinion that "the more justice, the more injustice", and that too strict application of the law is harmful to the society.[11] Seneca the Younger believed that capital punishment was the usual retribution in the army,[12] but he was also convicted of the negative impact of cruelty on maintaining military discipline.[13] In his opinion commanding officers were fully aware of the necessity of leniency when

---

5   The scope of his authority: Tac. *Ann.* 1.14.3; Suet. *Cal.* 1.2; Cass. Dio 56.25.2. As argued by Paweł Sawiński, from AD 11 *auspiciis Augusti* (Cass. Dio 56.25.2) and then, from AD 14 *auspiciis Tiberii* (Tac. *Ann.* 1.14.3); Sawiński (2007), 221–222; Sawiński (2021), 27–30. On Germanicus' campaigns against the Germanic peoples see the paper of Adam Ziółkowski in this volume.

6   Tac. *Ann.* 2.43.1; *TS* 1.15; *SCPP* 30–36.

7   Vell. Pat. 2.129.3; Joseph. *AJ* 18.2.5; Tac. *Ann.* 2.43.1, 3.12.1; *TS* 1.15.

8   On the course of the mutiny: Vell. Pat. 2.125.2–4; Tac. *Ann.* 1.31–49; Suet. *Tib.* 25. 2–3; *Cal.* 1.2; Cass. Dio 57. 5–7.

9   Mommsen (1899), 561 f.; Brecht (1938), 62–65; Arangio-Ruiz (1974), 3–6; Carcani (1981), 73; Santalucia (1994), 19 f.; Wolff (2009), XIV–XVI, 7–27.

10   D. 49.16.3.2, 49.16.3.5, 49.16.3.7. Cf. Isid. *Etym.* 9.3.39.

11   Cic. *Div.* 1.10.33.

12   Sen. *Ir.* 1.16.5.

13   Sen. *Clem.* 1.16.3. According to Celsus (D. 1.3.17), understanding laws is not a matter of sticking to their letter, but to their force and essence. Paulus (D. 50.17.144 praef.) also believed that not everything which is lawful is righteous. Both authors clearly relied on Seneca's reflections.

violation of discipline concerns large groups of soldiers.[14] If Germanicus judged that *emansores* should be treated with full severity, he must have perceived the situation as serious enough to react quickly and decisively.

As I have written above, the first probable date is AD 14, when the four legions of Germania Inferior raised a mutiny upon the news of Augustus' death. Germanicus' aim could have been either to tighten discipline loosened by the recent disturbances, or, on the contrary, to propose a sort veiled amnesty to at least some of the offenders. In the first case it would be an aggravation of the penalty by changing, or simply restoring the old legal qualification of the act. In this way, Germanicus could at the same time emphasize his lack of tolerance for roving caused by the lack of superiors' control, and be able to condemn to death mutineers hiding outside the camp as deserters. On the second interpretation Germanicus' edicts might be considered an attempt to persuade as many hiding legionaries as possible to return and rejoin troops loyal to the commander: in this way, as not belonging to the category of *qui diu afuissent*, they would be treated more leniently. In my opinion, the latter possibility is more probable. Germanicus had no means to suppress the mutiny by force, because he had come to the revolted legions with only closest associates;[15] this being the case, the plausibility of his trying to enforce stricter discipline immediately after the restoration of order is very slight. Velleius Paterculus' remark about Germanicus' having attempted to calm the rebellious mood with gentleness, whereas Drusus the Younger achieved the same effect with severity, may be taken as an additional hint:

> *Quo quidem tempore ut pleraque non ignave Germanicus, ita Drusus, qui a patre in id ipsum plurimo quidem igne emicans incendium militaris tumultus missus erat, prisca antiquaque severitate usus ancipitia sibi maluit tenere quam exemplo perniciosa, et his ipsis militum gladiis, quibus obsessus erat, obsidentes coercuit.*[16]

> In this crisis, while in many respects the conduct of Germanicus was not lacking in rigour, Drusus employed the severity of the Romans of old. Sent by his father into the very midst of the conflagration, when the flames of mutiny were aheady bursting forth, he preferred to hold to a course which involved danger to himself than one which might prove a ruinous precedent, and used the very swords of those by whom he had been besieged to coerce his besiegers (transl. Frederick W. Shipley).

In fact, as Tacitus attests, Germanicus could not afford to apply measures similar to those used by his brother;[17] it also goes without saying that Velleius Paterculus' descrip-

---

14   Sen. *Ir.* 2.10. 4. On the *utilitas* as the basic criterion for interpreting the law by the Romans: Valditara (2015), 65–76.

15   Tac. *Ann.* 1.34.1–2, 1.36.1.

16   Vell. Pat. 2.125.4–5.

17   Tac. *Ann.* 1.28–30; Rivière (2016), 173–175.

tion is a poorly disguised critique of Germanicus' conduct.[18] What really matters is that neither Velleius Paterculus, nor Tacitus indicates a particular severity of Germanicus in AD 14, which is an additional argument in favour of the partial amnesty interpretation.

The other possibility is to date Germanicus' edicts to the period of his Eastern mission. A passage from the *Senatus consultum de Cn. Pisone Patre* (*SCPP*) of AD 20 points to the question of military discipline in the Roman units stationed in Syria. The governor Gnaeus Calpurnius Piso was accused of undermining the discipline among soldiers, at the same time through acts of ferocity and laxity including excessive *donativa*:

> *perspecta etiam crudelitate unica, qui incognita causa, sine consili sententia plurimos capitis supplicio adfecisset neq(ue) externos tantummodo, sed etiam centurionem c(ivem) R(omanum) cruci fixsisset; qui militarem disciplinam a divo Aug(usto) institutam et servatam a Ti. Caesare Aug(usto) corrupisset, non solum indulgendo militibus, <ne> his, qui ipsis praesunt, more vetustissumo parerent, sed etiam donativa suo nomine ex fisco principis nostri dando, quo facto milites alios Pisonianos, alios Caesarianos dici laetatus sit, honorando etiam eos, qui post talis nominis usurpationem ipsi paruisse<n>t.[19]*

Also evidenced was the unexampled cruelty [of the man] who had inflicted capital punishment on many without their cases having been heard, without the recommendation of his advisors, and crucified not only noncitizen [soldiers] but even a centurion, a Roman citizen; who had corrupted the military discipline established by the deified Augustus and maintained by Ti. Caesar Augustus, not only by indulging the soldiers, <so that they would not> obey their superiors in accordance with our most venerable tradition, but also by giving donatives in his own name from the funds of our princeps, after which he took pleasure that some soldiers were called "Piso's men" and others "Caesar's men", and also by honouring those who, after assuming such a name, had obeyed himself (transl. Cynthia Damon).

The accusations against Piso should be treated with distrust, as they read like a set of offences of the archetypal "bad commander" in literature. Moreover, they closely duplicate the standard set of insults of the Republican political invective. There is little doubt that we are dealing with clichés rather than real offenses.[20] The highly stylized description of Piso's deeds makes it difficult to recognize any real disciplinary problems caused by him, if any, the more so as problems with desertions are typical for ongoing campaigns rather than for soldiers stationing in quarters, quite apart from the question whether the commander would really intent to act against the emperor's representative,[21] and thus against the emperor himself.[22]

---

18 Rivière (2016), 177 f.
19 *SCPP* 50–58.
20 Bauman (1970), 238; Bauman (1974), 109; Eck et al. (1996), 253; Rivière (2016), 391 f.
21 *SCPP* 55–57.
22 Bauman (1970), 238; Eck et al. (1996), 252–254.

Tacitus also writes about Piso's negative impact on the soldiers' discipline, although he does not accuse him of cruelty towards the subordinates:

> [...] et postquam Syriam ac legiones attigit, largitione, ambitu, infimos manipularium iuvando, cum veteres centuriones, severos tribunos demoveret locaque eorum clientibus suis vel deterrimo cuique attribueret, desidiam in castris, licentiam in urbibus, vagum ac lascivientem per agros militem sineret, eo usque corruptionis provectus est ut sermone vulgi parens legionum haberetur.[23]

> Then, the moment he reached Syria and the legions, by bounties and by bribery, by attentions to the humblest private, by dismissals of the veteran centurions and the stricter commanding officers, whom he replaced by dependants of his own or by men of the worst character, by permitting indolence in the camp, licence in the towns, and in the country a vagrant and riotous soldiery, he carried corruption to such a pitch that in the language of the rabble he was known as the Father of the Legions (transl. John Jackson).

Tacitus' list of Piso's offences is certainly more consistent than that we find in the *SCPP*, but this simply shows that he was a better writer than the latter's editors. But even if we take them at face value, the question is whether the soldiers' misdemeanors were serious enough to treat at least some *emansores* as deserters? Probably not. There are no strong arguments for the statement that the problem of roving among Piso's soldiers was impossible to eliminate by traditional methods and required introduction of new disciplinary regulations. It is worth noting that in the narrative of Tacitus, as well as in the *SCPP*, the real accusation is Piso's behaviour with regard to Germanicus, not to his subordinates. Unlike the mutineers of AD 14, "Syrian" legionaries are an anonymous, amorphous group whose main fault is being spoiled by the *legatus*. Piso's tolerance of the soldiers' bad habits seems to be mainly a part of his negative image. Therefore, in my opinion, the edicts of Germanicus were most likely issued in the context of mutiny of AD 14.[24]

Germanicus' edicts and the evolution of the Roman military discipline

The acts quoted by Arrius Menander are extremely important for the study of the Roman military discipline. During the reign of Augustus the *ius militiae*[25] was distinguished from the *ius publicum* as a separate scope of regulation. The first known jurist

---

23 Tac. *Ann.* 2.55.5. See also *Ann.* 3.12.3, 3.14.1.
24 Similarly: Rivière (2016), 499 (n9), but without a more detailed justification.
25 The earliest known definition of the Roman military law is very late and comes from the work of Isidore of Seville. Isid. *Etym.* 5.7.1: *Ius militare est belli inferendi sollemnitas, foederis faciendi nexus, signo data egressio in hostem vel commissio. Item signo dato receptio; item flagitii militaris disciplina, si locus deseratur; item stipendiorum modus, dignitatum gradus, praemiorum honor, veluti cum corona vel torques donantur.* In the English translation of Stephen A. Barney, Wendy J. Lewis, Jennifer A. Beach and Oliver Berghof: "Military law is the formalized practice of waging war, the bond of mak-

who specialized in this field was Lucius Cincius.[26] The creation of the military law was above all an aspect of the establishment of the professional army by Augustus, not to mention the necessity of putting military affairs in order after the period of devastating – and for the soldiers, demoralizing – civil wars.[27] The edicts of Germanicus belong to the oldest normative sources relative to the Roman military law, even if their content is known only indirectly through the work of Arrius Menander.

Modern authors reconstruct the military discipline of the Imperial Roman army largely from the narrative sources (especially Flavius Josephus, Tacitus and Suetonius) as well as from the *Digesta*, usually without a deeper reflection on their contradictions. In a widespread belief, the Romans were the counterparts of the 18th-century Prussians who are seen as an embodiment of discipline enforced by brutality.[28] A common mistake is treating the literary image of an ideal soldier as a reflection of reality, which leads to disregarding the unambiguous meaning of more pertinent information.[29] For example, those who present the legionaries as mere obedient, unthinking tools in the hands of their superiors,[30] deprived of any individual initiative, do not reflect on the popularity of single combats in the Roman army, often initiated without the permission of the commander; even Titus engaged in such combats during the suppression of the Jewish revolt (AD 66–74).[31]

Sara Elise Phang points out that the motif of the soldiers' blind obedience in literary works was a reflection not of the reality but of expectations of many civilians who feared alleged military brutality.[32] It was a side effect of the separation of the soldiers from a large part of the society, itself an effect of the creation of the professional army: as a result, in some parts of the Empire soldiers were perceived as potentially dangerous strangers. In her opinion this was the reason why some ancient authors believed that soldiers should be constantly fighting or working – it would be a form of protection against the threat posed by "idle" men-at-arms.[33] Even if her interpretation is a

---

ing treaties, the marching against or engagement with the foe at a given signal. Also the cessation of hostilities at a given signal, and the military discipline for the disgrace of deserting one's post; also the method of distributing military pay, the hierarchy of ranks, the honor of rewards, as when a crown or torques are given". It is doubtful that during the reign of Augustus, the Roman military law was defined in the same way, however, some elements could remain the same.

26 Gell. *NA* 16.4.2–6; Giuffrè (1974b), 39–41, 61; Giuffrè (1980), 20; Giuffrè (2013), 73; Nicolet (1980), 405 (n21).

27 *RGDA* 17; Suet. *Aug.* 49.1–3; Hdn. 2.11; Cass. Dio 40.23–25.

28 In fact, the Prussian severity is another historiographical myth. See a more balanced picture of the Prussian military discipline during the Age of Enlightenment: Duffy (1974), 35–53; Duffy (1987), 18, 55, 73 f.

29 Faszcza (2021).

30 E. g. Wiedemann (1996); Goldsworthy (1996), 7 f., 30, 264–271; Gilliver (2011), 9, 26, 121 f.

31 See Lendon (2005), 233–260.

32 Phang (2008), 74–76.

33 Phang (2008), 201–208, 221–226. This dependence is well illustrated by the works of Juvenal and Martial. About relations between soldiers and civilians, including conflicts and stereotypes, see

bit too far-reaching, there is no doubt that the establishment of the standing army of professionals led to the emergence of many harmful stereotypes about soldiers, which resulted in the half-belief, half-expectation that they should constantly be subjected to harsh discipline based on punishments.[34]

Apart from our fragment, the earliest military regulations contained in the *Digesta* are dated to the second half of the second century AD[35] and cannot be automatically transferred to the reign of Augustus, when the *ius militiae* was being created.[36] As far as I know, only Jakob Sulser attempted to present Roman military discipline of the first century AD with no reference to the material in the *Digesta*; and his inferences were quite different from those of other scholars.[37] Needless to say, the passage about Germanicus' legislative activity is insufficient for broader conclusions about the nature of Augustan military legislation, but it should not be disregarded as a source for studying it, and the working of the Principate in its early phase in general.

The acts of Germanicus are our only evidence on regulating military discipline by edicts. Due to the lack of analogies, it is uncertain whether they applied to Germanicus' troops only. The reference to their content made by Arrius Menander does not settle the problem, because it is difficult to establish what was the nature of his *De re militari* (theoretical treatise?; draft of legal regulations?; collection of legal acts and juridical answers?).[38] The answer to the question whether Germanicus' edicts became a part of the Imperial *ius militiae* is not obvious either. Their inclusion in the *Digesta* does not prove yet the continued validity of the edicts.

All preserved military edicts dated to the first century BC and the first century AD concern privileges for veterans. Between 37 and 31 BC young Caesar, the future Augustus, issued an act containing social and economic privileges for his soldiers.[39] In

---

especially MacMullen (1963); Campbell (2002). The influence of prejudices against soldiers on the perception of military discipline is an interesting, but not yet fully exploited issue.

34   Fear of soldiers is strictly dependent on the military participation ratio: Andreski (1968), 33 f.

35   D. 49.16.7, 50.6.7 (Publius Taruntenus Paternus); maybe also D. 49.16.9, 49.16.11 (Aelius Marcianus).

36   The Principate is usually treated by the scholars dealing with the military discipline as a homogeneous period. Due to the lack of awareness of complexity of the problem some authors arbitrarily select and compile sources from the reigns of different emperors. As a result, the dominant vision of the Imperial military discipline is largely ahistorical, see such works as Müller (1906); Jung (1982), 973–1008; Wesch-Klein (1998), 147–156; Phang (2008), 73–151. Moreover, many authors fail to confront juridical sources with the practice, which creates the illusion of an exceptionally strict military discipline.

37   Sulser (1923).

38   Vincenzo Giuffrè perceives the work of Arrius Menander as a set of various legal regulations, not a consistent vision of a "military code"; Giuffrè (1974a), 27–29; Giuffrè (1974b), 73. Other authors do not share his interpretation, probably because it does not go beyond speculations. Cf. Brand (1968), 125 f.

39   *FIRA*[2] 1, no. 56. The act may have been related with the unrest of veterans in 31 BC: Cass. Dio 51.3.1–6.

AD 46 Claudius granted certain rights to veterans originated from the Anauni and other tribes subjected to Tridentum, who had formally received the Roman citizenship.[40] In the third case, in AD 88/89 Domitian granted his veterans tax exemptions and regulated their family status.[41] In these three edicts there is not a single word about the military discipline. The choice of the legal form by Germanicus is thus unique, but considering the state of the evidence this lack of analogies from his and later periods does not exclude similar cases.

During the reign of Trajan legal military issues began to be regulated mainly by rescripts (*rescripta*), which was a part of the overall trend regarding imperial legislation.[42] Trajan's successors continued his practice.[43] The greatest number of rescripts date from the times of Severus Alexander and Gordian I, which prompted J. Brian Campbell to conclude that rescripts became the main tool of communication between emperors and soldiers, as was the case with regard to other parts of the Roman society.[44] Unfortunately, we do not know why one legal form replaced the other. Why did the emperors stop issuing military edicts is a question that would deserve a separate analysis in the framework of a larger theme devoted to changes in the Roman legal culture.[45]

Another way of regulating various aspects of military service in the early Principate were general laws (*leges*), just like during the Republic. One of them was the *lex Iulia maiestatis* (or *lex Iulia de maiestate*) of AD 8, about which Tacitus makes the following remarks:

> *nam legem maiestatis reduxerat, cui nomen apud veteres idem, sed alia in iudicium veniebant, si quis proditione exercitum aut plebem seditionibus, denique male gesta re publica maiestatem populi Romani minuisset: facta arguebantur, dicta inpune erant.[46]*

> For he had resuscitated the Lex Majestatis, a statute which among the ancients had carried the same name but covered a different type of offence – betrayal of the army; seditious incitement of the plebs; any act, in short, of official maladministration diminishing the 'majesty of the Roman people'. Deeds were prosecuted, words went immune (transl. John Jackson, with the author's modifications).

---

40 CIL 5.5050 = *FIRA*² 1, no. 71.
41 *FIRA*² 1, no. 76.
42 Plin. *Ep.* 29; D. 29.1.24, 49.16.4 praef., 49.16.4.5.
43 See the list of Hadrian's and Antoninus Pius' rescripts made by Campbell (1984), 436–438.
44 Campbell (1984), 281.
45 See Schulz (1946), 99–329; Guarino (1981), 404–450, 485–522; Bretone (1982), 127–331; Schiavone (2016), 262–294, 397–436. The impact of the Roman legal culture on military legislation is usually ignored by scholars. The key study still remains: Vendrand-Voyer (1983). Cf. Phang (2008), 131–139.
46 Tac. *Ann.* 1.72.3. Cf. D. 48.4.1.1.

106   MICHAŁ NORBERT FASZCZA

The same law was also described by Marcianus:

> [...] *lex autem Iulia maiestatis praecipit eum, qui maiestatem publicam laeserit, teneri: qualis est ille, qui in bellis cesserit aut arcem tenuerit aut castra concesserit. eadem lege tenetur et qui iniussu principis bellum gesserit dilectumve habuerit exercitum comparaverit: quive, cum ei in provincia successum esset, exercitum successori non tradidit: quive imperium exercitumve populi romani deseruerit* [...].[47]

> But the lex Julia on treason makes him liable who injures the public *majestas*, such as he who surrenders in war or recklessly yields a citadel or camp. Under the same law who, without the command of the emperor, wages war or raises a levy or prepares an army; or who, though he has been superseded in his province, has not handed his military command over to his successor; or who has abandoned his imperium or an army of the Roman people [...] (transl. Alan Watson).

The *lex Iulia maiestatis* and the edicts of Germanicus are the oldest extant Imperial legal acts on military discipline. The difference between them, however, is that Augustus' primary concern were commanders, while Germanicus focused on ordinary soldiers. The emperor's interest in the military discipline was not accidental, because its restoration was of particular importance in the new political reality. His army had been a "civil war army", and Augustus' bitter experience with the *seditio* of 36 BC showed the limits of his authority in the face of soldiers' discontent.[48] Obviously, legionaries posed no threat to Augustus' political power, but acting like a "well-organized trade union" they put pressure to gain additional benefits.[49] The edict of 37–31 BC, as well as the manner in which young Caesar solved the problem of mutinous veterans after Actium,[50] shows him gaining the subordinates' loyalty in a way quite different from imposing harsh discipline. The events of AD 14 were clearly of an entirely different nature.

Augustus' attitude to the ideal of strict discipline is in fact quite problematic. The only examples of severe punishments like decimation (*decimatio*) date back before 30 BC,[51] and so before the establishment of the new regime. According to Suetonius, his efforts to restore discipline were made under the banner of restoring the ancestral customs,[52]

---

47   D. 48.4.3.
48   Vell. Pat. 2.81.1; App. *B Civ.* 5.128–129; Cass. Dio 49.14.1–3.
49   The term used by: Alföldi (1976), 120; Ziolkowski (2010), 277 f.
50   Cass. Dio 51.3.1–6.
51   Suet. *Aug.* 24.2; App. *Ill.* 26; Cass. Dio 48.42.2, 49.38.4; Brice (2011).
52   Suet. *Aug.* 24.1: *In re militari et commutavit multa et instituit, atque etiam ad antiquum morem nonnulla revocavit. Disciplinam severissime rexit: ne legatorum quidem cuiquam, nisi gravate hibernisque demum mensibus, permisit uxorem intervisere.* In the English translation: "He made many changes and innovations in the army, besides reviving some usages of former times. He exacted the strictest discipline. It was with great reluctance that he allowed even his generals to visit their wives, and then only in the winter season" (transl. John C. Rolfe). Cf. *SCPP* 52–54.

presumably as a part of Augustus' wide ranging program of the "restitution of the Roman Republic".[53]

Valerius Maximus is the only extant Roman author who alleges that the army of his time was disciplined and strictly obedient,[54] but it is difficult to treat his statement in a different way than as an expression of his servility. The one thing that we know is that during the reign of Augustus flogging was commonly used, especially by centurions.[55] Even if it could lead to periodic tensions in the army and highlighted the imperfections of the promotion system,[56] it did not cause serious disturbances, e. g. mutinies. As a matter of fact, the first known example of significant tightening of the military law were Germanicus' edicts – one thing is to promote discipline as a value, and another to change the qualification of the offence (even if the primary intention of Germanicus was to minimize the category of offenders). Of course, we do not know how Augustus would have acted in similar circumstances.

In Suetonius' narrative, it was Augustus' successor, Tiberius, who had a particular inclination towards severe discipline, which might be taken as a suggestion of the difference between the two emperors:

> *Disciplinam acerrime exegit animadversionum et ignominiarum generibus ex antiquitate repetitis atque etiam legato legionis, quod paucos milites cum liberto suo trans ripam venatum misisset, ignominia notato.*[57]

> He required the strictest discipline, reviving bygone methods of punishment and ignominy, and even degrading the commander of a legion for sending a few soldiers across the river to accompany one of his freedmen on a hunting expedition (transl. John C. Rolfe).

An indirect proof of Suetonius' credibility is the *synkrisis* between the severity of Drusus the Younger and the gentleness of Germanicus, made by Velleius Paterculus.[58] Drusus the Younger, whose attitude was more like Tiberius', was presented in a more positive light, even though Velleius Paterculus surely knew that Germanicus had no means to crush the mutiny by force. The image of Augustus as a strict disciplinarian may have been an inspiration for the members of the Julio-Claudian dynasty, but the

---

53   *RGDA* 1–4; Zanker (1987); Guizzi (1999); Hurlet/Mineo (2009); Levick (2010), 202–287.
54   Val. Max. 2.7 praef.
55   Tac. *Ann.* 1.18.1, 1.21.1, 1.23.2–3, 1.26.2, 1.35.1; Papyrus from Qasr Ibrim, Reg. no. 80/11 = Inv. of inscriptions: GI/55, Neg. 80F113_026, published in: Derda et al. (forthcoming), no. 29 (I would like to thank Professor Adam Łajtar for information about the find and permission to use it in my article). The Papyrus from Qasr Ibrim contains a question of one soldier to another whether he had recovered after the whipping by centurion's rod.
56   See Faszcza (2020).
57   Suet. *Tib.* 19.1.
58   Vell. Pat. 2.125.4–5.

question arises when it was created: after the end of the civil wars or after his death?[59] As has been said above, the ideal of a "good ruler" popularized during the Empire was characterized among others by the ability to maintain strict discipline in the army and so protect the Roman citizens from the soldiers' *ferocia*.[60] Suetonius' descriptions may have been driven by this ideal, too, additionally increased by the dramatic events of the so-called "year of the four emperors" (AD 69).[61]

If Tiberius' attitude to the military discipline was not merely a literary creation, it would be surprising if the circumstances of his succession had not affected him. Germanicus' edicts might then be considered as an intermediate stage between the Augustan military heritage and the later changes. Be that as it may, his legal acts show that issuing military edicts was not yet an exclusive prerogative of the ruler and that in his time the *ius militiae* was being adapted to specific conditions of the new political and military order.

Why could Germanicus issue the edicts?

In the new reality, the emperor was the sole commander-in-chief, and the actual commanders were only his legates (*legati Augusti*).[62] However, Augustus, followed by some of his successors, also created a new category of commanders of higher rank than legates. His solution, followed by Tiberius in the first half of his reign, was to bestow on trusted close relatives an extraordinary *imperium* higher than that of legates of the provinces where they themselves exercised it.[63]

While facing the rebellious legionaries, Germanicus exercised the power granted to him in AD 13 as to highest commander in the Germanic theatre of war covering two provinces and eight legions.[64] The *imperium proconsulare* included the *ius edicendi*; the question is, however, whether the position held by Germanicus entitled him not only to issue military edicts, but also to change the legal status of legionaries. During the Republic, Roman soldiers swore the oath (*sacramentum*) to the commander, and not to the state, having to repeat it with each change of command.[65] After the establishment of the Empire, the only person to whom soldiers swore allegiance was the emperor.[66]

---

59   On the cult of military discipline during the Principate and its numismatic evidence: Ziolkowski (1990). The first coins with the legend DISCIPLINA AVG(VSTI) were issued under Hadrian.

60   Phang (2008), 46–49, 213–217, 239–242.

61   As in the works of Tacitus: Wellesley (1969), 80–84, 91 f.; Kajanto (1970), 702–709.

62   On the political side of Augustus' arrangements see Raaflaub (2009), 205–209, 214 f., 218 f.

63   Sawiński (2021).

64   See the papers of Adam Ziółkowski and Paweł Sawiński in this volume.

65   Brand (1968), 71; Giuffrè (1973), 6; Rüpke (1990), 78; Phang (2008), 119 f.

66   Premerstein (1937), 22–24, 73–76; Vendrand-Voyer (1983), 49 f.; Campbell (1984), 7, 20, 281–286; Raaflaub (2009), 205–209, 213–215.

In fact, apart from Germanicus' acts, all known military edicts of the first century AD were issued by the rulers. If dating the edicts to AD 14 is correct, there are apparently only two possibilities to explain Germanicus' initiative: the legal system of the early Empire was more flexible than is generally assumed, or he was endowed with some extra powers not mentioned in our sources.[67]

Less uncertain would be the legal position of Germanicus in AD 17–19, granted to him by the mandate (*mandatum*) of Tiberius *per transmarinas provincias*.[68] Considering the wide range of his competences, including, *inter alia*, conducting foreign policy and interfering in the dynastic affairs of neighbouring kingdoms,[69] the right to issue disciplinary edicts would not be surprising. Unfortunately, apart from the not very credible accusation of Piso, we do not have any information about disciplinary problems among units stationed in the East. Linking the edicts with Germanicus' Eastern mission remains a possibility, but, as has been stated above, much stronger is the argument which dates them to the time of the mutiny of AD 14. Is there an explanation of the legislative activity of Germanicus in Germania Inferior apparently encroaching on the sphere reserved for the emperors other than a specific competence granted to him by Augustus and/or Tiberius?

First of all, a mention should be made of his unique position in the Empire at that time. It resulted not only from the act of adoption made by Tiberius under the pressure of Augustus,[70] but also from his exact position in the succession scheme, evidently dynastic, envisaged by the first emperor. Tacitus and Suetonius inform us about Augustus' dilemma whether to omit Tiberius and designate Germanicus his direct successor.[71] Regardless of the truthfulness of this particular statement of the two historians and their strong anti-Tiberian attitude in general, the privileges granted to Germanicus by the first emperor were clearly perceived three generations later as signs of Augustus' intention to make him and his descendants rule the Empire after the death of Tiberius, the more when as contrasted with the *princeps'* reserved treatment of Drusus the Younger, Tiberius' natural son.[72] It is worth adding that being entrusted by the ageing emperor with responsible missions in various parts of the Empire not only gave him

---

67   On the powers granted by Tiberius in general: Tac. *Ann.* 1.25.2, 1.26.1, 1.36.2; but note *Ann.* 1.24.1: *Haec audita quamquam abstrusum et tristissima quaeque maxime occultantem Tiberium perpulere, ut Drusum filium cum primoribus civitatis duabusque praetoriis cohortibus mitteret, nullis satis certis mandatis, ex re consulturum.* In the English translation: "In spite of his secretiveness, always deepest when the news was blackest, Tiberius was driven by the reports from Pannonia to send out his son Drusus, with a staff of nobles and two praetorian cohorts. He had no instructions that could be called definite: he was to suit his measures to the emergency" (transl. John Jackson).

68   On the essence of powers related to the performance of tasks *per transmarinas provincias*: Arnaud (1994), 222–226, 244–253.

69   Arnaud (1994), 232–236; Rivière (2016), 277–338.

70   Suet. *Tib.* 15.2; Tac. *Ann.* 1.3.5; Cass. Dio 55.13.2.

71   Tac. *Ann.* 4.57.3; Suet. *Tib.* 21.2; *Cal.* 4.1.

72   Sawiński (2018), 87 f.

experience indispensable for the *princeps*, but also prepared the Romans and the subject communities for his future succession. A further hundred years later the perception of Augustus' wishes was pretty much the same, as evidenced by the *Feriale Duranum*, the calendar of religious observances of the Roman military garrison stationed in Dura-Europos in the third century AD, in which Germanicus figures as the only male non-emperor whose birthday was commemorated.[73] In AD 14 Augustus' long-run intentions in the matter of succession must have been common knowledge throughout the Empire and it cannot be ruled out that the soldiers who at the news of the emperor's death were encouraging Germanicus to bid for the supreme power, acted upon this belief, not upon their alleged aversion to Tiberius' severity.[74]

The change of rulers did not affect his position. Actually, whether or not Tiberius really favoured Drusus the Younger,[75] during his reign and on his initiative Germanicus' superior status was not only retained but also enhanced. In AD 15 Germanicus was first granted the title of *imperator*[76] and then given the right to triumph,[77] both officially by the senate, but at Tiberius' behest; and however we interpret the emperor's decision to recall his adopted son from Germania, the honours bestowed on him for his campaigns, the culmination of which was his magnificent triumph in AD 17, gave him – hailed as the avenger of the *clades Variana*, as the restorer of Rome's invincibility, but most of all as the one who had regained the military standards lost in the Teutoburg disaster[78] – additional prestige greater than any post could give.[79] Subsequent honours: not only the *imperium maius* in the East, but also consulship together with Tiberius[80] and *ovatio* for the Armenian settlement,[81] followed quasi-automatically. In view of all this the question arises whether not only during his Eastern command, but already in Germania he would have needed special powers to issue edicts such as those mentioned by Arrius Menander. Was it not enough to be *the* Germanicus, i. e. the embodiment of the Roman military virtues, the husband of Augusts' granddaughter and the adoptive son of the ruling emperor, and, on top of that, the holder of an *imperium* greater than that of ordinary *legati*?

---

73   *Feriale Duranum*, no. 117, col. II, lines 12–13: *VIIII kal(endas) iunias ob natalem G[er]mani[c]<i> Cae[sa]ris sup[pli]cat[i]o [me]mori[ae Ge]rm[anici]* | *C[a]esaris* (24 May). Women and gods also appear in the *Feriale Duranum*, but they form separate categories.

74   Suet. *Tib.* 25.2–3; *Cal.* 1.2. Severity as one of the reasons of Tiberius' unpopularity, cf. *Tib.* 19.1.

75   Thus Tac. *Ann.* 2.43.5–6.

76   Tac. *Ann.* 1.58.5–6.

77   Tac. *Ann.* 1.55.1, 2.41.1.

78   *TS* 1.13–15.

79   On the great popularity of Germanicus among the common people: Tac. *Ann.* 2.43.5–6.

80   Tac. *Ann.* 2.53.1.

81   Tac. *Ann.* 2.64.1.

Some modern scholars, basing on passages in Cassius Dio[82] and Paulus,[83] maintain that the emperors right from the beginning gave their *legati* detailed *mandata* which minutely defined the latter's tasks,[84] including the scope of their edicts; in that perspective, the right to issue edicts which changed the legal status of the Roman citizens would have had to be specified in *legatus'* instructions. Whether right or wrong, in Germanicus' case this view is irrelevant precisely because both in Germania and in the East he acted not as an ordinary *legatus Augusti*, but as the holder of an extraordinary *imperium*. Now, there is no doubt that each *imperium* of his was set in an appropriate legal form, but it is difficult to believe that the specification of powers which went with them had to go so far into detail. After all, the source of Germanicus' authority stemmed directly from belonging to the *familia Caesaris*,[85] more precisely, from being the only close relative of the ruling *princeps* with the full *cursus honorum* behind him and enough experience and achievement to his credit to undertake any task the emperor would have committed himself to perform, had he been able to split himself in two.[86]

This brings us back to the *arcanum imperii* of the reign of Augustus and the first decade of Tiberius (ca. 30 BC–AD 23), that *Zwischenzeit* between the Republic and the fully-developed Principate, when the new political order was still in the making, less with regard to the by then generally accepted monarchy than because the ways of matching *regnum* with the political institutions and phraseology of republican vintage were still at an experimental stage.[87]

One of the central solutions Augustus adopted consisted in duplicating, or sometimes even triplicating himself by mustering his nearest kin (we can safely include Marcus Agrippa in their ranks) to perform tasks far exceeding in scope those of the "regular" magistrates, proconsuls and legates, confined to their strictly defined, narrow

---

82 Cass. Dio 53.15.4.
83 D. 1.18.3.
84 Berger (1953), 575; Millar (1977), 157; Campbell (1984), 281.
85 The best proof is the succession policy under the Julio-Claudian dynasty; see Sawiński (2018), 21–159 (about the power and political position of potential successors during the reigns of Augustus and Tiberius).
86 See Tac. *Ann.* 2.43.1, how Tiberius explained in the senate the necessity to grant Germanicus his Eastern *imperium maius*: *Igitur haec et de Armenia quae supra memoravi apud patres disseruit, nec posse motum Orientem nisi Germanici sapientia conponi: nam suam aetatem vergere, Drusi nondum satis adolevisse. tunc decreto patrum per missae Germanico provinciae quae mari dividuntur, maiusque imperium, quoquo adisset, quam iis qui sorte aut missu principis obtinerent.* In the English translation: "These circumstances, then, and the events in Armenia, which I mentioned above, were discussed by Tiberius before the senate. 'The commotion in the East,' he added, "could only be settled by the wisdom of Germanicus: for his own years were trending to their autumn, and those of Drusus were as yet scarcely mature.' There followed a decree of the Fathers, delegating to Germanicus the provinces beyond the sea, with powers overriding, in all regions he might visit, those of the local governors holding office by allotment or imperial nomination" (transl. John Jackson).
87 With regard to military matters, see Campbell (1984), 32–43, 61–65.

provinces in the original sense of fields of activity. This solution, an integral element of Augustus' dynastic succession system as well,[88] which assumed total mutual loyalty within the extended imperial family and required of all its members, not only the emperor's designated heirs (except obvious misfits, Agrippa Postumus and Claudius), to achieve a military and administrative apprenticeship (which they did better or worse, and which at least one of them, the original heir apparent Caius Caesar, seemingly failed to pass), worked well for half-a-century with only one hitch (Tiberius' self-exile to Rhodos) and so can legitimately be rated an essential component of the political system of the early Principate. Needless to say, the emperors' appointees, exactly as the emperor himself, had to receive from the senate and the people the correspondingly high status expressed in traditional Republican terms, but just as the real power of the *princeps* was essentially of discretionary nature, they, his representatives in the strongest possible sense, must also have had a very large margin of freedom to decide and act as they thought fit in matters they encountered while holding their posts (as opposed to those they were expressly sent to cope with). Germanicus was placed at the head of one third of the Empire's military forces to reconquer Germania, not to deal with mutinous legionaries; but when faced with them, he surely acted at his own discretion.[89] As we learn from Arrius Menander, among the decisions taken on that occasion were apparently the edicts which treated long absent soldiers as deserters or, in other words, made them liable to the death penalty.

One more thing. As has been written above, what makes Germanicus' edicts unique, at least for us, is the fact that they were issued by someone else than the emperor (of course, barring some new sensational epigraphic discovery, we shall never know whether other holders of extraordinary *imperium* of his day ever did something similar). Now, this uniqueness largely stemmed from another, namely from the fact that the extraordinary *imperia* granted to the emperors' nearest kin were a relatively short-lived phenomenon which came to an end with the passing of Drusus the Younger, only four years after the death of his adoptive brother. Apart from the particular family situation which deterred Tiberius, and his successors as well, from giving his/their prospective heirs a suitable official standing and a chance to acquire experience indispensable for such posts, with the consolidation of the principate – and, one might add, with the imposition of the *pax Romana* – the need for these posts disappeared, and so did the discretionary power their holders were vested with, which enabled Germanicus to issue the edicts mentioned by Arrius Menander.

88 Ziolkowski (2010), 312 f.
89 In the same emergency Drusus the Younger was sent to deal with the mutiny of the "Pannonian" legions *nullis satis certis mandatis; ex re consulturum* (Tac. *Ann.* 1.24.1). For the English translation see n67.

Bibliography

Alföldi, Andreas (1976): Oktavians Aufstieg zur Macht. Bonn: Rudolf Habelt.

Andreski, Stanislav (1968): Military Organization and Society. 2nd edition. Berkeley, Los Angeles: University of California Press.

Arangio-Ruiz, Vincenzo (1974): "Sul reato di diserzione in diritto romano" (1919). In: Ibid.: Scritti di diritto romano. Napoli: Jovene, Vol. 2, 1–12.

Arnaud, Pascal (1994): *"Transmarinae provinciae*. Réflexions sur les limites géographiques et sur la nature des pouvoirs en Orient des 'corégents' sous les règnes d'Auguste et de Tibère". In: Cahiers du Centre Gustave Glotz 5, 221–253.

Bauman, Richard A. (1970): The *Crimen Maiestatis* in the Roman Republic and Augustan Principate. Johannesburg: Witwatersrand University Press.

Bauman, Richard A. (1974): *Impietas in principem*. A Study of Treason Against the Roman Emperor with Special Reference to the First Century A. D. München: C. H. Beck.

Berger, Adolf (1953): Encyclopedic Dictionary of Roman Law. Philadelphia: American Philosophical Society.

Brand, Clarence E. (1968): Roman Military Law. Austin: University of Texas Press.

Brecht, Christoph H. (1938): *Perduellio*. Eine Studie zu ihrer begrifflichen Abgrenzung im römischen Strafrecht bis zum Ausgang der Republik. München: C. H. Beck.

Bretone, Marco (1982): Tecniche e ideologie dei giuristi romani. 2nd edition. Napoli: Edizioni Scientifiche Italiane.

Brice, Lee L. (2011): "Disciplining Octavian. A Case Study of Roman Military Culture, 40–30 BCE". In: Lee, Wayne L. (ed.): Warfare and Culture in World History. New York: New York University Press, 35–59.

Campbell, J. Brian (1984): The Emperor and the Roman Army 31 BC–AD 235. Oxford: Clarendon Press.

Campbell, J. Brian (2002): War and Society in Imperial Rome 31 BC–AD 284. London, New York: Routledge.

Carcani, Michele (1981): Dei reati delle pene e dei giudizi militari presso i Romani. ed. Vincenzo Giuffrè. Napoli: Jovene.

Derda, Tomasz et al. (forthcoming): Roman Army on the Southern Limits of the Empire in the First Years of Augustus. Greek and Latin Papyri from Qasr Ibrim. Warszawa: Department of Papyrology of University of Warsaw.

Duffy, Christopher (1974): The Army of Frederick the Great. New York: The Emperor's Press.

Duffy, Christopher (1987): The Military Experience in the Age of Reason. London, New York: Routledge.

Eck, Werner et al. (1996): De senatus consultum de Cn. Pisone Patre. München: C. H. Beck.

Faszcza, Michał N. (2020): "*Cedo alteram*, or the Problem with Some Augustan Centurions in Times of Peace". In: Eos 107 (1–2), 109–125.

Faszcza, Michał N. (2021): "A Citizen-Soldier of the Roman Republic. Beyond the Literary Creation". In: Klio 58 (2), 25–41.

Gilliver, Catherine M. (2011): The Roman Art of War. 3rd edition. Stroud: The History Press.

Giuffrè, Vincenzo (1973): Aspetti costituzionali del potere dei militari nella tarda 'respublica'. Napoli: Jovene.

Giuffrè, Vincenzo (1974a): "Arrio Menandro e la letteratura 'de re militari'". In: Labeo 20, 27–63.

Giuffrè, Vincenzo (1974b): La letteratura 'de re militari'. Appunti per una storia degli ordinamenti militari. Napoli: Jovene.

Giuffrè, Vincenzo (1980): Il 'diritto militare' dei Romani. Bologna: Pàtron.

Giuffrè, Vincenzo (2013): *Homines militares e status Rei Publicae*. Torsioni di una constituzione. Napoli: Jovene.

Goldsworthy, Adrian K. (1996): The Roman Army at War 100 BC–AD 200. Oxford: Clarendon Press.

Guarino, Antonio (1981): Storia del diritto romano. 6th edition. Napoli: Jovene.

Guizzi, Francesco (1999): Augusto. La politica della memoria. Roma: Salerno.

Hurlet, Frédéric / Mineo, Bernard (2009): "*Res publica restituta*. Le pouvoir et ses représentations à Rome sous le principat d'Auguste". In: Hurlet, Frédéric / Mineo, Bernard (eds.): Le Principat d'Auguste. Réalités et représentations du pouvoir. Autour de la *Res publica restituita*. Rennes: Presses universitaires de Rennes, 9–22.

Jung, Jost H. (1982): "Die Rechtsstellung der römischen Soldaten. Ihre Entwicklung von den Anfängen Roms bis auf Diokletian". In: Temporini, Helga (ed.): Aufstieg und Niedergang der römischen Welt, Bd. II, T. 14, 882–1013.

Kajanto, Iiro (1970): "Tacitus' Attitude to War and the Soldier". In: Latomus 29 (3), 699–718.

Kunkel, Wolfgang (1952): Herkunft und soziale Stellung der römischen Juristen. Weimar: Hermann Böhlaus Nachfolger.

Lendon, Jon E. (2005): Soldiers & Ghosts. A History of Battle in Classical Antiquity. New Haven, London: Yale University Press.

Levick, Barbara (2010): Augustus. Image and Substance. London, New York: Routledge.

MacMullen, Ramsay (1963): Soldier and Civilian in the Later Roman Empire. Cambridge MA: Harvard University Press.

Millar, Fergus (1977): The Roman Emperor (31 BC–337 AD). London: Duckworth.

Mommsen, Theodor (1889): Digestia Iustiniani Augusti. In: Krüger, Paul / Mommsen, Theodor (eds.): Corpus Iuris Civilis. Institutiones et Digesta. Berolini: Weidmann.

Mommsen, Theodor (1899): Römisches Strafrecht. Leipzig: Duncker & Humblot.

Müller, Albert (1906): "Die Strafjustiz im römischen Heere". In: Neue Jahrbücher für das Klassische Altertum. Geschichte und Deutsche Literatur und für Pädagogik 17, 550–577.

Nicolet, Claude (1980): The World of the Citizen in Republican Rome. Berkeley, Los Angeles: University of California Press.

Phang, Sara E. (2008): Roman Military Service. Ideologies of Discipline in the Late Republic and Early Principate. Cambridge: Cambridge University Press.

Potter, David S. / Damon, Cynthia (1999): "The Senatus Consultum de Cn. Pisone Patre". In: American Journal of Philology 120 (1), 13–42.

Premerstein von, Anton (1937): Von Werden und Wesen des Prinzipats. München: C. H. Beck.

Raaflaub, Kurt (2009): "The Political Significance of Augustus Military Reforms". In: Edmondson, John (ed.): Augustus. Edinburgh: Edinburgh University Press, 203–228.

Rivière, Yann (2016): Germanicus. Prince romain 15 av. J.-C.–19 apr. J.-C. Paris: Perrin.

Rüpke, Jörg (1990): *Domi Militiae*. Die religiöse Konstruktion des Krieges in Rom, Stuttgart: Franz Steiner Verlag.

Santalucia, Bernardo (1994): Studi di diritto penale romano. Roma: L'Erma di Bretschneider.

Sawiński, Paweł (2007): "Some Comments on the Character of Germanicus' *imperium* During his Activity in Germany and in the East". In: Berdowski, Piotr / Blahaczek, Beata (eds.): *Haec mihi in animus vestris templa. Studia classica* in Memory of Professor Lesław Morawiecki. Rzeszów:

Institute of History at The University of Rzeszów and The Rzeszów Archaeological Foundation, 221–226.

Sawiński, Paweł (2018): The Succession of Imperial Power under the Julio-Claudian Dynasty (30 BC–AD 68). Berlin: Peter Lang Verlag.

Sawiński, Paweł (2021): Holders of Extraordinary *imperium* under Augustus and Tiberius. A Study into the Beginnings of the Principate. London, New York: Routledge.

Schiavone, Aldo (2016): Storia giuridica di Roma. Bologna: G. Giappichelli.

Schulz, Fritz (1946): History of Roman Legal Science. Oxford: Clarendon Press.

Sulser, Jakob (1923): *Disciplina*. Beitrage zur inneren Geschichte des römischen Heeres von Augustus bis Vespasian. Dachau: Bayerland.

Valditara, Giuseppe (2015): Riflessioni sulla pena nella Roma repubblicana. Torino: G. Giappichelli.

Vendrand-Voyer, Jacqueline (1983): Normes civiques et métier militaire à Rome sous le Principat. Clermont-Ferrand: Adosa.

Wellesley, Kenneth (1969): "Tacitus as a Military Historian". In: Dorey, Thomas A. (ed.): Tacitus. London: Duckworth, 63–97.

Wesch-Klein, Gabriele (1998): Soziale Aspekte des römischen Heerwesens in der Kaiserzeit. Stuttgart: Franz Steiner Verlag.

Wiedemann, Thomas (1996): "Single Combat and being Roman". In: Ancient Society 27, 91–103.

Wolff, Catherine (2009): Déserteurs et transfuges dans l'armée romaine à l'époque républicaine. Napoli: Jovene.

Zanker, Paul (1987): Augustus und die Macht der Bilder. München: C. H. Beck.

Ziolkowski, Adam (2010): Storia di Roma. 2nd edition. Milano, Torino: Bruno Mondadori.

Ziolkowski, Mariusz (1990): "Il culto della Disciplina nelle religione dell'esercito Romano". In: Rivisita storica dell'Antichità 20, 97–107.

Germanicus in Roman Numismatic Memory*

AGATA ALEKSANDRA KLUCZEK

Keywords: Germanicus' triumph, posthumous commemoration of Germanicus, "commemorative" coins, "restored" coins

The concept of Roman numismatic memory is obviously a modern construct. The ancients themselves did not leave any clear exposition of the relationship between *nummi* and *memoria*. Not that they were unaware of the link between the two. Actually, in the passage on the etymology of verbs in *De lingua Latina*, where Varro derives from *memoria* not only *meminisse* ("to remember") but also *monere* ("to remind"), *quod is qui monet, proinde sit ac memoria* ("because he who *monet* 'reminds', is just like a memory"), he writes that it is for this reason that the derivative *monimenta* applies to tombstones and other memorials of the dead, and adds: *ab eo cetera quae scripta ac facta memoriae causa monimenta dicta* ("from this, the other things that are written and done to preserve their *memoria* 'memory' are called *monimenta* 'monuments'").[1] Similarly, although in Paulus' definition of *monimentum*, of unmistakeably Varronian imprint – both what is erected for the dead and anything that is made to commemorate someone – only *fana, porticus, scripta* and *carmina* are quoted in the second sense[2], references to the past are such constant and prominent a feature in the legends and types of Imperial coins that for the modern student of antiquity they are just another historical source to an extent unparalleled in other numismatic systems, both in terms of what actually happened and what their issuers wanted to be remembered.

---

* I am grateful to Adam Ziółkowski for his pertinent remarks on the earlier draft of this paper. All illustrations come from www.cngcoins.com or www.kuenker.de. I thank the Classical Numismatic Group, Inc. and Fritz Rudolf Künker GmbH & Co. KG for their consent to my using the photographs of the coins free of charge. The research activities co-financed by the funds granted under the Research Excellence Initiative of the University of Silesia in Katowice.

1 Varro, *LL* 6.49, transl. by R. G. Kent.

2 Festus 123.7–10L.

As a matter of fact, all the numismatic issues (i. e. coins and medallions) of the Roman Empire can be considered elements of a consistent policy of commemoration. Their ever changing types and legends were constantly informing those who used them – and the Empire was monetized as no other political entity before the 16th c. – about the achievements, wishes and attitudes of the rulers. This was done both directly, by presenting their *res gestae*, and indirectly, through references to the past, sometimes in the form of the so-called restitution issues, copying those emitted long before and thereby alluding to the personages and circumstances the latter had commemorated in the first instance. Even coins advertising the ruling emperors' presumptive successors, and so to an extent referring not even to the present, but to the future, served this purpose, since they introduced the latter into the collective imaginary, and so into the collective memory as well. The Romans of the Empire may not have coined the term "numismatic memory", but they certainly practised it.

In modern literature, Roman numismatic memory takes on yet another meaning, and it is in that sense that it is understood in the present paper. It is the memory of a given person that can be extracted from posthumously issued coins. This is a contextual memory, because the exigencies of the present (the issuer's interest) determined the things which were to be extracted from the legendary or historical past – whether remote or more recent, or from the nooks and crannies of memory – and made manifest in coinage. Its expression in Roman Imperial coinage may be associated with the content of restituted or imitation-related issues, may be assigned to the "antiquarian" trend, or may be identified as simple instances of repetition or iconographical inspiration.[3] A numismatic representation that is developed or recalled becomes a witness of memory, which does not necessarily refer to a specific person but to an idea, and it is this idea that becomes the "key" referring back to a specific figure.

***

The concept of Roman numismatic memory thus covers several fields of association in which one may locate the memory of Germanicus Iulius Caesar. The coins in question, both provincial and imperial, are conveniently described in the relevant volumes of *Roman Imperial Coinage* (RIC) and *Roman Provincial Coinage* (RPC);[4] furthermore, Germanicus' presence in coinage has been the subject of particular studies by such authors as Simonetta Piattelli, Francesco Panvini Rosati, Arnaud Suspène, and Bernhard Weisser.[5] Some of these studies were stimulated by the bimillennial anniversary

---

3   Estiot (2009), 161; Grau (2022), *passim*.
4   RIC 2.1; RPC 1; RPC 2.
5   Piattelli (1986), 185–187; Piattelli (1987), 319–327; Panvini-Rosati (1987), 79–86; Suspène (2013), 175–195; Weisser (2015), 98–104; Weisser (2017), 71–90. See also Guilhembet (2013), 197–204.

of Germanicus' birth (15 BC), others by the progress of numismatic research in general. Nevertheless, there remain some uncertainties concerning the date of particular issues, starting with the question of whether a coin was struck during Germanicus' lifetime or after his death in AD 19, and their classification as imperial or provincial, as well as their attribution to specific mints.[6]

In the present study, I analyse Germanicus' image on coins in the sphere of numismatic memorisation, without attempting to settle questions concerning the chronology and provenance of (un)certain issues; neither do I attempt to elaborate on the problems of the origins of specific representations. My aim is to discuss concisely the presence of Germanicus in coinage during the reigns of the successive emperors and then to characterise the original coin types commemorating him. In this way, I search for the features (and perhaps the uniqueness) of the numismatic memory of Germanicus.

***

During the last decade of Augustus' rule and in the early years of Tiberius' reign Germanicus was one of the principal figures in the Roman Empire, apparently predestined to assume, sooner or later, the imperial power. Through the adoption by Tiberius in AD 4 he became a full-fledged member of the emperor's family, which at that moment, apart from Augustus himself, consisted of his two adopted sons – Tiberius and Agrippa Postumus, and the former's two sons, one natural – Drusus the Younger, and the other adopted – Germanicus. Now, in the dynasty's new order Germanicus' position was evidently just behind Tiberius, the indisputable heir apparent. The natural son of Drusus the Elder and Antonia the Younger, and thus the grandson of Octavia, Germanicus was married to Agrippina the Elder, the daughter of M. Agrippa and Julia, the daughter of Augustus. The fact that Augustus ordered Tiberius to adopt Germanicus, despite the fact that Tiberius already had a natural son, clearly indicated his resolve that, after the inevitable Tiberian interlude, it would be Germanicus' and Agrippina's children who would continue the Julian inheritance; in other words, that the imperial power would remain in the hands of the first emperor's natural descendants.[7]

Outwardly, however, Augustus plainly treated the new arrangement of his family as a private affair. Nevertheless, some time after his adoption by Tiberius, Germanicus' likeness appeared on coins from Corinth, one of the two most presigious Roman colonies outside Italy. His bare head appears on the obverse, with the legend GERMAN-

6   Cf. Suspène (2013), 176–178.
7   See Sawiński (2018), 86–91.

ICVS CAESAR COR (Fig. 1);[8] but other coins of this series featured the likenesses of the *princeps* himself, as well as Tiberius, Drusus and Agrippa Postumus,[9] in other words, all the adult Iulii Caesares. What is more, these are the only known coins featuring Germanicus during Augustus' reign.[10] Less certain is the case of some provincial coins, such as those minted at Tabae in Caria, on which the heads of Germanicus and Drusus the Younger are depicted, facing each other on the obverse, complemented by the legend ΓΕΡΜΑΝΙΚΟΣ ΔΡΟΥΣΟΣ ΦΙΛΑΔΕΛΦΟΙ; but their Augustan dating is not certain.[11]

***

The image and name of Germanicus first appeared on coins struck outside Italy, in mints belonging both to *coloniae* and *municipia*, and to peregrine communities. During the reign of Tiberius (AD 14–37) Germanicus was not present at all on imperial coins, but his name appeared on coins emitted by numerous provincial mints (twenty-two out *ca.* 145).[12] It is difficult to date most of these provincial coins: some were struck during Germanicus' lifetime; others were emitted *pro memoria* after his death. During Caligula's reign (AD 37–41) when, not surprisingly, a number of imperial issues commemorated his father (see below), the latter appeared on coins struck by nineteen

8   RPC 1, no. 1142. Cf. RPC 1: 252; Suspène (2013), 185 (AD 4–5); Weisser (2015), 99 f.; Weisser (2017), 72, 78 f. (AD 4–6).
9   RPC 1, nos 1139, 1144 (Augustus), 1139 (Tiberius), 1141 (Agrippa Postumus), 1143 (Drusus the Younger).
10   The problem with chronology of some issues, see RPC 1: 267, no. 1318 and 507, no. 3134 (under Tiberius), but cf. Weisser (2017), 72 f., 78 (under Augustus).
11   RPC 1: 471 and no. 2871 (dated to Augustus' reign). Cf. countermark CAESAR on *aes* coinage (particularly in Lower Gemany) – Augustan or Tiberian date – Giard (1976), 27; RIC 1: 10–11; Suspène (2013), 178. See also the following note.
12   *Coloniae civium Romanorum*: RPC 1, nos 74–75 (Romula, Hispania), 137 (Acci, Hispania), 232 (Tarraco, Hispania); *municipium civium Romanorum*: RPC 1, nos 68–70 (Italica, Hispania); *colonia Latinorum*: RPC 1, no. 123 (Carteia, Hispania); other provincial mints: RPC 1, nos 5452 (Panormus, Sicilia), cf. Frey-Kupper (1991), 90–95; RPC 1, nos 946–949 (Cyrenaica), 1318 (Tanagra, Boeotia), cf. Weisser (2017), 72 f., 78 (under Augustus); RPC 1, nos 1779C (Byzantium, Thrace), 2017 (Caesarea Germanica, Bithynia), 2064 (Nicomedia, Bithynia), 2367 (Pergamum, Mysia), 2538A, 2539–2540 (Hypaepa, Lydia), 2968 (Hierapolis, Phrygia), 2992–2995 (Sardis, Lydia), 3058 (Tripolis, Lydia), 3134 (Apamea, Phrygia), cf. Weisser (2017), 73, 78 (under Augustus); RPC 1, nos 3163A (Siblia, Phrygia), 3180 (Synnada, Phrygia), 3205–3206 (Prymnessus, Phrygia), 3623A–D (Caesarea, Cappadocia). See also RPC 1, no. 198 (*colonia* Ilici, Hispania): obv. TI CAESAR DIVI AVG F AVG(VSTVS) P M, head, l.; rev. C I I A L TER LON L PAP AVIT II VIR Q IVNCTIO, two *togati* standing with hands clasped over a thymiaterion. The *togati* have been identified as personifications of the cities of Ilici and Icosium, Tiberius and Seianus, Tiberius and Caligula, or Germanicus and Drusus, cf. RPC 1: 98; Weisser (2017), 74 (n19).

out of sixty-six provincial mints.[13] During Claudius' reign (AD 41–54) their number declined significantly: two or three out of *ca.* 120.[14]

In total, more than sixty provincial coin types issued by *ca.* forty mints referred to Germanicus. These mints were scattered over a number of provinces of the Empire, particularly in Spain and Asia Minor.

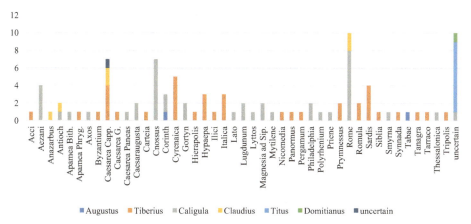

Graph 1 Geographical distribution of coin types propagating Germanicus (number of issues)

At first sight, the chronological and geographical distribution of imperial and provincial emissions (Graph 1) suggests widespread popularity of Germanicus in the Empire's *pars orientalis*, which can be linked with the fact that he spent the last two years of his life in this region. A second glance reveals a slightly different picture. That the relative frequency of his representations in local coinage cannot be treated as more than a by-product of his personal visits to given places is shown by the fact that, e. g., out of the many cities in Greece and Asia Minor he visited during his Oriental proconsulate, he indubitably appears on the issues of only two – Pergamum and Mytilene; others do not feature him in their issues.[15] However, the obverse of the Pergamum coins with

---

13   *Coloniae civium Romanorum*: RPC 1, nos 377, 384 (Caesaraugusta, Hispania), 1178–1179 (Corinth), 991–996, 999 (Cnossus, Crete), 2013 (Apamea, Bithynia); other provincial mints: RPC 1, nos 2347 (Mytilene, Lesbos), 3077, 3081–3083 (Aezani, Phrygia), 962 (Axos, Crete), 1022–1023 (Gortyn, Crete), 1026 (Lato, Crete), 1027 (Lyttos, Crete), 1028 (Polyrhenium, Crete), 1572 (Thessalonica, Macedonia), 2454–2455 (Magnesia ad Sipylum, Lydia), 2471 (Smyrna, Ionia), 2689 (Priene, Ionia), 3018–3019 (Philadelphia, Lydia), 4163 (Antioch, Syria), 5486 (uncertain), 4976 (Caesarea Paneas, Syria). Cf. BMCG, Lesbos, Methymna: 181, no. 38 (head of Germanicus) = RPC 1, no. 2340 (head of Caligula).

14   RPC 1, nos 4060 (Anazarbus, Cilicia), 4281 (Antioch, Syria). See also RPC 1, nos 3629–3630 (Caesarea, Cappadocia). Cf. Michel (2018), 213–216.

15   Cf. Suspène (2013), 186, a list of places that are likely to have been visited by Germanicus on the basis of the contemporary epigraphical and statuary monuments: Nicopolis, Patras, Athens, Euboea,

Germanicus' head and the legend ΓΕΡΜΑΝΙΚΟΣ ΚΑΙΣΑΡ, is counterbalanced by the reverse representation of Drusus and the legend ΔΡΟΥΣΟΣ ΚΑΙΣΑΡ;[16] so there is nothing which makes them specifically "his". More straightforward is the import of those from Mytilene, on which the obverse – Germanicus' head with the inscription ΘΕΟΝ ΓΕΡΜΑΝΙΚΟΝ ΜΥΤΙ – is juxtaposed with the reverse representation of Agrippina the Elder and the legend ΘΕΑΝ ΑΙΟΛΙΝ ΑΓΡΙΠΠΙΝΑΝ ΜΥΤΙ.[17] That the type alludes precisely to the stay of Germanicus and Agrippina on Lesbos in AD 18 is suggested by contemporary coins from Mytilene featuring Iulia Livilla, the couple's youngest child, born on that island.[18] The issue in question, however, dates from Caligula's reign.

In Syria, Germanikeia (Caesarea Germanica), founded by Germanicus as an autonomous community, is an uncertain case since the issue featuring him as *ktistes*, with the legend ΓΕΡΜΑΝΙΚΟΣ ΚΑΙΣΑΡ ΚΤΙΣΤΗΣ, is variously dated to the time just after his death or to Caligula's reign.[19] As for the capital of the Roman East, the following Antiochean issues belong to the reigns of Germanicus' son and brother, respectively: one with the legend ΓΑΙΟΣ ΚΑΙΣΑΡ ΣΕΒΑΣΤΟΣ ΓΕΡΜΑΝΙΚΟΣ, and the head of Caligula on the obverse, and ΓΕΡΜΑΝΙΚΟΣ ΚΑΙΣΑΡ and the head of Germanicus on the reverse;[20] and the other with NERO GERMANICVS CAESAR and the head of Germanicus on the obverse, and S C within a wreath on the reverse.[21] Since Germanicus died in Antioch, the commemorative aspect of these issues is self-evident.

As can be seen, instances of Germanicus' close association with a city in the coinage of which he appears are quite rare. One is therefore obliged to conclude that his commemoration in local issues was usually the result of other considerations, chief among which was the expression of loyalty to the ruling emperors, as shown by the fact that in the provincial coinage Germanicus was rarely presented unaccompanied (Figs. 2–3).[22] Usually, his likeness was coupled with the representations of Tiberius, Caligula, or Drusus the Younger. During Tiberius' reign, the likenesses of Germanicus and Drusus were regularly juxtaposed; they were shown together on the reverse (Fig. 4),[23] or one

---

Lesbos (Mytilene), Perinthus, Byzantium, Ilium, Assus, Pergamum?, Clazomenae?, Colophon, Ephesus?, Aphrodisias?, Eumenea? (Phrygia), Iasus?, Rhodes, Myra, Perge and Aspendus. Cf. also Blonce/Gangloff (2013), 113–131.

16 RPC 1, no. 2367 (AD 14–19).
17 RPC 1, no. 2347 (AD 37–41). Cf. Trillmich (1978), 116–121; Hekster (2015), 125.
18 RPC 1, no. 2348 (AD 37–41), obv. ΙΟΥΛΙΑΝ ΝΕΑΝ ΓΕΡΜΑΝΙΚΟΥ ΜΥΤΙ, bust of Julia Livilla, l.; rev. Γ ΚΑΙСΑΡΑ СΕΒΑСΤΟΝ ΜΥΤΙ, Caligula standing facing, holding patera.
19 RPC 1, no. 2017 (*ca.* AD 20?), rev. ΚΑΙΣΑΡΗΑ ΓΕΡΜΑΝΙΚΗ, view of city gate. Cf. Price/Trell (1977), 226 (but the coin is dated to AD 40).
20 RPC 1, no. 4163 (AD 37–41).
21 RPC 1, no. 4281 (AD 41–54, late in the reign of Claudius?).
22 See, e. g., coins of Corinth, RPC 1, nos 1178, 1179, obv. CAESAR, head of Germanicus, r. or l.
23 RPC 1, nos 68 (obv. head of Tiberius), 74, 137, 232, 2871, 2995. Cf. RPC 1, no. 198 (two *togati*). Cf. Weisser (2015), 101; Weisser (2017), 74.

was shown on the reverse and the other on the obverse of a coin (Fig. 5).[24] Some legends openly emphasised their relation; for example, in Sardes and Tabae they received the epithet *philadelphoi* (Fig. 6).[25] As is evident, in the provincial coinage Germanicus usually functioned as a "name" or a link in the chain of the ancestors or relatives of the rulers: son, father, brother and – exceptionally – husband of Agrippina the Elder.

Germanicus' image in the provincial coinage reinforces the above interpretation due to its lack of originality. Germanicus tended to be presented in a rather monotonous manner: his head or bust is depicted, sometimes juxtaposed with a portrait of the then ruling emperor or a different member of the imperial family. One of the exceptions to this rule is provided by the coins emitted during Caligula's reign in Magnesia ad Sipylum. On the reverse, Germanicus as a priest, *togatus*, *capite velato*, holding a patera in his hand, stands in the company of Agrippina the Elder, represented as Demeter with a sceptre and ears of corn (Fig. 7).[26] Scenes like this one, emphasising the idea of *pietas* and suggesting prosperity and the abundance of crops, are, however, extremely rare in the provincial coinage featuring Germanicus.

***

Germanicus appeared in imperial coinage during the reign of his son Caius (AD 37–41) better known as Caligula, the emperor who used coins to promote his family relationships on an unprecedented scale. As many as forty out of fifty-eight types of coins issued by the mints in Lugdunum and Rome honoured the members of the imperial family (cf. Graph 2). Three of them – Augustus and Caligula's parents – were honoured by issues struck in all the three metals, gold, silver and bronze: Augustus by sixteen types,[27] Germanicus by ten (Figs. 8–9),[28] Agrippina by eight.[29] Other relatives had to be contented with bronze types: three of them commemorated Caligula's elder brothers, Nero and Drusus Iulii Caesares, who are represented riding horses as *principes iuventutis*;[30] while two, with the legend AGRIPPINA DRVSILLA IVLIA, honoured

---

24 RPC 1, nos 69, 2367, 2968, 2992, 3058, 3205–3206, 5452. Cf. Weisser (2015), 101 f.; Weisser (2017), 75.
25 RPC 1, nos 2871, Tabae, 2994–2995, Sardes.
26 RPC 1, nos 2454, obv. ΓΑΙΟΝ ΚΑΙCΑΡΑ CΕΒΑCΤΟΝ, head of Caligula, r.; rev. ΓΕΡΜΑΝΙΚΟΝ ΚΑΙ ΑΓΡΙΠΠΙΝΑΝ ΜΑ ΑΠΟ CΙΠ(Υ); 2455, obv. ΓΑΙΟΝ ΚΑΙCΑΡΑ CΕΒΑCΤΟΝ, head of Caligula, r.; ΜΑΓΝΕΤΩΝ ΑΠΟ CΙΠΥΛΟΥ ΓΕΡΜ ΑΓΡΙΠ.
27 RIC 1, Cal., nos 1–4, 6, 8, 10 (au/d, Lugd.), 16–16, 23–24, 31 (au/d, Rome), 36, 44, 51 (ses, Rome), 56 (dp, Rome).
28 RIC 1, Cal., nos 11–12 (au/d, AD 37, Lugd.), 17–18 (au/d, AD 37–38, Rome), 25–26 (au/d, AD 40, Rome), 35 (as, AD 37–38, Rome), 43 (as, AD 39–40, Rome), 50 (as, AD 40–41, Rome), 57 (dp, Rome). For numismatic familial presentation on Caligula's coinage, with attention to Germanicus, see Suspène (2013), 178–180; Hekster (2015), 47 f., 122–127; Grau (2022), 88 f.
29 RIC 1, Cal., nos 7–8 (au/d, Lugd.), 13–14, 21–22, 30 (au/d, Rome), 55 (ses, Rome). Cf. Morelli (2009), 55–61.
30 RIC 1, Cal., nos 34, 42, 49 (dp, Rome).

Caligula's sisters – Iulia Drusilla, Iulia Agrippinilla (Agrippina the Younger) and Iulia Livilla;[31] finally, one bronze type, of admittedly very uncertain dating, commemorated M. Agrippa.[32]

In this way, Caligula created his own numismatic stemma of the *domus Augusta*, which excluded Tiberius, the murderer of his mother and brothers, and the latter's natural son, Drusus the Younger. Naturally, Augustus was assigned the primary position. As for Caligula's parents, particularly noteworthy is the position of Agrippina, whom during Germanicus' burial (which neither Tiberius nor Livia attended) the Roman plebs hailed as the sole surviving offspring of Augustus,[33] and whose bones Caligula, as one of the first acts of his reign, brought over to Rome from the island of Pandateria – where, exiled by Tiberius, she had died of starvation in AD 33[34] – and deposited in the Mausoleum Augusti.[35] Agrippina's surviving sepulchral inscription neatly encapsulates the reason for her exaltation in the numismatic memory: *ossa Agrippinae M. Agrippae [f.] divi Aug. neptis uxoris Germanici Caesaris matris C. Caesaris Aug. Germanici princip-is* [...] (The bones of Agrippina, daughter of Marcus Agrippa, granddaughter of the Deified Augustus, wife of Germanicus Caesar, mother of the princeps Caius Caesar Augustus Germanicus).[36] More difficult to interpret is the single bronze type depicting Agrippina's father, his first appearance in coinage since 12 BC, the year of his death:[37] against the banal explanation that, as the husband of Iulia, Augustus' only daughter, and Caligula's grandfather through Agrippina the Elder, he rounded out the circle of his ancestors,[38] one can juxtapose Suetonius' report that Caligula hated Agrippa be-

---

31   RIC 1, Cal., nos 33, 41 (ses, Rome). Three sisters of Caligula are represented with the attributes of Concordia, Securitas, and Fortuna. For the extravagant affection of Caligula for his sisters, cf. Suet. *Cal*. 15.3; Cass. Dio 59.3.4.
32   RIC 1, Cal., no. 58 (as, Rome). The coin was probably struck under Caligula: Nicols (1974), 65–86; Carter/Metcalf (1988), 145–147; attributed to the reign of Tiberius: BMCRE 1: cxxxiii ("the exact date of issue is a harder matter to decide"), and Tib., no. 161. This type was restored under Titus, Komnick (2001), no. 52.0 (AD 80–81), and Domitianus, Komnick (2001), no. 4.0 (AD 81–82).
33   Tac. *Ann*. 3.4.
34   Suet. *Tib*. 53.2.
35   Suet. *Cal*. 15.1; Cass. Dio 59.3.5.
36   CIL 6.886.
37   RIC 1, Aug., nos 412, 414 (d, 12 BC, Rome). This monetary type was restored under Trajan, see Komnick 2001, nos 50.0, 51.0 (d, *ca*. AD 112–113, Rome). The figure of Agrippa on coins, RRC, nos 534.1–3 (au/d, 38 BC); see also RIC 1, Aug., no. 154 (dp, Nemausus) = RPC 1, no. 522; RIC 1, Aug., nos 155–157 (as, Nemausus) = RPC 1, no. 523; RIC 1, Aug., no. 158 (as, Nemausus) = RPC 1, no. 524; RIC 1, Aug., nos 159–161 (as, Nemausus) = RPC 1, no. 525; RIC 1, Aug., nos 397, 400, 406–409 (au/d, Rome); RPC 1, nos 77–84 (Gades), 533 (Arausio), 864 (Tingi), 942 (Cyrenaica), 1106 (Sparta), 1366–1367 (Nicopolis), 2008, 2011 (Apamea), 2260 (Parium). Cf. Grant (1990), 9–17. The head of Agrippa is also on the obverse of the colonial coins of Caesaraugusta, RPC 1, nos 381, 386 (under Caligula). See also the copper piece, RPC 1, no. 5454 (mint uncertain): on obverse the head of Caligula acompanied by the legend C CAESAR GERMANICI F M AGRIPPAE N (*Caius Caesar Germanici filius M. Agrippae nepos*); cf. BMCRE 1: 397, no. 108bis (probably a Spanish mint); Grant (1948), 116; Grant (1950), 68 (probably a mint in Gallia).
38   See, e. g., Barrett (2015), 290 f.

cause of his low origin and flew into rage whenever someone referred to him as his ancestor, as well as the fact – also recorded by Suetonius – that he abolished the annual celebrations of the battles at Actium and Naulochos.[39] Together with the lack of clear chronological indicators of the type in question, which on the obverse proclaimed Agrippa's three consulships (M AGRIPPA L F COS III)[40] and on the reverse depicted the figure of Neptune, an allusion to the very naval victories which Caligula forbade to celebrate, its dating to the latter's reign is not certain at all, though it cannot be ruled out that this single type was issued on the Senate's own initiative at the beginning of Caligula's principate, before he revealed his attitude to his low-born grandfather.

Be that as it may, the numismatic memory of Germanicus during Caligula's reign was clearly situated on the genealogical and dynastic plane. The legends of relevant coins indicated his family affiliation with the preceding emperors – Augustus and Tiberius: GERMANICVS CAESAR TI AVGVST F DIVI AVG N (*Germanicus Caesar Tiberii Augusti filius Divi Augusti nepos*)[41] and with Caligula himself: GERMANICVS CAES P CA CAES AVG GERM (*Germanicus Caesar pater Caii Caesaris Augusti Germanici*).[42]

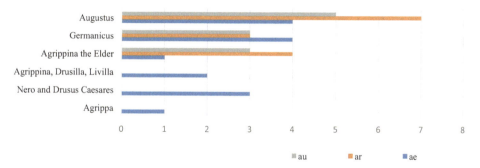

Graph 2 Proportions of Caligula's coin types propagating his family/ancestry: mints of Lugdunum and Rome (AD 37–41)

We learn from the literary sources and archaeological remains that the next emperor, Claudius, venerated his elder brother's memory;[43] yet in the numismatic material of

---

39   Suet. *Cal.* 23.1; cf. Cass. Dio 59.20.1.
40   The official form in which Agrippa was presented after his death, which we find in the Pantheon's inscription as well; see Ziolkowski (2007), 464–466.
41   RIC 1, Cal., nos 35, 43, 50.
42   RIC 1, Cal., nos 11–12, 17–18, 25–26.
43   For emphasis on family, and the celebration of the memory of Germanicus, see Suet. *Claud.* 11.2–3. The architectural decorations associated with this attitude to Germanicus have survived, see, e. g., the Julio-Claudian relief in Ravenna, cf. La Rocca (1992), 291–310; Hölscher (1994), 94–99; Osgood (2010), 62–65; figural decoration on the triumphal arch at Rome, celebrating Claudius' victory in Britain, cf. Barrett (1991), 1–19; Rose (1997), 113–115; monument in Verona, cf. Cavalieri-Manasse (1992), 9–41; figural decoration of the temple of Augustus and Rome at Leptis Magna; cf. Rose (1997), 184 f.; Hurlet (2000), 306–311. Cf. Michel (2018), 188–190, 199 f., 205–212.

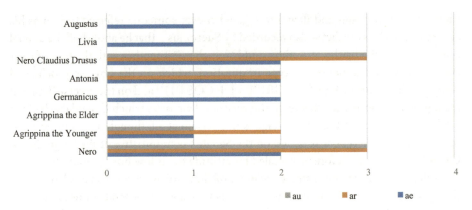

Graph 3 Proportions of Claudius' coin types propagating his family/ancestry: mint of Rome (AD 41–54)

his reign Germanicus is present on only four coin types, just two of which commemorate him directly. This, however, does not mean that there is contradiction between various kinds of evidence. First of all, references to the emperor's family are much less frequent in Claudius' imperial coinage, in spite of his considerably longer reign (thirteen years as opposed to Caligula's four) and a correspondingly higher number of coin types (thirty out of a hundred-fifteen types issued in Rome, cf. Graph 3). Almost a half of these types commemorated Claudius' parents, Drusus the Elder (eight types: three in gold, three in silver, two in bronze) and Antonia the Younger (six types: two in each metal). Among them, Drusus' Germanic victories of 12–9 BC were recalled on coins of the DE GERM(ANIS) type, with the representation of a triumphal arch surmounted by an equestrian statue or with a *vexillum* – two shields crossed, and two pairs of spears and two trumpets crossed.[44] Antonia Augusta (the *agnomen* conferred on her by her grandson Caligula) was honoured with Ceres' wreath: the reverses emphasised her as the model for Claudius' Constantia and the priestess of Divus Augustus.[45] Only slightly less numerous were the types honouring Claudius' last wife – Germanicus' daughter Agrippina the Younger (four),[46] and her son, adopted by Claudius as Nero Claudius Germanicus (eight).[47] Of the remaining types Augustus and Livia shared one *dupondius* (on the obverse Divus Augustus, on the reverse Diva Augusta[48]), Ger-

---

44   RIC 1, Claud., nos 93 (ses, AD 41–50, head of Nero Claudius Drusus), 109 (ses, *ca.* AD 50–54, head of Nero Claudius Drusus), and DE GERM(ANIS) type: RIC 1, Claud., nos 69–74 (au/d, AD 41–45). Drusus as *imperator*, cf. Tac. *Ann.* 1.3; Suet. *Claud.* 1: the senate voted him a marble arch, decorated with trophies, on the Appian way, and bestowed the name Germanicus on him and his descendants; cf. Cass. Dio 55.2.1–3.
45   RIC 1, Claud., nos 65–68 (au/d, AD 41–45), 92 (dp, AD 41–50), 104 (dp, *ca.* AD 50–54).
46   RIC 1, Claud., nos 75, 80–81 (au/d, AD 50–54), 103 (ses, *ca.* AD 50–54).
47   RIC 1, Claud., nos 76–79, 82–83 (au/d, AD 50–54), 107–108 (dp, *ca.* AD 50–54).
48   RIC 1, Claud., no. 101 (dp, *ca.* AD 41–50).

manicus was commemorated directly on one *as* and one *sestertius* (GERMANICVS CAESAR TI AVG F DIVI AVG N and the head of Germanicus),[49] while on another *sestertius* Agrippina the Elder was presented as the daughter of Marcus Agrippa and the wife of Germanicus (AGRIPPINA M F GERMANICI CAESARIS[50]); furthermore, on one of the coins featuring Agrippina the Younger, she is named Germanicus' daughter (AGRIPPINA AVG GERMANICI F CAESARIS AVG[51]). As can be seen, the two types referring directly to Germanicus are not unsatisfactory at all, especially when compared with the couple Augustus and Livia. Together with the separate type commemorating Agrippina the Elder, they are not only a manifestation of fraternal piety but also illustrate Claudius' emphasis of his connection with Augustus' family, and so help to explain why he chose Nero as his successor at the expense of his natural son.

***

After a long absence during Nero's reign (AD 54–68),[52] the Civil Wars of AD 68–69, and Vespasianus' reign (AD 69–79), the numismatic memory of Germanicus re-emerged under Titus (AD 79–81) and Domitianus (AD 81–96), in the obverses of *asses* featuring the head of Germanicus *en profil*, with an inscription which identified him and provided his filiation: GERMANICVS CAESAR TI AVG F DIVI AVG N;[53] the reverses, as on other restitution coins (see below), featured inscriptions which identified the issuers, first Titus, then Domitianus, sometimes with the filiation reference to *divus Vespasianus*, as well as information that the coin was issued *ex senatus consulto* (S C) or the *restituit* formula, which indicated the restitution of old numismatic types (*nummi restituti*). Some coins of Titus additionally provide the date of issue (*cos* VIII, i. e. AD 80). Domitianus' restitution coins were issued exclusively during the first two years of his reign (AD 81–82).

In general, the restitution series of Titus and Domitianus reproduced the types of original coins of the early Empire, especially portraits of the members of the first imperial dynasty (cf. Graph 4).[54] Titus' restitution coins featured, apart from Germanicus, eight other personages: Augustus, M. Agrippa, Tiberius, Drusus the Elder, Drusus

---

49 RIC 1, Claud., nos 105–106 (ses/as, *ca.* AD 50–54).
50 RIC 1, Claud., no. 102 (ses, *ca.* AD 50–54).
51 RIC 1, Claud., no. 103 (ses, *ca.* AD 50–54).
52 Germanicus was Nero's maternal grandfather, but no numismatic references were made to him during the latter's reign. Nero's formal imperial lineage can be found in the inscription (CIL 12.5471) on a milestone from the territory of Forum Iulii (Fréjus) Cf. Hekster (2015), 132.
53 Flavian restoration coinage attributed to Roman mint, see Komnick (2001), 87–90 (AD 80/81), 99 (AD 81/82); or to "Thracian" mint, see RPC 2, 87–88 (nos 511–525, AD 80–81; nos 534–542, AD 81–82); see also RIC 2.1, 187, 191–193, 242 (nos 399–497, AD 80–81, Rome, and nos 822–830, AD 81–82, Rome or "Thracian" mint).
54 Graph 4 was developed on the basis of the RIC 2.1 catalogue. I have taken account of both types and variants of coins. A different method of establishing the types of restitution coins was followed

the Younger, Agrippina the Elder, Claudius and Galba; additionally, a woman's bust on the coins PIETAS, IVSTITIA, SALVS AVGVSTA presented Livia in the guise of these divinities. The restitution coins of Domitianus replicated those commemorating Germanicus and five others: Augustus, M. Agrippa, Tiberius, Drusus the Younger and Claudius.

Germanicus was included in both groups and was mentioned in a total of nine variants of the Flavian restitution coins.[55] If we estimate popularity by the number of types, he yielded to Augustus, Livia and Tiberius but outranked the others, including Galba. In terms of style and content, the restored coins of Titus copied the issues of Caligula (Fig. 10)[56] and Claudius (Fig. 11),[57] whereas Domitianus' restoration series was strictly speaking a continuation of that of his brother.[58]

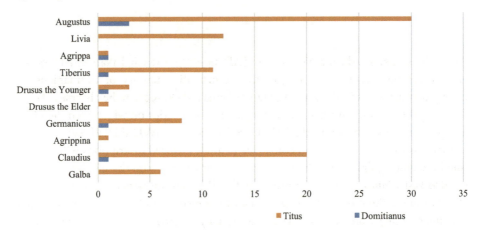

Graph 4 Flavian restitution coins featuring previous emperors and other members of the Julio-Claudian dynasty

The commemoration policy of the new dynasty as expressed in memorial coinage differed from one emperor to another. Broadly speaking, the selection of coin types "to

---

by H. Komnick, hence a slight discrepancy in figures, though the conclusions are not different. See Komnick (2001), 28–55, nos 1.0–62.0, and 91–96, nos 1.0–10.0.

55 Rev. IMP T CAES DIVI VESP F AVG P M TR P P P COS VIII RESTITV(IT), around S C, Komnick (2001), nos 10.0–10.1 = RIC 2.1, Tit., nos 417–418 = RPC 2, no. 518; rev. IMP T CAES DIVI VESP F AVG REST(ITVIT), around S C, Komnick (2001), no. 27.0–27.1 = RIC 2.1, Tit., nos 438–439; Komnick (2001), no. 25.0 = RIC 2.1, Tit., no. 442 = RPC 2, no. 519; RIC 2.1, Tit., no. 440; Komnick (2001), no. 28.0 = RIC 2.1, Tit., no. 441; Komnick (2001), no. 26.0 = RIC 2.1, Tit., no. 443; rev. IMP D CAES DIVI VESP F AVG REST, around S C, Komnick (2001), no. 7.0 = RIC 2.1, Dom., no. 828 = RPC 2, no. 539.

56 RIC 2.1, Tit., nos 417–418, 442–443. Prototype: RIC 1, Cal., no. 43.

57 RIC 2.1, Tit., nos 438–439, 441. Prototype: RIC 1, Claud., no. 106.

58 RIC 2.1, Dom., no. 828. Prototype, cf. RIC 2.1, Tit., no. 442.

be restored was so made as to throw light on current events of the day".[59] Vespasianus emitted "imitations" whose reverse designs were copied from earlier coins, those used in the Republic and those issued by his "good" imperial predecessors: mainly Augustus, but also Tiberius, Claudius and Galba.[60] The numismatic memory reflected in the *nummi restituti* of Titus and Domitianus also served the current political agenda of the Flavii, as Holger Komnick observes in his excellent monograph on the restoration issues of the emperors Titus, Domitianus, Nerva and Trajan;[61] but the main thrust of the message moved from the principle of the choice of the best to the dynastic ideology. This new policy of commemoration was clearly due to Titus' initiative; after his untimely death it was continued during the first two years of his brother's reign, and then stopped altogether.

Germanicus was the key figure linking the early and late Julio-Claudian emperors; in spite of the fact that he never acceded to the supreme power, he perfectly accentuated the dynastic principle. So did his wife, through whom the blood of Augustus was continued in the Claudii Nerones and Domitii Ahenobarbi (the legend of the restitution coin type commemorating her referred to her as Germanicus' wife and the daughter of M. Agrippa: AGRIPPINA M F GERMANICI CAESARIS; see above).[62] There was, however, another message which Flavian restitution coins featuring him conveyed. Germanicus was named on them *Tiberii Augusti filius Divi Augusti nepos*; the same filiation as that of Drusus the Younger (TI AVG F DIVI AVG N),[63] whose re-appearance was meant to stress the same family arrangement as that of the imperial Flavii – respectively, Tiberius and his sons – Germanicus and Drusus, and Vespasianus and his sons – Titus and Domitianus.[64] There is little doubt that the restitution coins featuring Drusus the Elder, Tiberius' natural brother, should be explained in the same way, even though in their case the parallel was not with the whole Flavian triad, but with the brothers Titus and Domitianus.

***

---

59   BMCRE 2, xliii; cf. RIC 2.1, 192.

60   There were as many as 33 of such repetitions: younger Caesar/Augustus: 19, Claudius: 4, Galba: 2, Tiberius: 1, and Republican coins: 7. Some of the coin types of the younger Caesar/Augustus imitated those which referred to the pivotal moments of his struggle for power: Philippi, the victory achieved under the auspices of Mars Ultor, Actium, the restitution of *res publica*, the recovery of *signa* from the Parthians; cf. Serra (2009), 1162–1177.

61   Komnick (2001), 158–180, on the historical value and possible contemporary purposes of these coin types. See also Hekster (2015), 56 f.

62   RIC 2.1, Tit., no. 419 = Komnick (2001), no. 11.0; prototype: RIC 1, Claud., no. 102.

63   RIC 2.1, Tit., no. 414 = Komnick (2001), no. 8.1, cf. ibid. no. 8.0; RIC 2.1, Tit., no. 437 = Komnick (2001), no. 24.0; prototype: RIC 1, Tib., no. 45; RIC 2.1, Dom., no. 827 = Komnick (2001), no. 6.0; prototype: RIC 1, Tib., no. 45.

64   Suspène (2013), 183.

The emissions commemorating Germanicus were overwhelmingly "civil" in character, in keeping with their main function of promoting the dynastic principle. Only two representations commemorated his military and diplomatic achievements, which is rather strange for the embodiment of an imperial *imperator* and especially *triumphator*.

One, of uncertain dating, introduced in the Roman coinage the motif of *rex datus*, the investiture of a foreign ruler performed by a Roman: in this particular case the crowning by Germanicus of L. Antonius Zeno, the son of Polemon, king of Pontus, and Pythodoris, as Artaxias (III), king of Armenia (AD 18–34).[65] The elevation of Artaxias III was commemorated in coinage by the issues of drachms and didrachms from Cappadocia, most likely from Caesarea.[66] The obverses show the head of Germanicus and the inscription GERMANICVS CAESAR TI AVG F COS II, which points to the year AD 18. The reverses present two figures in armour, identified by the legend: ARTAXIAS and GERMANICVS (Fig. 12). On the left-hand side, Artaxias is wearing an Armenian tiara with a diadem with ribbons hanging from the back and supports it with his right hand. On the right-hand side, Germanicus is standing, holding a spear and placing the diadem on Artaxias' head.[67] This reverse type might well have been an illustration of the crowning moment of Zeno's enthronement in Artaxata, the capital of Armenia in Tacitus' *Annales* 2.56: *Germanicus* [...] *insigne regium capiti eius imposuit* ("Germanicus placed on his [Artaxias'] head the emblem of royalty"[68]). The Roman superiority is signalled by Germanicus' gesture and the spear in his other hand, the two figures being of equal height.

The type had no precedent in the Roman coinage, its only distant analogue being that on *denarii* struck in the late sixties or early fifties of the 1st century BC by the *monetalis* M. Aemilius Lepidus, the future triumvir,[69] with the personification of Alexandria

---

65 See: Tac. *Ann.* 2.56 and 64; *TS* 1.16–17. See Sawiński (2021), 88–90; Olbrycht (2016), 605–633.

66 RIC 1, Cal., no. 59; RPC 1, nos 3629 (didrachm), 3630 (drachm). The dating of the issue is debated, the principates of Caligula or Claudius having the largest following. The discussion is a clash of numismatic, stylistic and historical arguments. The coins are thought to have been struck during Caligula's reign, the emperor commemorating his father (so BMCRE 1, cxlviii; RIC 1, 107), or during Claudius' reign, being associated with the Roman foreign policy in general and the 30th anniversary of Germanicus' operation in particular (thus RPC 1, 554 f.; Suspène (2013), 182). The idea of dating the coins to the reign of Tiberius has its supporters too. See Piattelli (1986), 185 f.; Piattelli (1987), 321–323; Olbrycht (2016), 625 f.

67 Cf. Krengel (2013), 63–71; Kropp (2013), 383. A tiara is presented both on the coins of Zeno Artaxias, see, e. g., Kovacs (2014), 19, nos 1–2, pl. 4.1, 4.2a–b. Obv. ΘΕΟΙ ϹϹΕΒΑϹΤΟΙϹ ΚΑΙϹΑΡΙ ΚΑΙ ΙΟΥΛΙΑ, Δ, tiara, star; rev. Β[ΑΣ] ΑΡΤΑΞΙΟΥ ΤΟΥ ΕΚ Β ΠΟΛΕ ΚΑΙ ΠΥΘΟΔΩΡΙ, horse. On the various Armenian tiara shapes see Nercessian (1985), 2–12; Nurpetlian/Kazarian (2016–2017), 225–238. The tiara is a symbol utilised frequently in the iconography of *Armenia capta* and *Armenia devicta* Roman coins' types, see RRC, nos 539.1 (d, 36 BC), 543.1 (d, 32 BC); RIC 1, Aug., nos 290–292 (d, 18 BC), 306–307 (d, 18 BC), 515–517 (d, ca. 19–18 BC).

68 Transl. by J. Jackson.

69 M. H. Crawford tentatively dates Lepidus' holding the office of *IIIvir monetalis* to 61 BC, see: RRC, 82–89 (esp. 87), 443 f. (a bit too early on historical grounds).

on the obverse and on the reverse a *togatus* crowning a chiton-clad figure, with the legend: PONT MAX TVTOR REG S C M LEPIDVS:[70] one of a series celebrating the deeds of the issuer's most famous ancestor, M. Aemilius Lepidus, cos. 187, 175, *pontifex maximus*, censor and *princeps senatus*, who, as the junior member of the embassy which went to Egypt in 201–200 BC, was appointed *tutor* of the young king Ptolemy V.[71] Although issued in a far-away provincial mint, the representation of Germanicus crowning Artaxias clearly served as a model for later coins with the *rex datus* theme.[72]

The other theme, first represented on Caligula's *dupondii* struck in Rome, celebrated Germanicus' achievements as the general. On the obverse, a bare-headed and cloaked figure, holding an eagle-tipped sceptre, is driving a quadriga adorned with the figure of Victory, the legend GERMANICVS CAESAR identifying the honoree. He is featured on the reverse as well, standing on a pedestal, bare-headed and cuirassed, with an eagle in his left hand, raising his right arm in the gesture of *salutatio*, with the legend SIGNIS RECEPT DEVICTIS GERM S C (Fig. 13).[73] The issue commemorated both Germanicus' triumph over the Germans, celebrated on 27 May AD 17, and the most acclaimed success of the campaigns of AD 14–16: the recovery of the *signa* lost by Varus, including two legionary eagles.[74]

Both themes – a triumphator driving the quadriga and recovery of the *signa* – had by the time the issue was struck a long tradition in Roman coinage, even though the latter had been used before only by Augustus to celebrate the recovery in 20 BC of the standards lost by Crassus to the Parthians at Carrhae.[75] The relevant issues, struck soon after the event, featured an inscription in three lines;[76] Capricorn;[77] Mars standing, holding an eagle and a standard;[78] an eagle, a standard and a shield;[79] a trium-

---

70 RRC, no. 419.2 (61 BC). Obv.: ALEXANDREA, a female head with a turreted diadem.

71 Just. *Epit.* 30.2.3–3.4. See also: Val. Max. 6.6.1 (*tutela*); Tac. *Ann.* 2.67 (*tutor*); the embassy: Liv. 31.2. On M. Aemilius Lepidus' role in Egypt and the question of the *tutor regis*, and on links between the Aemilii Lepidi and the Ptolemaic dynasty, see Otto (1934), 27–29, 120–123; Evans (1990), 103 f.; Meadows (1993), 56 f.

72 MIR 14, no. 594 (REX PARTHIS DATVS, ses, AD 116–117); RIC 3, Ant. P., nos 619 (REX ARMENIIS DATVS S C, ses, AD 140–144), 620, 1059 (REX QVADIS DATVS S C, ses, AD 140–144); MIR 18, nos 91–92 (REX ARMENIIS DATVS IMP II TRP IIII COS II (S C), au/ses/dp, AD 164).

73 RIC 1, Cal., no. 57 (Rome).

74 Triumph – see Tac. *Ann.* 2.41; Suet. *Cal.* 1.1; Vell. 2.129.2; Strab. 7.1.4. On the standards lost by Varus and recovered by Germanicus, see Tac. *Ann.* 1.60; 2.25; 2.41; on his victories, see Tac. *Ann.* 1.49–52, 55–71, 2.5–26.

75 Cf. Hor. *Epist.* 1.18.54–57; Hor. *Carm.* 4.15.4–9; Ov. *Fast.* 5.579–590; *RG* 29; Strab. 16.1.28; Vell. 2.91.1; Suet. *Aug.* 21.3; Suet. *Tib.* 9.1 etc. Augustus apparently also retrieved the standards lost by Decidius in 40 BC and Statianus in 36 BC: Cass. Dio 48.25; Plut. *Ant.* 38.5–6.

76 SIGNIS PARTHIC(IS) RECEPTIS, RIC 1, Aug., nos 523–526 (d, *ca.* 19–18 BC, Antioch).

77 SIGNIS RECEPTIS, RIC 1, Aug., no. 521 (au, *ca.* 19–18 BC, Antioch); SIGNIS PARTHICIS RECEPTIS, RIC 1, Aug., no. 522 (au, *ca.* 19–18 BC, Antioch).

78 SIGNIS RECEPTIS, RIC 1, Aug., nos 41 (d, *ca.* 20/19–17/16 BC, Colonia Caesaraugusta?), 58 (d, *ca.* 20/19–17/16 BC, Colonia Patricia?), 60, 80–84 (au/d, *c.* 19 BC, Colonia Patricia?).

79 SIGNIS RECEPTIS / SPQR / CL V, RIC 1, Aug., nos 85a–87b (au/d, *ca.* 19 BC, Colonia Patricia?).

phal arch surmounted by a quadriga in the centre plus figures to the right and left[80] or flanked by eagles;[81] and a kneeling Parthian extending a *vexillum*.[82] As for Germanicus, *signa recepta* were a major theme of the *monumenta* of his victories stipulated as a part of his posthumous honours in the *Tabula Siarensis*: the triumphal arch (*ianus*)[83] to be erected *in circo Flaminio* in Rome and decorated with statues of the conquered peoples (*cum signis devictarum gentium*), with the inscription reading: *Germanis bello superatis* [...] *receptisque signis militaribus*[84], and the other, to be built on the bank of the Rhine and decorated by the statue of Germanicus receiving the military standards from the Germans (*statua Germanici Caesaris* [...] *recipientis signa militaria a Germanis*).[85] This notwithstanding, it was only during the reign of his son that this achievement was announced on coins, in the form which highlighted his having been – unlike Augustus – the *auctor* of the standards' recovery (*signis receptis devictis Germanis*).

The iconography of the reverses of Caligula's *dupondii* was replicated on bronze coins from Amphipolis in Macedonia. The legends date the issues to the reigns of Claudius: ΤΙ ΚΛΑΥ(ΔΙΟ)(Σ) ΣΕΒΑΣ(ΤΟ)(Σ),[86] and Nero: ΝΕΡΩΝ ΚΛΑΥΔΙΟΣ ΚΑΙΣΑΡ and ΤΙ ΚΛΑΥΔΙΟC ΚΑΙCΑΡ ΝΑΡΩΝ CΕ.[87] The representation is very similar – a figure in military dress, standing and holding an *aquila* in his left hand, and extending his right hand in a gesture of *salutatio* – but without any reference to Germanicus in the legend. One might see in these coins a provincial echo of Germanicus' popularity, but it is much more probable that they are linked with the recovery from the Chauci of the third legionary eagle lost in the Teutoburg Forest (*ca.* AD 41), for which, and for other exploits of the governors of the two Germaniae, P. Gabinius and the future emperor Galba, Claudius received his first imperatorial salutation.[88] The details of the eagle's recovery are obscure, starting with the question of how it found its way to the land of the Chauci, but the propaganda of its recovery would have corresponded with the celebration of Claudius' triumph over the Britons in AD 44[89] and the concomitant creation of his image as the victorious emperor. The Amphipolitan coins from the reign of Nero appear to be a simple repetition of the motif.

---

80 CIVIB ET SIGN MILIT A PART RECVP(ER), RIC 1, Aug., nos. 131–137 (au/d, *ca.* 18 BC–17/16 BC, Colonia Patricia?).
81 S P R SIGNIS RECEPTIS, RIC 1, Aug., no. 508 = *RPC* 1, no. 2216 (IMP IX TR PO IV); RIC 1, Aug., nos 509–510 = RPC 1, no. 2218 (IMP IX TR PO(T) V), (cist, 19–18 BC, Antioch).
82 CAESAR AVGVSTVS SIGN RECE, RIC 1, Aug., nos 287–289, 314–315 (*ca.* 19 BC, Rome).
83 Cf. *TS* 1.9; 1.22; 1.26; Tac. *Ann.* 2.83.
84 *TS* 1.9–21. Cf. Castagnoli (1984), 330 f.; La Rocca (1993), 83–92.
85 *TS* 1.26–29.
86 RPC 1, nos 1639–1640.
87 RPC 1, nos 1641–1642.
88 Cass. Dio 60.8.7; see Bickel (1944), 302–305.
89 Suet. *Claud.* 17.3; Cass. Dio 60.23.1–6; Eutrop. 7.13.

The obverses of Caligula's *dupondii RIC* 57 present Germanicus in a horse-drawn quadriga. Among the iconographic motifs commemorating triumphs and military successes in general in the Republican and Imperial coinage (others presented a Roman on a horseback spearing or trampling a fallen enemy, Victory and a captive, a trophy and a captive, various arms, or a Roman performing sacrifice[90]), this one had the most obvious triumphal connotations. As *triumphatores* riding a quadriga were shown: Marius, the victor over the Cimbri and Teutones,[91] and after him Sulla,[92] Pompeius,[93] and the young Caesar (the triple triumph in 29 BC;[94] after 27 BC, the image of Augustus riding in a triumphal chariot appeared on coins only as a detail decorating triumphal arches commemorating the military achievements of the *princeps*[95]).

During the Julio-Claudian dynasty, "triumphal" emissions with a triumphing general riding a quadriga were a very small group which included, apart from Caligula's issue, the coins of Augustus honouring Tiberius,[96] probably struck in connection with the latter's second triumph *ex Pannonis Delmatisque* on 23 October AD 12,[97] Tiberius' coins probably commemorating the same triumph,[98] the coins of Claudius after his triumph *de Britannis*,[99] and a type issued by a client king, Agrippa I, during Caligula's reign.[100] The group is as follows:

90 Cf. Weisser (2005), 165–180 (Republican coinage) and Mittag (2009), 447–462; Mittag (2017), 419–452 (Imperial coinage).
91 Q C FVNDAN, *triumphator* in quadriga, r., holding laurel-branch in l. hand, on near horse, rider holding laurel-branch, the triumph over the Cimbri and the Teutones being indicated by a Celtic *carnyx*: RRC, no. 326.1 (101 BC, d, Rome).
92 L SVLLA IM(P(E)), *triumphator* in quadriga, r., holding caduceus in r. hand, crowned by flying Victory, RRC, nos 367.1–5 (82 BC, au/d, "mint-moving with Sulla").
93 PROCOS, *triumphator* in quadriga, r., holding branch in r. hand, on near horse, rider, above, flying Victory with wreath, RRC, nos 402.1a–b (71 BC, au, Rome).
94 CAESAR DIVI F or IMP CAESAR, *triumphator* in quadriga, r., holding branch in r. hand, RIC 1, Aug., nos 263 (d, 32–29 BC, mint uncertain) and 264 (d, 29–27 BC, mint uncertain). Octavian's *triumphus curulis* (13 August: Dalmatia, 14 August: *victoria Actiaca*, 15 August: Aegyptus), see, e.g., Liv. *per.* 133; Verg. *Aen.* 8.714; Hor. *Carm.* 1.37.22; *RG* 4; Vell. 2.89.1; Suet. *Aug.* 22; Suet. *Tib.* 6; Flor. *Epit.* 2.21.10; Cass. Dio 51.21–22; Oros. 6.20.3 *etc.* Cf. Lange (2009), 148–156.
95 See, e.g., RIC 1, Aug., nos 131–137, 144–145 (au/d, *ca.* 18 BC–17/16 BC, Colonia Patricia?), 267 (d, 29–27 BC, uncertain mint).
96 RIC 1, Aug., nos 221–223 (au/d, Lugd.). See also RPC 1, no. 3129, Apamea (Phrygia): ΓΑΙΟΣ ΚΑΙΣΑΡ ΓΑΙΟΣ ΜΑΣΩΝΙΟΣ ΡΟΥΦΟΣ ΑΠΑΜΕΩΝ, figure (Caius Caesar) in a facing quadriga, above, Nike crowning the charioteer. Augustus's grandson was depicted as a *triumphator* although he was never granted a triumph, cf. Rose (2005), 52; Sawiński (2018), 71. The coins publicised the successes of Caius Caesar's eastern expedition. The mission in the East: Sawiński (2021), 85–88; Dąbrowa (2021), 48 f.
97 Vell. 2.121.2; Suet. *Tib.* 20. Cf. Sawiński (2018), 102–107.
98 RIC 1, Tib., nos 1–4 (au/d, Lugd.).
99 RIC 1, Claud., no. 122 = RPC 1, no. 3625 (didr, Caesarea Capp.).
100 RPC 1, no. 4976 (Æ, Caesarea P.). Obv. ΓΑΙΩ ΚΑΙΣΑΡΙ ΣΕΒΑΣΤΩ ΓΕΡΜΑΝΙΚ[Ω], head of Caligula, l.

Emperor	Denominations and mint	Emission (chronology)	Coin legend and iconography	*Triumphus*
Augustus	*aurei, denarii,* Lugdunum	AD 13–14	TI CAESAR AVG F TR POT XV, figure, laureate and cloaked, standing in a quadriga, right, holding laurel branch in the right hand and sceptre in the left	AD 12; over Pannonia and Dalmatia
Tiberius	*aurei, denarii,* Lugdunum	AD 14–15	TR POT XVI IMP VII, figure, laureate and cloaked, standing in a quadriga, right, holding a laurel-branch in the right hand and eagle-tipped sceptre in the left	AD 12; over Pannonia and Dalmatia
Tiberius	*aurei, denarii,* Lugdunum	AD 15–16	TR POT XVII IMP VII, figure, laureate and cloaked, standing in a quadriga, right, holding a laurel-branch in the right hand and an eagle-tipped sceptre in the left	AD 12; over Pannonia and Dalmatia
Caligula	*dupondii*, Rome	[AD 37–41]	GERMANICVS CAESAR: figure, bare-headed and cloaked, standing in a quadriga, right, holding an eagle-tipped sceptre in the left hand	AD 17; over the Cherusci, Chatti, and Angrivarii
Caligula [Agrippa I]	Æ, Caesarea Paneas	AD 40/41	ΝΟΜΙΣ ΒΑΣΙΛΕΩΣ ΑΓΡΙΠΠΑ LE, figure, bare-headed, standing in a quadriga, right, holding an eagle-tipped sceptre in the left hand	–
Claudius	didrachms, Caesarea Cappadociae	*ca.* AD 45	DE BRITANNIS: figure, bare-headed, standing in a quadriga, right, holding an eagle-tipped sceptre in the left hand	AD 44; over the Britons

When compared with other coins of this category, Caligula's *dupondii* with the depiction of Germanicus as *triumphator* have certain unique features. First, unlike the others, struck ideally at the same time as the triumphs they commemorated, they were issued some twenty years after his death. As such, they alone served the issuer's interests, not by advertising his own achievements but indirectly, through a reference, both on the obverse and the reverse, to a personage, and an event, from the past, and so alone were carriers of numismatic memory in the aforementioned restricted sense. The identity of those to whom their message was addressed in the first place is revealed in the second unique feature of Caligula's *dupondii*: unlike the earlier imperial issues with this theme, *aurei* and *denarii* minted in Lugdunum, they were token money minted in Rome; in other words, they were intended to circulate mainly in the City and the rest of Italy. That they stuck in the collective imaginary is shown by the fact that Agrippa I, who spent in Rome the greater part of his imperial friend's reign, included their type, copied even to smallest details (with Caligula's depiction on the obverse and the legend ΓΑΙΩ ΚΑΙΣΑΡΙ ΣΕΒΑΣΤΩ ΓΣΡΜΑΝΙΚ[Ω]), among the bronze issues copying and imitating Roman themes minted in Caesarea Philippi (Fig. 14). What is more, whereas Claudius' coins minted in Rome on the occasion of his triumph over the Britons featured a triumphal arch surmounted by a *statua equestris* and two trophies,[101] in the didrachms from Caesarea Cappadociae celebrating the same triumph (*de Britannis*) the theme of the *triumphator* riding a quadriga was used, closely copying the type used by his predecessor to commemorate his father, and the ruling emperor's' brother (Fig. 15).

***

To sum up. First and foremost, although Germanicus never became *princeps*, and although almost all the issues featuring him were struck long after his death, these issues were minted for around eighty years, in numbers whose total approached those of some emperors and exceeded by a long way those which commemorated other non-rulers. Admittedly, they constitute a relatively undifferentiated set, at least typologically; but the fact that later rulers – not only his son and his brother – thought it worthwhile to commemorate him for so long in their coinage is testimony to the fact that the ancients did remember him.

The monotonous, derivative and schematic character of the overwhelming majority of Germanicus' numismatic presentations (basically his head in profile and name, sometimes accompanied by filiation) is not surprising, considering that their function was to accentuate relations within the imperial family (the Julio-Claudians) and the dynastic principle in general (the Flavii). Distinctly original were the coin types referring to his particular achievements, of which the one featuring the coronation of Artaxias became the prototype of issues commemorating an investiture of a client king by a

---

101 RIC 1, Claud., nos 30, 33–34 (au/d, AD 46–47, TR P VI IMP X, TR P VI IMP XI), 44–45 (au/d, AD 49–50, TR P VIIII IMP XVI).

Roman emperor.[102] The *rex datus* group is chronologically dispersed (1st–3rd centuries AD) and, while not numerous,[103] varies from one issue to another in the size of the figures, their postures and poses; but they all repeat the gestural code of the ARTAXIAS GERMANICVS type: the act of a Roman crowning the future king.

The only coin type referring openly to Germanicus' triumph is exceptional in presenting both the *triumphator* riding a quadriga and the *signa recepta* theme, and, with regard to the latter, in the unity of the message (SIGNIS RECEPT[IS] DEVICTIS GERM[ANIS]) and the uniqueness of its form. The theme itself appeared in the coinage of only three emperors: Augustus, Caligula, and Vespasianus.[104] The novelty of Caligula's *dupondii* consisted in their representing neither the deities, nor the *signa* themselves or the defeated enemy, but the figure of the one who retrieved the standards with the legionary eagle in his hand (SIGNIS RECEPT DEVICTIS GERM). The repetition of the type on the coins from Amphipolis, struck under Claudius and Nero, is a clear case of numismatic memory in the broad sense.

The main originality of the *triumphator* theme of Caligula's *dupondii* was its being depicted for the first time on coins minted in Rome, which created a precedent followed by both Claudius and the Flavii. In spite of its popularity, reflected in its being copied by Agrippa I, Claudius' triumph was commemorated with an entirely different type. Under the late Julio-Claudians, Germanicus' imagery was used exclusively on the provincial coins from Caesarea Cappadociae. It should be noted, however, that the Flavian triumphal types, commemorating Titus' triumph *de Iudaeis* (June, AD 71)[105] and Domitianus' over the Dacians (AD 86) and over the Dacians and the Chatti (AD 89),[106] reverted to the Germanicus-like presentation of the *triumphator* riding a quadriga, though with both the sceptre and a palm branch, as on coins earlier than Caligula's

---

102 Damsky (1990), 97 f.; Kropp (2013), 383. A paraphrase of a crowning gesture – two persons (kings Agrippa and Herod) crown the *togatus* (Claudius) – on the coins from Caesarea Maritima, RPC 1, no. 4982 (AD 37–44), obv. ΒΑΣ ΑΓΡΙΠΠΑΣ ΣΕΒ ΚΑΙΣΑΡ ΒΑΣ ΗΡΩ[ΔΗΣ], and Chalcis, RPC 1, no. 4777, Chalcis, AD 43/44, obv. ΒΑΣΙΛ ΗΡΩΔΗΣ ΒΑΣΙΛ ΑΓΡΙΠΠΑΣ, ΚΛΑΥΔΙΟΣ ΚΑΙΣΑΡ ΣΕΒΑΣΤΟΣ. Cf. Burnett (1987), 25–38; Kropp (2013), 377–389.

103 The small number and chronological dispersal of relevant issues make it difficult to trace the iconographic evolution of the *rex datus* motif. Cf. Göbl (1961), 70–80; Kluczek (2009), 151–158; Suspène (2012), 259–279; Kéfélian (2021), 117–120.

104 Cf. Vojvoda (2015), 43–52. See RIC 2.1, Vesp., nos 119–120, 138 (ses, Rome, AD 71), SIGNIS RECEPTIS S C, Victory flying and offering *aquila* to emperor, standing on platform. See also RIC 2.1, Vesp. (Dom.), no. 959 (au, Rome, 77–78), COS V, captive kneeling, offering standard with *vexillum* attached. This reverse type repeats the iconography of Augustus' coins, RIC 1, Aug., nos 287–289.

105 Figure (Vespasianus or Titus) in a quadriga, r. or l., holding a branch and sceptre: RIC 2.1, Vesp., nos 49, 250 (d/ses, AD 71), 364, 388 (au/ses, AD 72–73), 577, 595 (ses/as, AD 73), 688 (d, AD 74); RIC 2.1, Vesp. (Tit.), nos 370–371, 498 (au/d/ses, AD 72–73), 431, 451, 462, 475–476 (ses/as, AD 72), 531, 611, 635 (d/ses/as, AD 73), 697 (d, AD 74); RIC 2.1, Vesp. (Dom.), nos 490 (as, AD 72), 673 (as, AD 73–74). Cf. RIC 2.1, Vesp., no. 1127 (AD 71, au, Lugd.), rev. TRIVMP AVG, an emperor in a quadriga, holding a branch and sceptre, crowned by Victory, accompanied by a trumpeter, soldier, and captive.

106 Domitianus in a quadriga, l., holding a branch and sceptre: RIC 2.1, Dom., nos 561 (au, AD 88), 700–701 (au, AD 90–91), 748–749 (au, AD 92–94), 750 (au, undated), 783 (au, AD 95–96).

dupondii. This representation, sometimes with only one of the insignia, started to appear more frequently from the middle of the second century on coins struck in Rome and depicting, apart from triumphs, the categories of imperial processions which used triumphal symbolism, *adventus* and *processus consularis*.

Whether or not we treat the latter as a legacy of Caligula's type commemorating Germanicus' triumph, the numerous monetary issues discussed above enable us to refer to the coins depicting him as, to quote *Tabula Siarensis*, "monumentum aeternae dedicasse memoriae Germanici Caesaris" ("dedicated this monument to the eternal memory of Germanicus Caesar"),[107] the more so as the image of Germanicus they convey closely matches his figure in other sources. Germanicus, though not an emperor, was present in the numismatic memory of the later generations of the Romans as if he had been one.

Figures

Fig. 1 Æ, Corinth, AD 4–6. Obv. GERMANICVS CAESAR COR, bare head of Germanicus, r.; rev. C HEIO POL/LIONE ITER / C MVSSIO P[R]/ISCO IIVIR, inscription within wreath. RPC 1, no. 1142.
© Classical Numismatic Group, Inc., Auction 343, Lot 327.

Fig. 2 Æ, Italica, [AD 14–19]. Obv. GERMANICVS CAESAR TI AVG F, bare head of Germanicus, l.; rev. MVNIC ITALIC PER AVG, *aquila* and *vexillum* between two *signa*; RPC 1, no. 70.
© Classical Numismatic Group, Inc., CNG 76, Lot 1022.

---

107 See *TS* 1.12–13, transl. J. Bert Lott. Germanicus's commemoration, cf. McIntyre (2017), 78–92; Sawiński (2018), 128–140.

Fig. 3 Æ, Tanagra, [AD 14–19]. Obv. ΓЄΡΜΑΝΙΚΟC, bare head of Germanicus, r.; rev. TANA, Apollo standing. RPC 1, no. 1318.
© Classical Numismatic Group, Inc., Triton IX, Lot 310.

Fig. 4 Æ, Romula, [AD 14–37]. Obv. PERM DIVI AVG COL ROM, laureate head of Tiberius, l.; rev. GERMANICVS CAESAR DRVSVS CAESAR, facing heads of Germanicus and Drusus. RPC 1, no. 74.
© Classical Numismatic Group, Inc., Auction 379, Lot 271.

Fig. 5 Æ, Pergamum, [AD 14–37]. Obv. ΓΕΡΜΑΝΙΚΟΣ ΚΑΙΣΑΡ, bare head of Germanicus, r.; rev. ΔΡΟΥΣΟΣ ΚΑΙΣΑΡ, bare head of Drusus, r. RPC 1, no. 2367.
© Classical Numismatic Group, Inc., Auction 163, Lot 168.

Fig. 6 Æ, Sardis, [AD 23–37?]. Obv. ΔΡΟΥΣΟΣ ΚΑΙ ΓΕΡΜΑΝΙΚΟΣ ΚΑΙΣΑΡΕΣ ΝΕΟΙ ΘΕΟΙ ΦΙΛΑΔΕΛΦΟΙ, two *togati* (Germanicus and Drusus) seated, l., on curule chairs; rev. ΕΠΙ ΑΡΧΙΕΡΕΩΣ ΑΛΕΞΑΝΔΡΟΥ ΚΛΕΩΝΟΣ ΣΑΡΔΙΑΝΟΥ ΚΟΙΝΟΥ ΑΣΙΑΣ, inscription within wreath. RPC 1, no. 2994.
© Classical Numismatic Group, Inc., Auction 375, Lot 554.

Fig. 7 Æ, Magnesia ad Sipylum, [AD 37–41]. Obv. ΓΑΙΟΝ ΚΑΙΣΑΡΑ ϹΕΒΑϹΤΟΝ, radiate head of Caligula, r.; rev. ΓΕΡΜΑΝΙΚΟΝ ΚΑΙ ΑΓΡΙΠΠΙΝΑΝ ΜΑ ΑΠΟ ϹΙΠ(Υ), Germanicus *capite velato* stands, behind him stands Agrippina as Demeter. RPC 1, no. 2454.
© Classical Numismatic Group, Inc., CNG 94, Lot 892.

Fig. 8 Au, Caligula, Rome, AD 37–38. Obv. C CAESAR AVG GERM P M TR POT, laureate head of Caligula, r.; rev. GERMANICVS CAES P C CAES AVG GERM, bare head of Germanicus, r. RIC 1, Cal., no. 17.
© Classical Numismatic Group, Inc., Triton IX, Lot 1390.

Fig. 9 As, Caligula, Rome, AD 37–38. Obv. GERMANICVS CAESAR TI AVGVST F
DIVI AVG N, bare head of Germanicus, l.; rev. C CAESAR AVG GERMANICVS PON
M TR POT / S C. RIC 1, Cal., no. 35.
© Classical Numismatic Group, Inc., no. 419340.

Fig. 10 As, Titus, mint?, AD 80–81. Obv. GERMANICVS CAESAR TI AVG F DIVI AVG
N, bare head of Germanicus, l.; rev. IMP T CAES DIVI VESP F AVG REST /
S C. RIC 2.1, Tit., no. 442.
© Classical Numismatic Group, Inc., Auction 389, Lot 590.

Fig. 11 As, Claudius, Rome, *ca.* AD 50–54. Obv. GERMANICVS CAESAR TI AVG F
DIVI AVG N, bare head of Germanicus, r.; rev. TI CLAVDIVS CAESAR AVG GERM P
M TR P IMP P P / S C. RIC 1, Claud., no. 106.
© Classical Numismatic Group, Inc., no. 788915.

Fig. 12 Didr, Caligula, Caesarea Cappadociae, [AD 37–41]. Obv. GERMANICVS CAESAR TI AVG F COS [II], bare head of Germanicus, r.; rev. ARTAXIAS GERMANICVS, Germanicus and Artaxias standing. RPC 1, no. 3629.
© Fritz Rudolf Künker GmbH & Co. KG, Osnabrück and Lübke & Wiedemann KG, Leonberg

Fig. 13 Dp, Caligula, Rome, [AD 37–41]. Obv. GERMANICVS CAESAR, Germanicus in quadriga, r., holding eagle-tipped sceptre; rev. SIGNIS RECEPT DEVICTIS GERM S C, Germanicus standing, right hand raised, left holding *aquila*. RIC 1, Cal., no. 57.
© Classical Numismatic Group, Inc., CNG 93, Lot 1140.

Fig. 14 Æ, Agrippa I, with Caligula, Caesarea Paneas, AD 40/41. Obv. ΓΑΙΩ ΚΑΙΣΑΡΙ ΣΕΒΑΣΤΩ ΓΕΡΜΑΝΙΚ[Ω], laureate head of Caligula, l.; rev. ΝΟΜΙΣ ΒΑΣΙΛΕΩΣ ΑΓΡΙΠΠΑ LE, figure in a quadriga, r., holding an eagle-tipped sceptre. RPC 1, no. 4976.
© Classical Numismatic Group, Inc., Triton XI, Lot 519.

Fig. 15 Didr, Claudius, Caesarea Cappadociae, [AD 41–54]. Obv. TI CLAVD CAESAR AVG GERM P M TR P, laureate head of Claudius, l.; rev. DE BRITANNIS, figure in a quadriga, r., holding an eagle-tipped sceptre. RPC 1, no. 3625. © Classical Numismatic Group, Inc., Triton XX, Lot 459.

Bibliography

Barrett, Anthony A. (1991): "Claudius' British Victory Arch in Rome". In: Britannia 22, 1–19.

Barrett, Anthony A. (2015): Caligula. The Abuse of Power. (2nd Edition, 1989). Abington–New York: Routledge.

Bickel, Ernst (1944): "Der Mythus um die Adler der Varusschlacht". In: Rheinisches Museum für Philologie 92, 302–318.

Blonce, Caroline / Gangloff, Anne (2013): "Mémoire du voyage de Germanicus en Orient". In: Cahiers du Centre Gustave Glotz 24, 113–134.

Burnett, Andrew (1987): "The Coinage of King Agrippa I of Judaea and a New Coin of King Herod of Chalcis". In: Huvelin, Hélène et al. (eds.): Mélanges de numismatique offerts à Pierre Bastien à l'occasion de son 75e anniversaire. Wetteren: Editions Numismatique Romaine, 25–38.

Burnett, Andrew et al. (1992): Roman Provincial Coinage. Vol. 1. From the Death of Caesar to the Death of Vitellius (44 BC–AD 69). London–Paris: The British Museum Press / Bibliothèque nationale de France.

Burnett, Andrew et al. (1999): Roman Provincial Coinage. Vol. 2. From Vespasian to Domitian (AD 69–96). London–Paris 1999: British Museum Press / Bibliothèque nationale de France.

Carradice, Ian A. / Buttrey, Theodore V. (2007): The Roman Imperial Coinage. Vol. 2.1. From AD 69–96 Vespasian to Domitian. London: Spink and Son Ltd.

Carter, Giles F. / Metcalf, William E. (1988): "The Dating of the M. Agrippa Asses". In: The Numismatic Chronicle 148, 145–147.

Castagnoli, Ferdinando (1984): "L' arco di Germanico in Circo Flaminio". In: Archeologia Classica 36, 329–332.

Cavalieri-Manasse, Giuliana (1992): "L'imperatore Claudio e Verona". In: Epigraphica 54, 9–41.

Crawford, Michael H. (1974): Roman Republican Coinage. Cambridge: Cambridge University Press.

Damsky, Ben L. (1990): "The Stadium Aureus of Septimius Severus". In: American Journal of Numismatics 2, 77–105.

Dąbrowa, Edward (2021): "Parthian-Armenian Relations from the 2nd Century BCE to the Second Half of the 1st Century CE". In: Electrum 28, 41–57.

Estiot, Sylviane (2009): "De Pertinax à la réforme de Dioclétien". In: Amandry, Michel / Bateson, Donald (eds.): A Survey of Numismatic Research 2002–2007. Glasgow: International Association of Professional Numismatists, 159–174.

Evans, Richard J. (1990): "The Moneyership of Marcus Lepidus Triumvir". In: Acta Classica 33, 103–108.

Frey-Kupper, Susanne (1991): "Germanicus und Drusus auf einer Münze von Panormos". In: Schweizer Münzblätter = Gazette numismatique suisse 164, 90–95.

Giard, Jean B. (1976): Catalogue des monnaies de l'Empire romain de la Bibliothèque nationale. Vol. 1. Auguste. Paris: Bibliothèque nationale de France.

Göbl, Robert (1961): "Rex … datus. Ein Kapitel von der Interpretation numismatischer Zeugnisse und ihren Grundlagen". In: Rheinisches Museum für Philologie 104 (1), 70–80.

Grant, Michael (1948): "The Colonial Mints of Gaius". In: The Numismatic Chronicle 8 (3/4), 113–130.

Grant, Michael (1950): Roman Anniversary Issues, An Exploratory Study of the Numismatic and Medallic Commemoration of Anniversary Years, 49 B. C. to A. D. 375. Cambridge: University Press.

Grant, Michael (1990): "Agrippa's Coins". In: Ceresa-Gastaldo, Aldo (ed.): Il bimillenario di Agrippa. Genova: Università di Genova. Facoltà di Lettere. Dipartimento di Archeologia, Filologia Classica e loro Tradizioni, 9–17.

Grau, Donatien (2022): La mémoire numismatique de l'Empire romaine. Paris: Les Belles Lettres.

Guilhembet, Jean P. (2013): "Germanicus: les facettes de la mémoire". In: Cahiers du Centre Gustave Glotz 24, 197–204.

Hekster, Olivier (2015): Emperors and Ancestors: Roman Rulers and the Constraints of Tradition. Oxford: Oxford University Press.

Hölscher, Tonio (1994): "Claudische Staatsdenkmäler in Rom und Italien". In: Strocka, Volker M. (ed.): Die Regierungszeit des Kaisers Claudius (41–54 n. Chr.). Umbruch oder Episode? Internationales interdisziplinäres Symposion aus Anlass des hundertjährigen Jubiläums des Archäologischen Instituts der Universität Freiburg i. Br. 16.–18. Februar 1991. Mainz: Ph. von Zabern, 91–102.

Hurlet, Frédéric (2000): "Pouvoir des images, images du pouvoir impérial. La province d'Afrique aux deux premiers siècles de notre ère". In: Mélanges de l'École française de Rome, Antiquité 112, 297–364.

Kéfélian, Anahide (2021): "Armenia and Armenians in Roman Numismatics". In: Electrum 28, 105–134.

Kluczek, Agata A. (2009): VNDIQVE VICTORES. Wizja rzymskiego władztwa nad światem w mennictwie złotego wieku Antoninów i doby kryzysu III wieku – studium porównawcze. Katowice: Wydawnictwo Uniwersytetu Śląskiego.

Komnick, Holger (2001): Die Restitutionsmünzen der frühen Kaiserzeit. Aspekte der Kaiserlegitimation. Berlin–New York: De Gruyter.

Kovacs, Frank L. (2014): "Artaxias III and a Numismatic Enigma". In: Armenian Numismatic Journal 10 (40), 19–27.

Krengel, Elke (2013): "Die erste armenische Münzprägung für Zenon/Artaxias aus Pontus". In: Jahrbuch für Numismatik und Geldgeschichte 63, 59–74.

Kropp, Andreas J. (2013): "Crowning the Emperor an Unorthodox Image of Claudius, Agrippa I and Herod of Chalkis". In: Syria. Archéologie, art et histoire 90, 377–389.

La Rocca, Eugenio (1992): "Claudio a Ravenna". In: La Parola del Passato 47, 265–314.

La Rocca, Eugenio (1993): "L'arco di Germanico 'in Circo Flaminio'". In: Bullettino della Commissione Archeologica Comunale di Roma 95 (1), 83–92.

Lange, Carsten H. (2009): Res publica constituta. Actium, Apollo and the Accomplishment of the Triumviral Assignment. Leiden–Boston: Brill.

Mattingly, Harold (1965): Coins of the Roman Empire in the British Museum. Vol. 1. Augustus to Vitellius. (2nd Edition, 1923). London: The Trustes of The British Museum.

Mattingly, Harold (1966): Coins of the Roman Empire in the British Museum. Vol. 2. Vespasian to Domitian. (2nd Edition, 1930). London: The Trustes of The British Museum.

Mattingly, Harold / Sydenham, Edward A. (1968): The Roman Imperial Coinage. Vol. 3. Antoninus Pius to Commodus. (2nd Edition, 1930). London: Spink and Son Ltd.

McIntyre, Gwynaeth (2017): "Uniting the Army. The Use of Rituals Commemorating Germanicus to Create an Imperial Identity". In: Vanacker, Wouter / Zuiderhoek, Arjan (eds.): Imperial Identities in the Roman World. Abington/New York: Routledge, 78–92.

Meadows, Andrew R. (1993): "Greek and Roman Diplomacy on the Eve of the Second Macedonian War". In: Historia. Zeitschrift für Alte Geschichte 42 (1), 40–60.

Michel, Anne C. (2018): "L'affirmation d'un pouvoir dynastique sous le principat de Claude". In: Chillet, Clément et al. (eds.): Arcana Imperii. Mélanges d'histoire économique, sociale et politique, offerts au Professeur Yves Roman. Vol. 2. Paris: Editions de Boccard, 183–244.

Mittag, Peter F. (2009): "Processus Consularis, Adventus und Herrschaftsjubiläum. Zur Verwendung von Triumphsymbolik in der Mittleren Kaiserzeit". In: Hermes 137 (4), 447–462.

Mittag, Peter F. (2017): "Die Triumphatordarstellung auf Münzen und Medaillons in Prinzipat und Spätantike". In: Goldbeck, Fabian / Wienand, Johannes (eds.): Der römische Triumph in Prinzipat und Spätantike. Berlin: De Gruyter, 419–452.

Morelli, Anna L. (2009): Madri di uomini e di dèi: la rappresentazione della maternità attraverso la documentazione numismatica di epoca romana. Bologna: Ante Quem soc. coop.

Nercessian, Yeghia T. (1985): "The Evolution of the Armenian Tiara". In: Armenian Numismatic Journal 11 (1), 2–12.

Nicols, John (1974): "The Chronology and Significance of the M. Agrippa Asses". In: Museum Notes. American Numismatic Society 19, 65–86.

Nurpetlian, Jack / Kazarian, Eduard (2016–2017): "The Shape of the Armenian Tiara". In: Revue des Études Arméniennes 37, 225–238.

Olbrycht, Marek J. (2016): "Germanicus, Artabanos II of Parthia, and Zeno Artaxias in Armenia". In: Klio 98 (2), 605–633.

Osgood, Josiah (2010): Claudius Caesar. Image and Power in the Early Roman Empire. Cambridge: Cambridge University Press.

Otto, Walter G. (1934): Zur Geschichte der Zeit des 6. Ptolemäers. Ein Beitrag zur Politik und zum Staatsrecht des Hellenismus. München: Verlag der Bayerischen Akademie der Wissenschaften.

Panvini-Rosati, Franco (1987): "La monetazione di Germanico nel quadro della politica monetaria giulio-claudia". In: Bonamente, Giorgio / Segolini Maria P. (eds.): Germanico. La persona, la personalità, il personaggio nel bimillenario dalla nascita. Atti del convegno 4 (Macerata – Perugia 9–11 maggio 1986). Pubblicazioni Facoltà di Lettere e Filosofia dell'Università degli studi di Macerata 39. Roma: Giorgio Bretschneider Editore, 79–86.

Piattelli, Simonetta (1986): "L'iconografia monetale di Germanico". In: Carradice, Ian / Attwood, Philip (eds.): Proceedings of the 10th International Congress of Numismatics. London: International Association of Professional Numismatists in association with the UK Numismatic Trust, 185–187.

Piattelli, Simonetta (1987): "La monetazione di Germanico". In: Annali della Facoltà di lettere e filosofia dell'Università di Macerata 20, 319–327.

Price, Martin J. / Trell, Bluma L. (1977): Coins and Their Cities. Architecture on the Ancient Coins of Greece, Rome and Palestine. London: V. C. Vecchi and Sons.

Rose, Charles B. (1997): Dynastic Commemoration and Imperial Portraiture in the Julio-Claudian Period. Cambridge: Cambridge University Press.

Rose, Charles B. (2005): "The Parthians in Augustan Rome". In: American Journal of Archaeology 109 (1), 21–75.

Sawiński, Paweł (2018): The Succession of Imperial Power under the Julio-Claudian Dynasty (30 BC–AD 68). Berlin: Peter Lang.

Sawiński, Paweł (2021): Holders of Extraordinary Imperium under Augustus and Tiberius. A Study into the Beginning of the Principate. London–New York: Routledge.

Serra, Alessandra (2009): "Le monete di 'restituzione o imitazione' di Vespasiano: gusto antiquario o esigenza politica?". In: Braidotti, Cecilia et al. (eds.): Ou pān ephēmeron. Scritti in memoria di Roberto Pretagostini, offerti da colleghi, dottori e dottorandi di ricerca della Facoltà di lettere e filosofia. Roma: Edizioni Quasar, 1159–1184.

Suspène, Arnaud (2012): "Images royales en contexte romain. Les rois étrangers sur les monnaies romaines (IIᵉ siècle a. C.–IIᵉ siècle p. C.)". In: Cahiers des études anciennes 49: Le Charaktèr du prince, 259–279.

Suspène, Arnaud (2013): "Germanicus. Les témoignages numismatiques". In: Cahiers du Centre Gustave Glotz 24, 175–195.

Sutherland, Carol H. (1984): The Roman Imperial Coinage. Vol. 1. From 31 BC to AD 69. (Revised Edition). London: Spink and Son Ltd.

Szaivert, Wolfgang (1986): Die Münzprägung der Kaiser Marcus Aurelius, Lucius Verus und Commodus (161–192). [Moneta Imperii Romani 18]. Wien: Verlag der Österreichischen Akademie der Wissenschaften.

Trillmich, Walter (1978): Familienpropaganda der Kaiser Caligula und Claudius. Agrippina Maior und Antonia Augusta auf Münzen. Berlin: Walter de Gruyter & Co.

Vojvoda, Mirjana (2015): "Signis Receptis as a Reverse Motive on Roman Imperial Coins". In: Arheologija i Prirodne Nauke 11, 43–52.

Weisser, Bernhard (2005): "Szenen des Triumphes auf republikanischen Münzen". In: Minda Numismatica. Festschrift der Münzfreunde Minden und Umgebung e. V. zum 2. Deutschen und 50. Norddeutschen Münzsammlertreffen und 50 Jahre Münzfreunde Minden und Umgebung e. V., 1965–2005, vom 3. bis 5. Juni 2005 in Minden. Minden: Münzfreunde Minden und Umgebung e. V., 165–180.

Weisser, Bernhard (2015): "Germanicus Caesar. Zur Inszenierung eines Nachkommen im Medium der Münzen zwischen 4 und 19 n. Chr.". In: Burmeister, Stefan / Rottmann, Joseph (eds.): Ich Germanicus – Feldherr – Priester – Superstar. Darmstadt: Konrad Theiss Verlag, 98–104.

Weisser, Bernhard (2017): "Germanicus als Mitglied der augusteischen Familie und Zwilling des Drusus minor. Lebenszeitliche Münzbilder zwischen 4 und 19 n. Chr.". In: Flecker, Manuel et al. (eds.): Augustus ist tot – Lang lebe der Kaiser!. Rahden/Westf.: Verlag Marie Leidorf GmbH, 71–90.

Woytek, Bernhard (2010): Die Reichsprägung des Kaisers Traianus (98–117). [Moneta Imperii Romani 14]. Wien: Verlag der Österreichischen Akademie der Wissenschaften.

Ziolkowski, Adam (2007): "Prolegomena to any Future Metaphysics on Agrippa's Pantheon". In: Leone, Anna et al. (eds.): Res bene gestae. Ricerche di storia urbana su Roma antica in onore di Eva Margareta Steinby. Roma: Edizioni Quasar, 464–475.

The Secret Life of Things
The statua loricata *from Ameria*

LECHOSŁAW OLSZEWSKI

Keywords: Germanicus, Amelia, honorific statues, statua loricata, Roman Empire

Current research on honorary statues from the Roman Empire is based on the conviction that initially (from the time of Augustus to the reign of the Severan dynasty) their reuse, transformation or other types of intervention were the result of rather rare actions undertaken to disgrace the depicted (*memoria damnata*), and thus stemmed from a desire to dishonor the memory of the condemned.[1] With time, especially after the so-called crisis of the third century CE, this phenomenon not only became more widespread, as a result of the economic crisis and the growing influence of Christianity, but also changed its character and exploited the good name of the people originally honored with the statue.[2] However, the creation of such narratives was only possible by depriving these Roman honorary statues of their materiality.

Contemporary scholarship has transformed ancient "statues" into "sculptures," thereby pushing them out of the world of matter into an aesthetic sphere.[3] This tendency has entailed that too much significance has been assigned to their "finished" form, and all kinds of transformations have come to be perceived as attempts to destroy the original effect and deprive them of their original artistic value.[4] Such recycling of materials and repurposing of statues, according to many of those who have failed to see indications of this type of practice in earlier periods, is even supposed to provide clear

---

1 Marina Prusac (2011), 13: "The recarving of portraits was thus a phenomenon which began as a social sanction against a disgraced individual, but in time also became a way to express an ideology of power." See, e. g., Varner (2001); Varner (2004); Pollini (2010).
2 Brenk (1987); cf. Elsner (2000).
3 Stewart (2003), 9.
4 For the function and meaning of bronze statue fragments, see Croxford (2016).

evidence of the decline of the Empire's culture. As a result, Roman honorary statues came to be treated more as objects from the world of art than from the world of people.

Honorary statues, however, were fundamentally different from the majority of the sculptural artifacts that constitute the focus of interest in art history. Their public display was never a decision of the client and/or creator, but rather the result of a complex process subordinate to certain rules, which involved individuals, institutions and sometimes even the entire civic community. Although Roman statues were indeed objects made of a specific material, and they sometimes depicted individualized faces atop characteristic bodies, an integral part of the statues was also the base, which featured inscriptions. The public display of statues was decided under concrete circumstances, and as a result, they had definite functions and were connected with specific rituals and practices of everyday life. The statues had particular relations with other objects, architecture and space, which were supposed to evoke desired reactions among the people and had their own history. Thus, they both embodied social norms (i. e., the system of honoring outstanding individuals) and contributed to their further reproduction (e. g., the objectification of social hierarchy).

Honorary statues consolidated and commemorated the relationship between the community as a whole and its individual members or patrons, including local officials and the emperor himself.[5] Their location, size, material, and scheme of depiction reflected the position of the honored individual in the current social hierarchy. This position was expressed in the form of the statue and was repeated or emphasized in the inscription. In the case of men, the inscription also presented their *cursus honorum,* and in the case of women: their public activity, family affinities and individual virtues.[6] Honorary statues, however, did not perpetuate social relations indefinitely. Therefore, both they and their inscriptions used to be transferred and transformed, and their purpose was often changed. Thus it can be said that they had their "secret life"[7] or individual biographies.[8] While this practice has been recognized and well documented in the case of Late Antiquity,[9] for the Early Empire it would appear to have been a marginal phenomenon. It is most often referred to only in the context of the negative emotions associated with *memoria damnata.* However, the statues may have been transformed for various reasons.[10] An object that had its own history could be used to satisfy the needs of the present in different ways, taking different forms and serving different purposes.

---

5   Stewart (2003); Hallett (2005); Fejfer (2008). Imperial statues in context: Deppmeyr (2008); Højte (2005); Boschung (2002).
6   Murer (2017); Hamerlrijk (2015); Ma (2013).
7   Kristensen (2013); see Schiffer (1987). I define what Kristensen/Stirling (2016), 6–8 (Fig. 2) call the "live and afterlive of sculpture" as the "secret life" of statues.
8   Chaniotis (2017); Joy (2009); see Kopytoff (1986).
9   E. g., Prusac (2011); Brillant/Kinney (2011); Deichmann (1975); Blanck (1969); Esch (1969).
10   Galinsky (2008).

Recent research has emphasized those motivations that are related to ideology, but ideology did not play any role in the transformations of many statues.[11] Some transformations could simply have been the result of repairs caused by natural disasters, such as earthquakes, others may have been the effect of conservation work, or could have been related to the value of the materials used. Changing the physical form of certain objects – by transforming, rebuilding, mimicking, replenishing, rededicating or simply destroying them – allowed the Romans, at a particular time and in a particular social context, to give the physical world a shape that corresponded to their imaginations at that time and to actualize their own place in the world. This was not a phenomenon limited to a specific period.[12]

An interesting example of such activity is – as analyzed by Julia L. Shear – a collection of statues that were repurposed on the Acropolis of Athens to honor the Romans during the late Republic and early Empire.[13] The dedications of private individuals from the time of Athens' glory were replaced with dedications of the people (*demos*) and/or council (*boule*). The reason for this secondary use was in no sense economic, since the collection in question represents only a small part of the monuments dedicated to the Romans by the Athenians. It was their form that was important, as it embodied the values that were crucial for the entire civic community. Adding a new inscription to the statues gave them an exceptional status. For example, in the times of Augustus, the statue of Archinos was turned into the monument of Publius Cornelius Lentulus.[14] Not only the name of the original owner was left on the statue, but also the name of its creator (i. e., Cephisodotos); which probably means that the original image of a naked or armored Greek was also used. The Athenians thereby inscribed their conquerors into the history of the Athenian community. This is also evidenced by the inscription, which – unlike its Roman equivalents – does not mention offices, affiliations or dates. The statue and the Greek inscription, therefore, depicted the Roman as a member of the Athenian community who had acted devotedly on its behalf, or was expected to act in such a way.[15]

Statues were also treated in a similar way in Italy, as exemplified by the statue of Marcus Holconius Rufus (the earliest securely dated and identified cuirassed statue of a private person preserved in the West) (Fig. 1).[16] Holconius had held the most important offices in Pompeii under Augustus and had been involved in major construction

---

11 See Ward-Perkins (1999).
12 This phenomenon concerned both the imperial family and the depictions of private individuals: Matheson (2000).
13 Shear (2007).
14 IG 2².4102 (most likely son of Cn. Cornelius Lentulus, cos. 14 BCE).
15 Shear (2007), 225–229.
16 Naples, Museo Archeologico Nazionale di Napoli, inv. no. 6233; see Fejfer (2008), 212 f.

projects.[17] The Pompeian decurions repeatedly expressed their gratitude for Holconius' local involvement. One of them was the statue mentioned above,[18] which stood, together with other statues of members of the Holconian family, in a tetrapylon along the southern *decumanus* (Via dell'Abbondanza) and near its intersection with the *cardo maximus* (Via Stabiana).[19]

Due to the quality of workmanship, according to Paul Zanker the statue must have been produced in a workshop that worked on imperial commissions. He suggested that the original statue was created between 2 BCE and 14 CE. During the earthquake of 62 CE,[20] the original head is said to have been destroyed and replaced by the current image, which was recarved from an imperial portrait. According to John D'Arms, it was precisely then that the statue from the Pompeian forum was moved to the tetrapylon.[21] The new head of Holconius was of course made from the portrait of Caligula, who was disgraced after his death.

However, there are arguments that support a completely different interpretation. It seems that the statue received its final form at the beginning of the first century CE. The quality of the workmanship and the iconography of the armor, similar to that of the statue of Mars Ultor from the Forum of Augustus,[22] indicate that not only the head, but the whole statue – as Brenda Longfellow suggests – may have originally belonged to someone from the family of the first princeps and been used to honor Holconius Rufus.[23] If only the head had been matched to the body, it would have been possible to maintain the proportions. However, the adaptation of the existing figure did not allow this. The traces of this transformation can be seen in fragments of the original figure's hairstyle, still visible in the form of curls on the nape of the neck; they clearly contrast with the hair arrangement on the top of the head (which itself is too small in relation to the body). The connection between the statue and the imperial family is also shown by the quality of the marble used, the distinctive patrician footwear (*calcei patricii*), and the purple of the cloak.[24] The public display of a statue recarved from the image of a member of the imperial family, which was no longer relevant to the current imperial genealogy, was a far greater distinction than the use of the head of a posthumously condemned tyrant.[25]

---

17   CIL 10.787 (expansion of the sanctuary of Apollon); CIL 10.841 (co-financing the renovation of the Large Theatre).
18   CIL 10.830.
19   Gasparini (2009), 73.
20   Zanker (1981).
21   D'Arms (1988).
22   Zanker (1981), 349 f.
23   Longfellow (2019), 35–40.
24   Fiorelli (1860–1864), vol. 2: 563.
25   The private reusing of the imperial family images, even the emperors themselves, was not at all unusual. During the time of Hadrian, one of the portraits of Nero was recarved into an image of

If in the case of Holconius we can only guess at the course of the "secret life" of the statue, we do have evidence that the repurposing of statues could concern not only the disgraced, but also those without descendants who could take care of their memory. Such was the case with Augustus' sister. Although three of Octavia's descendants became emperors (Caligula, Claudius and Nero), it was only during her brother's reign that her likenesses were a significant element of the imperial visual communication. One of Octavia's portraits, which was probably created at the end of the first century BCE and is now in a private collection,[26] bears the traces of an attempt at an interesting transformation. Unlike with Nero or Domitian, nobody tried to replace her face with a new image; the portrait was simply reused for another statue. Around the base of the portrait's neck, there are traces of chiseling that had been aimed at separating the head from the marble pivot (it apparently must have been too big to be set on a new body or elsewhere). Ultimately, the work was not finished.

The statues discussed above (of Publius Cornelius Lentulus, Marcus Holconius Rufus and Octavia) show how wide the spectrum of motivations behind the transformations or reusing of honorary statues could be at the beginning of the Empire. The changing forms of statues did not only reflect the dynamic relationship between those honoring and the honored, but also social and cultural changes. Above all, this puts into question the existence of a process initiated by the practice of *memoria damnata*, which later developed into various activities using old creations as *spolia*.[27] Both in the Early Empire and in Late Antiquity, various motivations lay behind the transformations. This is because Roman statues were not created as works of art (although they can be seen as such) but rather as things with their own lives immersed in the social world, connected to people and responding to their diverse needs.

One of the most interesting Roman honorary statues is the bronze *statua loricata*, which is now on display in the Museo Archeologico di Amelia (Fig. 2).[28] The statue, with a fragment of the original travertine base, was found in 1963, just off the Via Rimembranze, over a hundred meters behind the southern gate (Porta Romana) of modern Amelia (ancient Ameria) in Umbria.[29] Along with the statue was found a column capital decorated with trophies and ships' prows,[30] an altar decorated with bucrania, and other architectural elements.[31]

---

    a private person, as was one of the images of the Domitian; see Varner 2004, 256 (no. 2.65); Prusac (2011), 138 f. (no. 149 and 151).

26   The Chalmin Octavia, see Pollini (2002).

27   Kinney (1995); Kinney (1997).

28   Amelia, Museo Archeologico di Amelia, inv. no. 50207.

29   Feruglio (1987), 20 f.

30   Amelia, Museo Archeologico, cat. II, no. 158 (the period of Augustus).

31   Rocco (2008a), 481–485. In 2012, a slab with relief (186 × 69.5 cm) from the time of Augustus was found in San Giovani (1 km from the walls of the ancient city) Rocco (2012). Amelia, Museo Archeologico, inv. no. 678726.

The supernatural size statue,[32] referring in form to the marble image of Augustus of Prima Porta (perhaps based on the bronze original),[33] depicts a Roman commander; over a tunic, he wears a breastplate with the scene of the fight between Achilles and Troilus, and with other elements of military kit. The young man raises – perhaps too low in the current reconstruction – his right hand in a gesture of ceremonial speech (*adlocutio*).[34] In his left hand, he holds a spear (*hasta*) pointing downwards, which leans against his shoulder. A sword (*parazonium*) hides under the left armpit, which, tightly tied, hangs on a tasseled sash (*balteus*) placed over his shoulder. The commander's feet are protected by double tied patrician boots (*calcei patricii*).

From the moment it was found, the identification of the statue did not give rise to any doubts. There is a consensus that the statue depicts Germanicus, presented in his last portrait of the "Gabii" type.[35] Although the dating of this type varies,[36] since it is identified by coins issued by Caligula, it must have been created between the triumph of Germanicus and the death of his son (17–41 CE). The real question is whether the statue represented Germanicus from the start, and if not, who it originally represented, and under what circumstances the original portrait was replaced with the current one.

Matteo Cadario, who analyzed the evolution of cuirassed statues of the "Hellenistic" type from the time of Alexander the Great until the second century CE, was convinced that the statue was created during the Julian-Claudian. There is no doubt that it was created after the statues of Augustus and Agrippa, which were found in the theatre at Butrint, and which postdate the battle of Actium.[37] Unlike the statue from Ameria, they do not have decorations on the breastplate, but both the form and motifs of ornament (lion's head and palmettes) are identical. Cadario concluded that the statue of Germanicus was his posthumous portrayal, which was created in the time of Tiberius.[38]

Giulia Rocco, who published the first – and as yet only – monograph on the statue, focused her research – unlike Cadario – on a stylistic analysis of the sculpture and its

---

32 The total height of the statue: approx. 2.09 m (Rocco (2008a), 493 (Figs. 11–14)); the dimensions of the base: height 0.88 × width 0.755 m (Rocco (2008a), 657–660 (Figs. 124–129)); see Rocco (2008b); Laube (2006), 206 f., 227 (no. 1); Manconi/Danesi (2002), 133–135; Lahusen/Formigli (2001), 90 f. (no. 41).

33 Pollini (2012), 190; see Squire (2013).

34 Germanicus appears on Caligula's coins in the *adlocutio* pose, reminiscent of the triumph of 26 May 17 CE (Germanicus in a quadriga with the legend GERMANICUS CAESAR) on the obverse, while on the reverse, the recovery of the legion eagles lost as a result of defeat in the Teutoburg Forest (Germanicus in armor with a legionary eagle and with the legend SIGNIS RECEPT DEVICTIS GERM SC); see, e. g., *RIC* I² *Cal.* 57 (*dupondius*).

35 Boschung (1993), 61; cf. Rocco (2008a), 539–554.

36 Rocco (2008a), 554 (37–41 CE); Fittschen/Zanker (1985), 30 (after 19 CE); Hertel (1982), 120 (17–19 CE); Massner (1982), 104 f. (30 CE).

37 Cadario (2004), 120–135; cf. Rocco (2008a), 587.

38 Cadario (2004), 174–179; cf. Rocco (2008a), 671–681.

iconographic motifs. On this basis, she came to the conclusion that the statue must have been created between the end of the second century and the middle of the first century BCE,[39] in Asia Minor. And, judging from the central motif of the breastplate, it must have originally belonged to someone who saw himself as the new Achilles. This could only have been Mithridates VI of Pontus,[40] who, in her opinion, was thereby alluding to victories over the Romans, who considered themselves descendants of the Trojans. After his defeat, the statue went to Rome as spoils, where in 81–79 BCE its breastplate, along with new elements, was incorporated into Sulla's statue.[41] Eventually, a hundred years later, in the time of Caligula, the portrait of the dictator was replaced by the image of Germanicus.[42]

A close analysis of the parts of the statue revealed that the connection of Germanicus' head with the torso was not perfect, and that on the inside of the breastplate there are rivet stumps; they most probably held the original portrait in place (Fig. 3). It must have been set on a slightly wider and longer neck than the present one.[43] Bearing this in mind, Cadario came to the conclusion that this mismatch indicates the statue was created in Caligula's time, and after his death, it was transformed into a statue of Germanicus.[44] On the other hand, Andrea Salcuni, focusing on the techniques employed in making bronze statues, argued that the statue could have been an original creation. The "mismatch" between the head and the body was simply the result of the lost wax method of making bronze sculptures. Individual elements were usually produced separately and were later matched during assembly. Thanks to cooperation it was possible to avoid mistakes, but they were inevitable when forms from two different prototypes were used.[45]

In turn, John Pollini, criticizing Rocco's theory, was, like Cadario,[46] of the view that the original statue represented Caligula. In Pollini's opinion the informal *memoria damnata* caused depictions of Caligula to be removed from public spaces, to be destroyed or intentionally damaged, or the material to be recycled.[47] Thus, he suggests that, in all likelihood, it was at this time that the original portrait (i. e., Caligula's) was replaced with the image of Germanicus. Pollini is convinced that the iconography of the breastplate reflects the achievements of both Caligula and his father.[48] Between

---

39 Rocco (2008a), 648–655.
40 Rocco (2008a), 661–668.
41 Rocco (2008a), 695–706.
42 Rocco (2008a), 670, 706–714.
43 Rocco (2008a), 528–531 (Figs. 57–58).
44 Cadario (2011).
45 Salcuni (2014), 140–142; Salcuni (2017), 128 f.
46 Pollini (2017), 431 n. 38: "My colleague Matteo Cadario and I independently came to the conclusion that the head of Caligula was later replaced with that of his father, Germanicus."
47 Cass. Dio 59.26.3; 59.30.1C; 60.4.5–6; cf. Joseph. *AJ* 19.185; see Flower (2006), 148–159; Varner (2004), 21–45, 225–236.
48 Pollini (2017), 435.

2017 and 2018, the statue itself and fragments from the Museo Archeologico Nazionale dell'Umbria in Perugia were examined using X-ray fluorescence spectrometry (XRF) and inductively coupled plasma mass spectrometry (ICP),[49] which, in his opinion, confirmed his earlier hypotheses. The breastplate, as Rocco had already concluded,[50] was made from a different alloy than the other elements, which had probably been intended for fire gilding. Eventually, however, they were combined with the breast-plate, which, due to its higher lead and tin content, was not suitable for this type of treatment.[51]

All the participants in this discussion, except for Salcuni, following the currently accepted narrative of art history, assume that the transformation of imperial statues could only have taken place if the depicted person had been disgraced. Thus, it follows that in this case, it could only have been Caligula. However, as I argued above, other motivations should be considered even for the period of the Early Empire. The more so because the interpretation of the iconography of the statue's breastplate has not been properly considered.

The connection between the iconographic features of the breastplate and Germanicus is not in doubt, but is there really any connection with his son's deeds? In my opinion, there is nothing to support such a conclusion. Pollini is convinced that the inspiration for the statue from Ameria was the statue of Augustus which probably stood in Nicopolis after the Battle of Actium. Caligula is thereby supposed to have tried to emulate the first princeps and his commemoration of victory on land and sea (*terra marique*).[52] Without paying any attention to the relationship between the figures depicted on the breastplate and the emperor, Pollini claims that the figure of Scylla, heralding the sea victory, corresponds well with both Caligula's "invasion" of Great Britain and the actions of Germanicus in Germany near the North Sea. But could this background and merely decorative figure really have been decisive for shaping the entire iconography of the statue?

First, let us consider the breastplate (*thorax*) itself.[53] Thanks to the most recent research, we know that the elements featured in the relief (Scylla, Achilles and Troilus) were an integral part of the breastplate decoration, while all the others, in the form of application, were probably added later.[54] The main element of the breastplate is a scene depicting Achilles and Troilus. Achilles holds a large round shield, wears an Attic helmet with a crest, and has a chlamys slung over his left arm, as he ambushes and grabs an unarmed Troilus by the hair, who rides on horseback, naked apart from high

49 Pollini/Giumlia-Mair (2019), 678–681.
50 Rocco (2008a), 668–670.
51 Pollini/Giumlia-Mair (2019), 681.
52 Pollini/Giumlia-Mair (2019), 677.
53 Franken (2000), 217–219.
54 Pollini/Giumlia-Mair (2019), 682.

riding boots (Fig. 4). The Trojan, from whose neck flutters a chlamys fastened under his chin, tries to free himself from the grip of the Greek hero by grabbing his forearm with his right hand. With his left hand he makes a dramatic move towards his pursuer. The galloping horse rears up, raising its front hooves, and Troilus is unable to stop it, due to the lack of a harness. The scene takes place on a small hill decorated with a palmette and flanked by acanthus leaves that roll into spirals on either side.

In the background, above the fighting figures, a winged Scylla emerges from the schematically designed sea waves, raising her right hand to throw a stone at Achilles. A winged Victoria is located on both sides of this central motif, below the shoulders. Two rows of *pteryges* are attached to the lower edge of the breastplate: the upper one consists of short, semi-circular lappets arranged in a row of alternating heads of lions and of the god Pan, while the lower row of long lappets is inlaid with a palmette motif. The backplate, in turn, is decorated in an antithetical arrangement, with a representation of a pair of Spartan women (*saltantes Lacaenae*) with baskets (*kalathiskos*) on their heads, performing a victory dance around a tall incense burner (*thymanatherion*). The shoulder straps are decorated with acanthus growing out of a lion's head.[55]

Many of the motifs used in armor decorations refer to classical and Hellenistic themes.[56] This adoption and adaptation of previously created elements, to combine them into eclectic compositions, was a characteristic practice of the artists (especially Greek craftsmen from mainland Greece and Asia Minor) who had been working in Rome and Italy since the Late Republic.[57] Among all the elements of the iconographic program of the armor, the most crucial is the death of Troilus, who in Greek mythology was the youngest son of Hecuba and Priam. According to a prophecy, Troy would not fall if Troilus turned twenty. However, Achilles surprised him by the fountain behind the city walls, where the young man had gone to water his horses. Yet Troilus managed to escape and took refuge in the sanctuary of Apollo. Nevertheless, Achilles managed to kill the boy there, which led Apollo to swear that he would take his revenge. The death of Troilus sealed both the fall of Troy and the death of the greatest hero of the Trojan War. In the Greek world, of course, there were many different variants of this myth,[58] which featured in different genres of art.

The story of Troilus was not a common subject in art, but we can find it in nearly two hundred classical representations, which most often depict the young man at the

---

55   Particularly noteworthy are the black inlays in the form of palmettes and the stylized inlay of sea waves under the Scylla element, which was made of a special alloy (*Corinthium aes*). Due to the small amount of gold and silver, it took on a black patina after a chemical bath in an aqueous solution containing copper salts and other ingredients; see Pollini/Giumlia-Mair (2019), 683 f.; cf. Emanuele (1989).

56   Queyrel (2012), 427–431.

57   Colin (1997), 27–44; see Hölscher (1987).

58   Scaife (1995), 189–191; Sistakou (2008), 57 f., 110, 154, 166.

moment of his tragic fight for life.[59] On Greek vases and wall paintings, he is most often portrayed on horseback, alluding to Homer's description of him as an excellent rider.[60] In the Hellenistic period and in the Roman world, a model representation became established, which the armor of the statue from Ameria repeats.[61] According to Roland Smith and Christopher Hallett, the similarity of these representations, even at the level of detail, suggests that there was an object that influenced the standardization of Troilus' iconography. The marble sculpture they identified in Aphrodisias, along with other circumstantial evidence, indicate that it was (like other Hellenistic creations such as Achilles and Penthesilea, or Scylla and Odysseus) a statuary group that was exhibited in one of the major cities in Asia Minor.[62]

In the Hellenistic period, the inhabitants of towns in Asia Minor asserted their identity in local history and expressed their attachment in the form of various monuments. In all likelihood, it was then that the new image of Troilus, different from that established in early Greek art, was consolidated. The defenseless young man was replaced by a brave and valiant warrior. A significant role in this regard was played by literature referring to the events of the Trojan War, whose authors tried to improve on Homer's version. This literary trend had been born much earlier, but it was during the Hellenistic period that the perspective of the inhabitants of Troy, and thus unfavorable to the Greeks, came to be clearly articulated.[63] Works such as the *Chronicle of the Trojan War* of Dictys Cretensis[64] and *The Fall of Troy* by Dares Phrygius prove the existence of a completely different image of Troilus. Here, he becomes one of the bravest Trojan warriors who, after Hector's death, commanded the defenders of Troy.[65] A similar interpretation of Priam's son is also presented in Vergil's *Aeneid*, where he is a brave warrior who dies while riding a chariot in battle.[66] Both literature and the visual arts began to commemorate the heroism of this Trojan, who still eventually died at the hands of Achilles, but as a local hero equal to the greatest figures of Greece. The question is whether the son of Germanicus could have played such a role.

Caligula came from a line of prominent Roman military leaders. Both his father and grandfather had exceptional reputations as soldiers. Campaigns on the Rhine

---

59 The iconography of the death of Troilus at the hands of Achilles: Kossatz-Deissmann (1981); see Smith/Hallett (2015), 154–161.

60 Hom. *Il.* 24.257.

61 Rocco (2008a), 605–624. From the beginning of the Empire, there is a fragment of an identical Achilles-Troilus group from Opitergium (modern Oderzo, Italy). The bronze figure of Achilles, in the same pose as in Amelia, proves the Romans' acceptance of this motif; see Beschi (1994), 279 f., 282–285, figs. 1–2; Rocco (2008a), 609 f., figs. 95–96; Cadario (2011), 229.

62 Smith/Hallett (2015), 155–161.

63 Bobrowski (2006), 176 f. Correcting "Homer's mistakes": Bobrowski (2009), 47–64.

64 See Merkele (1988).

65 See Beschorner (1992); Smith/Hallett (2015), 162–164.

66 Verg. *Aen.* 1.474–478.

front brought Drusus, brother of Tiberius, imperial acclamation,[67] *ornamenta triumphalia* and *ovatio*;[68] and his son, Germanicus, received the title of imperator twice,[69] a triumph,[70] and a triumphal arch at the Roman Forum.[71] Earlier, for his mission in Illyricum, he had received *ornamenta triumphalia*.[72] His successes in the East brought Germanicus another honor: an ovation and a triumphal arch at the Augustus Forum.[73] Although Caligula certainly wanted to match his ancestors, his military achievements were largely symbolic. The greatest success of the activities carried out in the years 39–40 CE, in Germany and the attempted invasion of Great Britain,[74] turned out to be the suppression of the alleged conspiracy of Gnaeus Cornelius Lentulus Gaetulicus.[75] Upon his return to Rome, on the last day of August 40 CE, he only received *ovatio*.[76] It was therefore difficult to see him as a candidate for the role of a heroic leader. It is no coincidence that we know of only one representation in full sculpture (and this in the form of a bust) where Caligula was presented in a cuirass.[77] However, this is not the only reason to doubt that he was the owner of this breastplate.

The practice of reusing sculptures usually involved changing the original image to a depiction of the contemporary ruler, and rarely referred to historical figures. Nevertheless, in the case of Caligula we are dealing with just such a situation. Although not all his images had been destroyed or reused,[78] of the more than sixty that have survived to our times more than half were transformed. In fact, the image of Caligula was most often replaced by portraits of his successor, Claudius. A dozen or so portraits were given the face of Augustus, and one of Tiberius. None of them was replaced by a portrait of Germanicus.[79] In the imperial statue groups, Caligula appeared most often with his father, so if this was the case in Ameria, there would have been no need to change the image of the son for the father.

---

67 RIC 1², Claud., no. 70–73.
68 Cass. Dio 54.33.5; Suet. *Claud.* 1.3.
69 CIL 13.1036.
70 Tac. *Ann.* 2.41.2–3; Vell. Pat. 2.129.2; Suet. *Calig.* 1.1; Strab. 7.1.4.
71 Tac. *Ann.*1.55.1; 2.41.1; see Koestermann (1957).
72 Cass. Dio 56.17.2.
73 Tac. *Ann.* 2.64.1; see Genzert (1997).
74 Germany and Britain: Suet. *Calig.* 43–47; Cass. Dio 59.21–23.6, 59.25.1–3; Oros. 7.5.5. On the subject of the "invasion" of Britain, see Malloch (2001).
75 Cassius Dio (59.22.2) claims he received seven imperial acclamations at the time, but they are not confirmed by any other source. He probably also rejected the ovation that the Senate offered him after suppressing the conspiracy (Cass. Dio 59.23.2).
76 Suet. *Calig.* 49.2.
77 Copenhagen, Ny Carlsberg Glyptotek, inv. no. 637; see Boschung (1989), 118 (no. 43). We are familiar with Caligula's image only from the private context, small bronze busts and cameos: Boschung (1989), 115 (no. 30, 32), 117 (no. 40), 118 (no. 42a); see Hoff (2009), 250–256; Cadario (2004), 179–180; Boschung (1987), 243–245.
78 Varner (2004), 42–44.
79 For the full set, see Varner (2004), 25–34.

However, the decisive argument against identifying the original portrait with Caligula is that he cannot in any way be identified with the figure of Troilus. On the other hand, the story of Priam's son perfectly matches the events associated with Germanicus, the adopted son of Tiberius, who embarked on his last mission after his triumph in 17 CE. When he reached Asia Minor, he visited Troy,[80] among other places, and then went by sea to Syria, from where he went to Armenia[81] to install Artaxias on the throne.[82] After meeting in Syria with the envoy of Artabanus, king of the Parthians,[83] he went to Egypt in early 19 CE.[84] The background for his actions at that time was the conflict with Gnaeus Calpurnius Piso, the governor of Syria,[85] who asserted his strength when Germanicus returned to his province. When Germanicus unexpectedly fell ill, he suspected that Piso was the one who had tried to poison him and broke off their friendship.[86] Germanicus died on 10 October 19 CE, in Antioch.[87]

Who else – if we exclude Caligula – could we consider as the personification of Troilus, the young man who was the son of a ruler, a brave leader, and who died, surprised by the enemy's deceit, in the eastern part of the Roman Empire? The only candidate is Gaius Caesar, son of Agrippa and Julia, who was adopted by Augustus in 17 BCE. Both he and Germanicus were considered as potential successors and were sent to the East to inspect the eastern provinces, settle relations with Parthia and strengthen Roman influence in Armenia. It was widely believed that both of them had suffered a treacherous death in the East.

As part of the eastern expedition which began in 1 BCE, Gaius met with the Parthian ruler Phraates V,[88] and then installed Ariobarzanes on the Armenian throne.[89] However, a rebellion against Rome broke out in August 2 CE. The following year, Gaius captured Artagira, the fortress of the insurgents, and was acclaimed by the army as *imperator*.[90] However, before the city was besieged, under the pretext of revealing confidential information about the Parthian king, Gaius was persuaded to a meeting at the Abbadon fortress on 9 September, during which the commander treacherously wounded him.[91] Although at first the wound did not seem serious, and in fact did not prevent him from suppressing the pro-Parthian rebellion, it caused a disease that influ-

---

80 Tac. *Ann*. 2.54.2.
81 Tac. *Ann*. 2.53–55; see Damon/Palazzolo (2019).
82 Tac. *Ann*. 2.56; *SCPP* 346–362; *Tab. Siar.* 113–114; see Low (2016).
83 Tac. *Ann*. 2.57.1.
84 Tac. *Ann* 2.59; Suet. *Tib*. 52.
85 On the relationship between Germanicus and Piso: Drogula (2015).
86 Tac. *Ann*. 2.69; *SCPP* 28–29.
87 *Tab. Siar.* I 35–38; Tac. *Ann*. 2.83.2; Suet. *Calig*. 1.2.
88 Vell. Pat. 2.101; Cass. Dio 55.10a.4; see Luther (2010).
89 RGDA 27; Tac. *Ann*. 2.4.1.
90 Vell. Pat. 2.102; Cass. Dio 55.10a.5–7; see Romer (1979).
91 Cass. Dio 55.10a.6; Insc. Ital. 13.1.245; cf. Strab. 11.14.6 (Ador); Vell. 2.102.2 (Adduus); see Herz (1984), 125.

enced Gaius' decision to withdraw from public life. He died in Limyra, on his way to Rome, on 21 February 4 CE.[92]

His death, like that of Lucius before him, was a severe blow to Augustus. Evidence of this is provided by the decision of the Senate to commemorate Gaius not only in Rome itself,[93] but also throughout the whole empire, which was reflected by the cities' posthumous honoring (the best known comes from Pisa[94]). Some of the cities decided to dedicate temples (e. g., Nemausus[95]), others to establish altars (e. g., Rheims[96] or Kos[97]), and others to erect honorary statues (e. g., Casinum,[98] Corinth,[99] Eresus,[100] and Aphrodisias[101]). However, after this extensive wave of distinctions, the interest in Gaius faded.[102] No children had been born from his marriage to Livilla, which was probably concluded before his departure to the East. After his death, Livilla became the wife of Drusus Caesar, son of Tiberius.[103] Once Augustus was gone, there was no one to cherish his memory. However, the posthumous honors awarded to Lucius and Gaius became a model for the honoring of further prematurely deceased candidates for the imperial purple, above all Germanicus and Drusus Caesar.[104] Bearing this in mind, it would not have been surprising, therefore, if allusions were made to this not so ancient history. Using a part of the statue of Gaius Caesar to commemorate the adopted son of Tiberius would not have signaled disrespect for the former in this context but would rather have been a distinction that recalled the tragic death of another young successor.

An argument in favor of this supposition is not only the connection between Gaius' biography and the mythical Troilus, but also his other portraits that have been recarved. This is most likely to have been the case with the portrait which is now in the Vatican Museum (Fig. 5).[105] Klaus Fittschen's thesis that the current face of Nero was created from the portrait of Gaius is widely accepted.[106] Other identifications had pre-

---

92 Vell. Pat. 2.102; Cass. Dio 55.10a.8–9 Tac. *Ann.* 1.3.3; *Insc. Ital.* 13.1.128, 13.2.164–165; see Ganzert (1984).
93 Sawiński (2018), 71–81.
94 CIL 11.1421; see Lott (2012), 67–77, 192–209.
95 CIL 12.3156; see Rose (1997), 129 (no. 55).
96 Vassileiou (1982).
97 IGR 4.1094 (Halasarna).
98 Notizie degli Scavi di Antichità 1939, 127–128, no. 157; see Rose (1997), 86–87 (no. 6).
99 Boschung (2002), 64–66 (no. 17); Rose (1997), 138–139 (no. 69).
100 IG I² Suppl. 124, 11–18; see Rose (1997), 151f. (no. 84).
101 Rose (1997), 163–164 (no. 103).
102 However, e. g., from Ephesus from the time of Trajan we know the priestly cult of Gaius and Lucius Caesar: SEG 4.521 (T. Statilius Crito); see Pollini (1987), 5f. (n18).
103 Raepsaet-Charlier (1987), 216–218 (no. 239).
104 *Tab. Siar.* IIa 1–7; IIc 1–7; IIc 18–20; see Sawiński (2018), 129–142.
105 Rome, Vatican Museums, Sala dei Busti 385, inv. no. 591.
106 Fittschen (1977), 35–39; see Varner (2004), 69f.; Pollini (1987), 66f., 101 (no. 20).

viously been made,[107] but this seems to be the most likely one. The portrait of young Nero in the "Cagliari" type, which began to appear after he took the imperial throne or a little later, is now set on a modern bust. However, when making a comparison with other realizations of this type, one can see a certain inconsistency in the hairstyle, in the form of double fringes. This additional wave of hair at the top of the forehead was a characteristic feature of Gaius' last type of depiction: "Modena-Capitol,"[108] which was created before or in the beginning of his expedition to the East. It is probably a remnant of a depiction from that period.

The research carried out by Pollini proved that the cuirass of *statua loricata* from Ameria was made of a different bronze alloy than the other parts of the Germanicus statue. Most probably the original intention was for them to be gilded. However, it was decided that these parts should be combined with the breastplate from another statue, with an image of Troilus' struggling with Achilles. The reason for this could not have been trivial. Cadario and Pollini are convinced that the breastplate belonged to Caligula, who, in my opinion, cannot be convincingly connected with the iconography of the statue. However, the motif of Troilus, as I have argued above, corresponds well with the tragic death of another young man from the imperial family, namely Gaius Caesar. Although he had ceased to be an important element of the dynastic genealogy, he could have become important when Germanicus died, or in 23 CE, after the death of Drusus Caesar. The deceased sons of Tiberius were presented and honored, also on the initiative of the Senate, in a way similar to that of the sons of Augustus. In Rome, the statue of Drusus was added to the posthumous statue of Germanicus,[109] in Spoletium the statues of the brothers stood on a one-passage honorary arch,[110] in Apollonia Sozopolis they were presented together with the statues of Augustus, Tiberius and Livia,[111] and in Leptis Magna their statues stood together in a quadriga.[112] The Koinon of Asia even minted coins with their figures on the obverse: young men, wearing togas and sitting on curule seats, are accompanied by the description: νέοι Θεοὶ φιλάδελφοι.[113]

It remains an unresolved question whether, at the time the statue of Germanicus was set up, the "secret life" (i. e., the origin of the cuirass from Gaius' statue) would have been noticed by onlookers, and whether it could have influenced their attitude

---

107 Jucker (1981), 284–295: Nero recarved from Octavian; Hiesinger (1975), 116: Nero; Kiss (1976), 130: Germanicus (?); Poulsen (1951), 120 (no. 4): Nero; Amelung (1908) vol. 2: 570 f. (no. 385): young Claudius; Bernoulli (1886), 169 (no. 6): Caligula (?).

108 Boschung (1993), 54; cf. Pollini (1987), 59–75 ("Type V").

109 CIL 6.909–910; see Rose (1997), 111 (no. 39).

110 CIL 11.4776–4777; see Rose (1997), 119 (no. 46).

111 *MAMA* IV 143A; see Rose (1997), 169 f. (no. 107).

112 Boschung (2002), 8–24 (particularly 14–18); Rose (1997), 182–184 (no. 125). The memory of Germanicus survived in the calendar of one of the military units in the East until the third century CE; see *Fer. Dur.* II 12–13.

113 RPC 1, no. 2994=BMC Sardis 104.

towards the image of Germanicus.[114] Assuming that the public display of the statue was a local initiative, it must have been common knowledge that a fragment of the depiction of Augustus' son had been incorporated into the statue. Certainly, the bronze statue itself had to indicate the special significance of the honored one. In Italy, the surviving representations of the Julian-Claudian imperial family in the public space were usually made of marble, which of course does not have to correspond to the situation in the Early Empire. In Herculaneum, a place of exceptional archaeological status, we know the bronze statues of the *divus Iulius* and the *divus Augustus* from the seat of *Augustales*,[115] and from the so-called basilica, among others, supernatural-sized bronze statues of Agrippina Minor, Tiberius, Claudius and Augustus as *divus*.[116] We can suppose that the place and form of the statue must have made an impression on the audience, reinforced both by the content of the inscription and the representation of Troilus fighting Achilles; it made clear that Germanicus was equal to the bravest heroes of the Trojan War and their heirs.

In the Roman Empire, honorary statues functioned in the same way during its beginnings, in the crisis of the third century CE, and much later. Their form was always adapted to the needs of Roman society at a given time, and their transformations were by no means all linked at certain times to any specific motivations. These were always of a diverse nature and were simply related to the transformation of the material world in such a way that it corresponded to the ideas of people at a given time. During the Early Empire, the reasons for the transformation of statues were not limited to actions related to the formal or informal *memoria damnata*. An analysis of the iconography of the armor of the statue of Germanicus of Amelia proves that we are simply unable to associate its original form with Caligula, but rather with another member of the imperial family – Gaius, the son of Agrippa adopted by Augustus. This is because the transformations of honorary sculptures could at this time already function like late antique *spolia* and use the name of the originally honored persons to honor their successors.

---

114   Liverani (2011).
115   Boschung (2002), 121–125; Rose (1997), 91 (no. 14).
116   Najbjerg (2002); Boschung (2002), 119–121; Rose (1997), 91f. (no. 15).

Fig. 1 Statue of. M. Holconius Rufus, Pompeii, Naples, Museo Archeologico inv. no. 6233.

The Secret Life of Things

Fig. 2 Statue of Germanicus from Amelia,
Museo Archeologico inv. no. 50207.

Fig. 3 Detail view of statue of Germanicus from Amelia: three bronze posts around the interior rim of the cuirass collar (after Rocco 2008a, fig. 57).

Fig. 4 Detail view of statue of Germanicus from Amelia: breastplate showing the death of Troilus at the hands of Achilles.

Fig. 5 Portrait of Nero recut from Gaius Caesar, Vatican City, Musei Vaticani (Sala dei Busti 385) inv. no. 591.

Bibliography

Amelung, Walter (1908): Die Sculpturen des Vaticanischen Museums, vol. 2. Berlin: Georg Reimer Verlag.
Bernoulli, Johann J. (1886): Römische Ikonographie, vol. 2.1. Berlin: Wilhelm Spemann Verlag.
Beschi, Luigi (1994): "Un guerriero bronzeo da Oderzo (IV)". In: Scarfì, Bianca M. (ed.): Studi di archeologia della X Regio in ricordo di Michele Tombolani. Roma: L'Erma di Bretschneider, 279–290.
Beschorner, Andreas (1992): Untersuchungen zu Dares Phrygius. Tübingen: Gunter Narr Verlag.
Blanck, Horst (1969): Wiederverwendung alter Statuen als Ehrendenkmäler bei Griechen und Römern. Roma: L'Erma di Bretschneider.
Bobrowski, Antoni (2006): "Racjonalizacja tradycji mitologicznej w 'Dzienniku wojny trojańskiej' Diktysa z Krety". In: Collectanea Philologica 9, 175–191.

Bobrowski, Antoni (2009): 'Dziennik wojny trojańskiej' Diktysa z Krety. Studium history-czno-literackie. Kraków: Wydawnictwo Uniwersytetu Jagiellońskiego.

Boschung, Dietrich (1987): "Römische Glasphalerae mit Porträtbüsten". In: Bonner Jahrbücher 187, 193–258.

Boschung, Dietrich (1989): Die Bildnisse des Caligula. Berlin: Deutsches Archäologisches Institut / Mann Verlag.

Boschung, Dietrich (1993): "Die Bildnistypen der iulisch-claudischen Kaiserfamilie: ein kritischer Forschungsbericht". In: Journal of Roman Archaeology 6, 39–79.

Boschung, Dietrich (2002): Gens Augusta. Untersuchungen zur Aufstellung, Wirkung und Bedeutung der Statuengruppen des julisch-claudischen Kaiserhauses. Mainz am Rhein: Philipp von Zabern Verlag.

Brenk, Beat (1987): "Spolia from Constantine to Charlemagne. Aesthetics versus Ideology". In: Dumbarton Oaks Papers 41, 103–109.

Brilliant, Richard / Kinney, Dale (eds.) (2011): Reuse Value. Spolia and Appropriation in Art and Architecture from Constantine to Sherrie Levine. Farnham: Ashgate Publishing.

Cadario, Matteo (2004): La corazza di Alessandro. Loricati di tipo ellenistico dal IV secolo a. C. al II d. C. Milan: LED Edizioni Universitarie.

Cadario, Matteo (2011): "Statua loricata di Germanico". In: La Rocca, Eugenio et al. (eds.): Ritratti le tante facce del potere. Roma: Mondo Mostre, 228–229.

Chaniotis, Angelos (2017): "The Life of Statues of Gods in the Greek World". In: Kernos 20, 91–112.

Colin, Diane A. (1997): The Artist of Ara Pacis. The Process of Hellenization in Roman Relief Sculpture. Chapel Hill: University of North Carolina Press.

Croxford, Ben (2016): "Metal Sculpture from Roman Britain. Scraps but Not Always Scrap". In: Kristensen, Troels M. / Stirling, Lea (eds.): The Afterlife of Greek and Roman Sculpture. Late Antique Responses and Practices. Ann Arbor: University of Michigan Press, 27–46.

D'Arms, John (1988): "Pompeii and Rome in the Augustan Age and Beyond. The Eminence of the Gens Holconia". In: Curtis, Robert I. (ed.): Studia Pompeiana & Classica. In honor of Wilhelmina Jashemski. New Rochelle: Aristide D. Caratzas, 51–73.

Damon, Cynthia / Palazzolo, Elizabeth (2019): "Defining Home, Defining Rome. Germanicus' Eastern Tour". In: Biggs, Thomas / Blum, Jessica (eds.): The Epic Journey in Greek and Roman Literature. Cambridge: Cambridge University Press, 194–210.

Deichmann, Friedrich W. (1975): Die Spolien in der spätantiken Architektur. München: Beck.

Deppmeyr, Korana (2008): Kaisergruppen von Vespasian bis Konstantin. Eine Untersuchung zu Aufstellungskontexten und Intentionen der statuarischen Präsentation kaiserlicher Familien. Hamburg: Dr Kovač Verlag.

Drogula, Fred K. (2015): "Who Was Watching Whom?. A Reassessment of the Conflict between Germanicus and Piso". In: American Journal of Philology 136, 121–153.

Elsner, Jaś (2000): "From the Culture of Spolia to the Cult of Relics. The Arch of Constantine and the Genesis of Late Antique Forms". In: Papers of the British School at Rome 68, 149–184.

Emanuele, Daniel (1989): "Aes Corinthium. Fact, Fiction, and Fake". In: Phoenix 43, 347–358.

Esch, Arnold (1969): "Spolien. Zur Wiederverwendung antiker Baustücke und Skulpturen im mittelalterlichen Italien". In: Archiv für Kulturgeschichte 51, 1–64.

Fejfer, Jane (2008): Roman Portraits in Context. Berlin/New York: De Gruyter.

Feruglio, Anna E. et al. (1987): Il volto di Germanico. A proposito del restauro del bronzo. Roma: Cedis.

Fiorelli, Giuseppe (1862): Pompeianarum Antiquitatum Historia, vol. 2. Naples.

Fittschen, Klaus (1977): Katalog der antiken Skulpturen in Schloss Erbach. Berlin: Mann Verlag.

Fittschen, Klaus / Zanker, Paul (1985): Katalog der römischen Porträts in den Capitolinischen Museen und den anderen kommunalen Sammlungen der Stadt Rom, Bd. 1: Kaiser- und Prinzenbildnisse. Mainz am Rhein: Philip von Zabern Verlag.

Flower, Harriet I. (2006): The Art of Forgetting. Disgrace and Oblivion in Roman Political Culture. Chapel Hill: University of North Carolina Press.

Franken, Norbert (2000): "Zu Bildschmuck und Attributen antiker Bronzestatuen". In: Kölner Jahrbuch 33, 215–229.

Galinsky, Karl (2008): "Recarved Imperial Portraits. Nuances and Wider Context". In: Memoirs of the American Academy in Rome 53, 1–25.

Ganzert, Joachim (1984): Das Kenotaph für Gaius Caesar in Lymyra. Tübingen: Ernst Wasmuth Verlag.

Ganzert, Joachim (1997): "Zu den Ehrenbögen für Germanicus und Drusus auf dem Augustusforum: '... arcus circum latera templi Martis Ultoris ...'". In: Mitteilungen des Deutschen Archäologischen Instituts, Römische Abteilung 104, 193–206.

Gasparini, Valentino (2009): "Gli archi onorari di Pompei. Una nuova interpretazione". In: Živa Antika. Antiquité vivante 59, 41–78.

Hallet, Christopher H. (2005): The Roman Nude. Heroic Portrait Statuary 200 BC–AD 300. Oxford: Oxford University Press.

Hamelrijk, Emily (2015): Hidden Lives, Public Personae. Women and Civic Life in the Roman West. Oxford: Oxford University Press.

Hertel, Ernst D. (1982): Untersuchungen zu Stil und Chronologie des Kaiser und Prinzenporträts von Augustus bis Claudius. Bonn: Rheinischen Friedrich-Wilhelmis Universität zu Bonn (Diss.).

Herz, Peter (1984): "Gaius Caesar und Artavasdes". In: Ganzert, Joachim: Das Kenotaph für Gaius Caesar in Lymyra. Tübingen: Ernst Wasmuth Verlag, 118–127.

Hiesinger, Ulrich (1975): "The Portraits of Nero". In: American Journal of Archaeology 79, 113–124.

Hoff, Ralf von den (2009): "Caligula. Zur visuellen Repräsentation eines römischen Kaisers". In: Archäologischer Anzeiger, 237–263.

Højte, Jakob M. (2005): Roman Imperial Statue Bases. From Augustus to Commodus. Aarhus/ Oxford/Oakville: Aarhus University Press.

Hölscher, Tonio (1987): Römische Bildsprache als semantisches System. Heidelberg: Carl Winter Verlag.

Joy, Jody (2009): "Reinvigorating Object Biography. Reproducing the Drama of Object Live". In: World Archaeology 41, 540–556.

Jucker, Hans (1981): "Iulisch-claudische Kaiser- und Prinzenporträts als 'Palimpsete'". In: Jahrbuch des Deutschen Archäologischen Instituts 96, 236–316.

Kinney, Dale (1995): "Rape or Restitution of the Past? Interpreting *spolia*". In: Scott, Susan (ed.), The Art of Interpreting. University Park: Penn State University Press, 53–67.

Kinney, Dale (1997): "*Spolia. Damnatio* and *renovatio memoriae*". In: Memoirs of the American Academy in Rome 42, 117–148.

Kiss, Zsolt (1976): L'Iconographie des princes Julio-claudiens au temps d'Auguste et de Tibère. Warsaw: Éditions scientifiques de Pologne.

Kopytoff, Igor (1986): "The Cultural Biography of Things". In: Appadurai, Arjun (ed.): The Social Life of Things. Commodities in Cultural Perspective. Cambridge: Cambridge University Press, 64–94.

Kossatz-Deissmann, Anneliese (1981): "Achilleus. VII Das Troilosabenteuer". In: Lexicon Iconographicum Mythologiae Classicae, vol. 1, 72–95.

Koestermann, Erich (1957): "Die Feldzüge des Germanicus 14–16 n. Chr.". In: Historia 6, 429–479.

Lahusen, Götz / Formigli, Edilberto (2001): Römische Bildnisse aus Bronze. Kunst und Technik. München: Hirmer Verlag.

Kristensen, Troels M. (2013): "The Life Histories of Roman Statuary and Some Aspects of Sculptural Spoliation in Late Antiquity". In: Altekamp, Stefan et al. (eds.): Perspektiven der Spolienforschung 1. Spoliierung und Transposition. Berlin/Boston: De Gruyter, 23–46.

Kristensen, Troels M. / Stirling, Lea (2016): "The Lives and Afterlives of Greek and Roman Sculpture. From Use to Reuse". In: Kristensen, Troels M. / Stirling, Lea (eds.): The Afterlife of Greek and Roman Sculpture. Late Antique Responses and Practices. Ann Arbor: University of Michigan Press, 3–24.

Laube, Ingrid (2006): Thorakophoroi. Gestalt und Semantik des Brustpanzers in der Darstellung des 4.–1. Jhs. v. Chr. Rahden: Marie Leidorf Verlag.

Liverani, Paolo (2011): "Reading Spolia in Late Antiquity and Contemporary Perception". In: Brilliant, Richard / Kinney, Dale (eds.): Reuse Value. Spolia and Appropriation in Art and Architecture from Constantine to Sherrie Levine. Farnham: Ashgate Publishing, 32–52.

Longfellow, Brenda (2018): "The Reuse and Redisplay of Honorific Statues in Pompeii". In: Ng, Diana Y. / Swetnam-Burland, Molly (eds.): Reuse and Renovation in Roman Material Culture. Functions, Aesthetics, Interpretations. Cambridge: Cambridge University Press, 24–50.

Lott, John B. (2012): Death and Dynasty in Early Imperial Rome. Key Sources, with Text, Translations, and Commentary. Cambridge: Cambridge University Press.

Low, Katie (2016): "Germanicus on Tour. History, Diplomacy and the Promotion of Dynasty". In: The Classical Quarterly 66, 222–238.

Luther, Andreas (2010): "Zum Orientfeldzug des Gaius Caesar". In: Gymnasium 117, 103–127.

Ma, John (2013): Statues and Cities. Honorific Portraits and Civic Identity in the Hellenistic World. Oxford: Oxford University Press.

Malloch, Simon J. V. (2001): "Gaius on the Channel Coast". In: The Classical Quarterly 51, 551–556.

Manconi, Dorica / Danesi, Alessandro (2002), "Statua di Germanico (nr 24)". In: De Marinis, Giuliano et al. (eds.): Bronzi e Marmi della Flamina. Modena: Artioli Editore, 133–135.

Matheson, Susan B. (2000): "The Private Sector. Reworked Portraits Outside the Imperial Circle". In: Varner, Eric / Bundrick, Sheramy D. (eds.): From Caligula to Constantine. Tyranny and Transformation in Roman Portraiture. Atlanta: Michael C. Carlos Museum, 70–80.

Merkele, Stefan (1988): Die Ephemeris belli Troiani des Diktys von Kreta. Frankfurt am Main/New York: Peter Lang.

Massner, Anne-Kathrein (1982): Bildnisangleichung. Untersuchungen zur Entstehungs- und Wirkungsgeschichte der Augustusporträts (43 v. Chr.–68 n. Chr.). Berlin: Mann Verlag.

Murer, Cristina (2017): Stadtraum und Bürgerin. Aufstellungsorte kaiserzeitlichen Ehrenstatuen in Italien und Nordafrika. Berlin: De Gruyter.

Najbjerg, Tina (2002): "A Reconstruction and Reconsideration of the So-Called Basilica in Herculaneum". In: McGinn, Thomas A. J. (ed.): Pompeian Brothels, Pompeii's Ancient History, Mirrors and Mysteries, Art and Nature at Oplontis and the Herculaneum "Basilica". Portsmouth: Journal of Roman Archaeology, 122–165.

Pollini, John (2002): "A New Portrait of Octavia and the Iconography of Octavia Minor and Julia Maior". In: Mitteilungen des Deutschen Archäologischen Instituts, Römische Mitteilungen 109, 11–42.

Pollini, John (1987): The Portraiture of Gaius and Lucius Caesar. New York: Fordham University Press.

Pollini, John (2010): "Recutting Roman Portraits. Problems in Interpretation and the New Technology in Finding Possible Solutions". In: Memoirs of the American Academy in Rome 55, 23–44.

Pollini, John (2012): From Republic to Empire. Rhetoric, Religion and Power in the Visual Culture of Ancient Rome. Norman: University of Oklahoma Press.

Pollini, John (2017): "The Bronze Statue of Germanicus from Ameria (Amelia)". In: American Journal of Archaeology 121, 425–437.

Pollini, John / Giumlia-Mair, Alessandra (2019): "The Statue of Germanicus from Amelia. New Discoveries". In: American Journal of Archaeology 123, 675–686.

Poulsen, Vagn (1951): "Nero, Britanicus, and Others". In: Acta Archaeologica 22, 119–135.

Prusac, Marina (2011): From Face to Face. Recarving of Roman Portraits and the Late-Antique Portraits Arts. Leiden/Boston: Brill.

Queyrel, François (2012): "Modes de représentation des Julio-Claudiens dans les Cyclades. Traditions régionales et reprises de schémas iconographiques". In: Stephanidou-Tiveriou, Theodosia et al. (eds.): Κλασική παράδοση και νεωτερικά στοιχεία στην πλαστική της ρωμαϊκής Ελλάδας. Thessaloniki: University Studio Press, 417–431.

Raepsaet-Charlier, Marie Th. (1987): Prosopographie des femmes de l'ordre sénatorial (Ier-IIe siècles), vol. 1–2. Louvain: Peeters Publishers.

Rocco, Giulia (2008a): La statua bronzea con ritratto di Germanico da Ameria (Umbria). Roma: Bardi.

Rocco, Giulia (2008b): "Il Germanico di America. Un bronzo ellenistico tra Grecia e Roma", Bollettino d'Arte 108, 2–28.

Rocco, Giulia (2012): "Un bassorilievo da Amelia di età augustea". In: Bollettino d'Arte 16, 1–22.

Romer, Frank E. (1979): "Gaius Caesar's Military Diplomacy in the East". In: Transactions of the American Philological Association 109, 199–214.

Rose, Charles Brian (1997): Dynastic Commemoration and Imperial Portraiture in the Julio-Claudian Period. Cambridge: Cambridge University Press.

Salcuni, Andrea (2014): "Le incongruenze della statua loricata di Germanico da Amelia. Note sull'uso di modelli parziali nella produzione di grande plastica in bronzo in epoca romana". In: Kemmers, Fleur et al. (eds.): Lege Artis. Festschrift für Hans-Markus von Kaenel. Bonn: Dr. Rudolf Habelt Verlag, 129–144.

Salcuni, Andrea (2017): "Zum Umgang mit Modellen bei der Herstellung römischer Großbronzen in Italien". In: Kemkes, Martin (ed.): Römische Großbronzen am UNESCO-Welterbe Limes. Beiträge zum Welterbe. Darmstadt: Konrad Theiss Verlag, 125–131.

Sawiński, Paweł (2018): The Succession of Imperial Power under the Julio-Claudian Dynasty (30 BC–AD 68). Berlin: Peter Lang.

Scaife, Ross (1995): "The Kypria and its Early Reception". In: Classical Antiquity 14, 164–191.

Schiffer, Michael B. (1987): Formation Processes of the Archaeological Record. Albuquerque: University of New Mexico Press.

Shear, Julia L. (2007): "Reusing Statues, Rewriting Inscriptions and Bestowing Honours in Roman Athens". In: Newby, Zahra / Leader-Newby, Ruth (eds.): Art and Inscriptions in the Ancient World. Cambridge: Cambridge University Press, 221–246.

Sistakou, Evina (2008): Reconstructing the Epic. Cross-Readings of the Trojan Myth in Hellenistic Poetry. Leuven: Peeters Publishers.

Smith, Roland R. R. / Hallett, Christopher H. (2015): "Troilus and Achilles. A Monumental Statue Group from Aphrodisias". In: Journal of Roman Studies 105, 124–182.

Stewart, Peter (2003): Statues in Roman Society. Representation and Response. Oxford: Oxford University Press.

Squire, Michael (2013): "Embodied Ambiguities on the Prima Porta Augustus". In: Art History 36, 242–279.

Varner, Eric (2001): "Portraits, Plots and Politics. *Damnatio memoriae* and the Images of Imperial Women". In: Memoirs of the American Academy in Rome 46, 41–93.

Varner, Eric (2004): Mutilation and Transformation. *Damnatio memoriae* and Roman Imperial Portraiture. Leiden/Boston: Brill.

Vassileiou, Alain (1982): "La dédicace d'un monument de Reims elevé en l'honneur de Caius et Lucius Caesar". In: Zeitschrift für Papyrologie und Epigraphik 47, 119–129.

Ward-Perkins, Bryan (1999): "Re-Using the Architectural Legacy of the Past, *entre ideologie et pragmatisme*". In: Brogiolo, Gian P. / Ward-Perkins, Bryan (eds.): The Idea and Ideal of the Town between Late Antiquity and Early Middle Ages. Leiden/Boston: Brill, 225–244.

Zanker, Paul (1981): "Das Bildnis des M. Holconius Rufus". In: Archäologischer Anzeiger, 349–361.